Also by Larry Schweikart

Reagan: The American President

Dragonslayers

SIX PRESIDENTS *and* THEIR WAR *with the* SWAMP

LARRY SCHWEIKART

BOMBARDIER
BOOKS

Published by Bombardier Books
An Imprint of Post Hill Press
ISBN: 978-1-63758-188-9
ISBN (eBook): 978-1-63758-189-6

Dragonslayers:
Six Presidents and Their War with the Swamp
© 2022 by Larry Schweikart
All Rights Reserved

Cover Design by Tiffani Shea

Post Hill Press
New York • Nashville
posthillpress.com

Published in the United States of America
2 3 4 5 6 7 8 9 10

To the imprisoned martyrs of Patriot Day, January 6, 2021, who reminded us that the US Congress still is the "People's House," if only for a few hours.

CONTENTS

INTRODUCTION

When I first started this project, I thought I had six themes, all bound by a common concept of "the Swamp." Nevertheless, I considered these largely separate and distinct topics. As I delved into the research, it became immediately clear that all six of these Swamp-related issues were intertwined. Slavery had been protected by the Spoils System, which became the target of reformers in the late 1800s—the same reformers who set their sights on the trusts. By the end of World War II, Americans' inability to control the Spoils Beast and the war-created bureaucracies led to the rise of quasi-independent agencies, such as the Federal Bureau of Investigation and the Central Intelligence Agency—each of which, due to claims of "national security," could hide many of their activities behind the cloak of national security. John Kennedy was unable to control them: whether they controlled him is a part of our story. No greater opponent of "big government" existed than Ronald Reagan, who, at the end of two terms, had scarcely put a dent in the "shadow government." By the time Donald Trump came into office, vowing to "drain the Swamp," it was beyond the ability of any administration, let alone any president who lacked 100 percent support in his effort, to do so.

Our presidents had much in common. They were all big men: four of the six were over six feet tall, and the shortest two (Theodore Roosevelt at 5'10" and Grover Cleveland at 5'11") were nevertheless stocky. Roosevelt had worked to become tough and muscular; Cleveland was portly. Abraham Lincoln, John Kennedy, Ronald Reagan, and Donald Trump were all tall with Reagan and Lincoln being physically athletic. Kennedy's public relations machine created an image of him as physically active, though much of that was a myth. All but perhaps Cleveland had an aura that commanded a room when they walked in. Three—Lincoln, Trump, and Roosevelt—suffered business failure, though Roosevelt's cattle ranch was a hobby he never personally managed. Two had studied law (Lincoln, Cleveland), four had been in the military, though neither Lincoln nor Reagan ever really saw combat. (Lincoln joked that he was wounded in the Black Hawk War...by a mosquito). Reagan spent World War II making training films and inspirational movies in Hollywood for the army. Only Roosevelt and Kennedy had truly tasted war on the front lines, and both emerged as heroes.

Of the six, only Kennedy and Cleveland were "insiders." Roosevelt had the upbringing and connections, but he wanted to upset the Swamp apple cart, leaving him in the vice presidency until fate cast him into a higher role. Cleveland, while part of the Democrat Party machine, nevertheless stood well outside the party's mainstream as a "gold" Democrat. Had the Swamp had its way, none of the six would have come anywhere close to the presidency.

An awareness of the growing size and power of the unelected bureaucracy started long before any of our six Presidents were even born. In the 1670s, for example, freemen began to complain about the number of burgesses, their daily pay, and the number of meetings. According to historian Edmund Morgan, they wanted "an end to fruitless government expenditures. Much of their tax money, they suspected, was going to line the pockets of a pack of officials."[1] Similar charges were repeated in the Declaration of Independence, wherein Thomas Jefferson wrote of the king: "He has erected a multitude of New Offices, and sent hither swarms of Officers to harass our people, and eat out their substance."[2] George Washington sought permission from Congress to create a body of assistants who could help with running the government, and the Departments of War, Treasury, and the State Department were established. Those remained quite small: Hamilton had, at times, only three secretaries or assistants and Jefferson only thirty for a worldwide effort in the State Department. Some growth would be expected. Yet it was kept small. President Jefferson still answered the White House door himself—in his slippers. During the War of 1812, at one time Secretary of State James Monroe was doing his own job, that of the secretary of war, and filling in for President James Madison, who was engaged in a ride of almost thirty hours trying to catch up to the army.

But by Lincoln's time, the growing spoils monster created by Martin Van Buren when he originated the Democrat Party to protect and preserve slavery was out of control. As we will see, Lincoln dealt with job seekers constantly. They interfered with his ability to run a war; they diverted his attention from reuniting the nation. Subsequent presidents (finally) acknowledged the problems posed by armies of job seekers descending on a chief executive and absorbing his time and attention. Washington, DC's answer to anything is "reform," and usually the reform is as bad as the problem itself. While the Pendleton Act removed the immediate burden for presidents of naming thousands of people to federal jobs, it quietly started another Swamp of its own, the perpetual lobbyists for interest groups, who changed the nature of campaigning from offering a few specific jobs to individuals to offering masses of group jobs to the special interests. Notice, this was neither anti-constitutional, nor would it have been a surprise to the Founders, particularly James Madison, who expected "factions" to appear. I doubt, however, Madison ever dreamed they would be camped out perpetually in Washington, DC, spending their entire time trying to bribe senators and representatives.

As politicians attempted to reform the Spoils Swamp, the Trust Swamp grew under their noses. Theodore Roosevelt rapidly moved from a neutral position on these to being the "Trust Buster" dedicated to breaking up the big business combinations. As we will see, TR did this largely with the best interests of big business in mind (or so he believed), perceptively seeing the national sensationalistic press as a problem equally destructive as the trusts themselves. Preventing the Yellow Journalists from starting a class war against big business and the rich was as noble an objective as Van Buren's goal of preventing a civil war, but in each case badly imagined and ineptly structured. Each, in a sense, only accelerated the end they hoped to avoid. One wonders what Theodore

Roosevelt would say about today's Hoax News that generates an endless waterfall of lies.

Much changed after Roosevelt, especially during the Great Depression and World War II, when the Spoils System gained new muscular, nearly bionic, legs. Under Theodore's cousin, Franklin, the unelected bureaucracy exploded with agencies such as the Agricultural Adjustment Administration, the Works Project Administration, the Public Works Administration, the Securities and Exchange Commission, the Civilian Conservation Corps and hundreds of others. Some of these would disappear after the Depression and the war, others would assume near immortality. World War II further expanded the bureaucracies, especially those related to national defense and security, to the point that by the end of General, President Dwight D. Eisenhower's second term, he sternly warned Americans about the "Military-Industrial Complex." While on a specific basis there is some question as to the extent of the defense contractors' powers (my own study of the National Aero-Space Plane showed that some of the biggest contractors wanted nothing to do with the program), the near-universal influence of military contractors in Washington is undeniable.[3] Ike was right in that the perpetual lobbying by these groups for more or better weapons began to drive policy decisions by itself. Donald Trump would discover the influence of the military-industrial complex in his term when he attempted to withdraw American forces from the war zones in Afghanistan and Iraq.

At least much of the military's budget was public and could be reviewed and challenged. But after World War II, a new agency, the Central Intelligence Agency—created by President Harry Truman specifically to gather information about foreign enemies—took on a life of its own when it came to dictating foreign policy. Using coups, assassinations, and other covert means seldom with the direct approval of a president, the CIA literally changed foreign governments and directed events abroad in ways that a president, such as John Kennedy, could be hemmed into a policy such as the fiasco at the Bay of Pigs. The question of whether the CIA tied JFK to Vietnam, however, is a different story, and as we will see, Kennedy needed little prodding to increase the American presence there. If the CIA was in charge of the Vietnam buildup, as some suggest, then the logic of a CIA-assisted assassination of the president by a "secret team" is sound; but if JFK was "going there" anyway, the CIA certainly would have had no reason to remove someone who was going their way.

Ronald Reagan came into office less concerned about the CIA's activities than about the pernicious, destructive, and paralyzing effect a nameless, faceless, unelected bureaucracy was having on the United States. He made reducing the size of government his third highest priority behind restoring the American economy and rebuilding the military sufficient to defeat the Soviet threat. Unfortunately for Reagan, the first two overwhelmed the third, and he never got close to attacking the "administrative state" as it had by then become known. This parasitic network inside the US government had by Reagan's time grown so large and powerful that it literally wrote its own laws, had its own armed police forces, and stood beyond Congress's ability to control it. By 1980, virtually all authority over the administrative state had been handed over to the courts, who essentially allowed the bureaucracy to write its own performance standards and its own definitions of legality. Courts gave these agencies the widest of latitudes, enabling them to wield a power the Founders never intended. As Ronald Reagan quipped, "The closest thing to eternal life I have seen on the earth is a government agency."

Two and a half decades after Reagan abandoned his war with "big government," Donald Trump ran on the promise of "draining the Swamp." His actual program, as we shall see, was far less ambitious than many thought at the time: he never promised to eliminate or even downscale the FBI, the CIA, or any government agency. Rather he promised to attack the lobbyist culture from a number of directions. Left unsaid by Trump was the fact that his energy program alone threatened to eliminate or severely weaken a number of energy-related lobbyists, who would have to return to old-fashioned competition—rather than begging the government for protection—to survive.

But Trump quickly found out that the more substantial changes he wanted to make in bringing equality to the justice system; in putting America first in all policies; in tightening border controls; and many others all ran afoul of some large, entrenched element of the Swamp, by then known as the Deep State. The administrative state had given up merely carrying out the orders of the president and instead had gone into full "resistance" mode to stop his every policy. Never in our history had so many unelected despots tried to undo the results of a legitimate election. At least the Confederates had the courage to leave the Union and fight; but the Deep State cabalistas remained as a Communist underground, torpedoing personnel choices, slow-walking clearances, refusing to obey direct White House commands, and, in the case of the Department of Justice, joining in the attempt to impeach Trump himself.

None of this would have been possible without the complete or partial failure of Cleveland, Kennedy, and Reagan to regain control of the government. But Trump also was opposed by "Big Tech," in the form of outright election tampering by Google, Facebook, Twitter, and other social media sites. Whereas TR fretted that the Yellow Journalists would provoke mobs to assault corporations, the same "news" media, which by Trump's time did not even pretend to be objective or fair, now joined with Big Tech to try to take down a president. They failed in 2016, but succeeded in 2020. TR may have "busted" the big trusts of the day, but he did so in such a way that new ones easily sprang up and perpetuated four years' worth of lies against Trump. Multiple scholarly analyses of the "news" coverage of the 2016 race showed that at best Trump got 7 percent favorable coverage. It was worse in 2020.

Is the Swamp now beyond all control? It is evident that while conservatives in the 1980s, 1990s, and the first decade of the twenty-first century agonized over the left's domination of Hollywood, academia, and the media, they had completely been blind to similar takeovers of the military, the Deep State institutions such as the CIA and FBI, and the seizure of America's corporations by "woke" CEOs and marketing departments. Despite the fact that Trump won over 74 million votes in 2020 (and the data for even that is contested: suggestions are that there was corruption in the system at the state level of Arizona, Georgia, Michigan, Nevada, Pennsylvania and Wisconsin—just to name a few) and may have won far more, half of America's electorate was already being demonized in 2021 as "white racists" and "hate groups."

In short, for almost 200 years the American people have been at war with one group of elites or another. These groups have embraced positions from supporting slavery to seeking governance by a corporatist network to policy by an agency whose purpose is to remain mostly secret. Even a popular president like Ronald Reagan found it impossible to even make a significant dent in the administrative state, which by the twenty-first century had united the law enforcement agencies, the military, and much of corporate America under its control along with media, entertainment, and tech giants. That Trump got as far as he did against this coalition was itself a miracle.

Producing this book, as with all my others, required a great deal of help from my agent, Roger Williams, my editors at Post Hill Press, and publisher Anthony Ziccardi. Thanks to my support team at Wild World of History (www.wildworldofhistory.com) for adjusting my schedule to have the time to produce this; to Charles Calomiris for excellent suggestions on the Trust Swamp; and to Steve Bannon and Sebastian Gorka for their insights on the Trump administration.

Part 1

Successes

Defeating the Slave Swamp constituted a titanic victory for everyday people in American history. As even defenders of the Confederate South often say, ordinary soldiers in the Southern army were not fighting for slavery but either for their homes or for their understanding of States' Rights. Those who actively sought to perpetuate a slave-based economy were in the very distinct minority. Nevertheless, the Slave Power had great influence nationally, and near total control in the Deep South. Nationally, its tentacles reached into the Senate, the House of Representatives, and the US Supreme Court, and compromise after compromise showed that the Slave Swamp would not be threatened in its ultimate ability to hold humans as property. Lincoln overcame that.

He was, of our six presidents, the most successful. But even as he defeated the Slave Swamp, the Spoils System that had been created thirty years earlier not only survived but flowered in the Civil War and after. Only courageous presidents such as James Garfield (who paid with his life), Chester Arthur, and Grover Cleveland seemed to triumph in controlling the "Spoils Beast." Or did they?

Instead, the Spoils Swamp merely underwent a metamorphosis into a larger, less manageable creature wherein jobs were promised to interest groups rather than individuals. Meanwhile, Theodore Roosevelt obsessed by the twin evils of a lying press and gigantic corporations, feared that the former would incite national mob action against the latter. By containing the trusts, TR may (or may not) have avoided what he feared, but his Justice Department's interpretations of antitrust law, adopted by the United States Supreme Court, was so nebulous as to become a political stick waved at any company the government at the time didn't particularly like. Worse, some of the most egregious offenders of monopoly power would come on the scene after Roosevelt's time in the form of the "news" monopolies and the giant tech companies that had moved into the news business via "social networking." As of the present, these have successfully avoided federal control—which Roosevelt certainly would have sought had he seen what they have become.

To one degree or another, however, all three saw some success against the Swamp. The resourcefulness of the now-labeled Deep State would prove remarkable in its ability to defy popular control and to grasp victory from the jaws of defeat.

CHAPTER 1

Abraham Lincoln and
the Slave Swamp

*I*n the fictional Lilliput of *Gulliver's Travels*, a great divide existed between those who opened their eggs at the little end and those who opened their eggs at the big end. To some in antebellum America, the debate over slavery was little more than "Big Endism" vs. "Little Endism." For example, both Illinois senator Stephen Douglas, who defeated Abraham Lincoln for the Senate in 1858 (then lost to him in the presidential race two years later) and the founder of the Democrat Party, Martin Van Buren, both believed that essentially the slavery crisis in America was a difference over which end you opened the egg.

In other words, ultimately, neither saw it as a fundamental truth that was, as Jefferson himself wrote, "self evident," but of how one pronounces tomato.

Of course, Stephen Douglas and Martin Van Buren, separated by thirty years—and Van Buren would die in the second year of the war—believed in *something*. They were neither groundless nor shallow. Both held revolutionary ideas that were ultimately unsound and destructive. Van Buren was the originator and essentially the founder of the modern two-party system and the present Democrat Party; Douglas espoused a view even widely held today of an institutionless America governed by "the people," or, in his words "popular sovereignty." (Much more will be said of Van Buren in the next chapter on the Patronage Swamp). By the 1850s, though, both their views came together oddly enough as a counter position to that of Abraham Lincoln.

It is somewhat ironic that of our six presidents and the swamps they faced, Lincoln was by far the most successful, yet at the same time the ideas that should have been crushed and demolished with his victory over the Slave Swamp not only reside in America today, but have morphed, metastasized, and now are ascendant. Both positions—those of Douglas and Van Buren—are alive and thriving today. Douglas's view, that only the people through a popular vote should be enabled to make law, is a foundation of the modern liberal playbook that calls for the end of the Electoral College and ultimately the Senate. Van Buren's position, that there are no absolutes, but rather that people can be effectively bribed to give up their principles, is rampant in the modern United States. If someone is rich and powerful enough, who cares what they do? They make great movies, or sing well, or pass bills that I happen to favor.

Abraham Lincoln stood in diametric opposition to both positions. "He believed," as Harry Jaffa wrote in his seminal *Crisis of the House Divided*, that "free government was…incompatible with chattel slavery. The sheet-anchor of American republicanism," he held, "was that no man was good enough to govern another without that other's consent."[4] All principles that might be invoked to enslave blacks, Lincoln insisted, could and would be used to enslave whites. Douglas advocated self-government for whites, but not for slaves. Any presence of a master-slave relationship contradicted the essence of free government.

Even before he met Douglas or debated him, Lincoln repudiated the notion of mob rule as defined by popular sovereignty. To those who advocated letting the voters decide the issue of slavery, in 1854 Lincoln said it meant there was "no right principle of action but *self-interest*" (his emphasis).[5] In short, Lincoln refused to hand over constitutional liberties either to ideology or bribes.

The fact that *Northerners* erected such convoluted theoretical obstacles to removing slavery speaks to the incredible grip the Peculiar Institution had on America, or at least on part of it. James Oakes, in *Freedom National*, explained the constitutional basis in the proslavery position that bewitched some Northerners for nearly forty years. Where the Constitution read *"persons* held in service" (by which slavery existed by state or local law as a servile status), Southerners and some Northerners insisted that slaves were *property*, which, of course, would have been protected by the Constitution.[6] For Lincoln and the Republicans to defeat slavery, they had to develop "a constitutionally viable argument for restricting the rights of property."[7] And there it was, right in front of them. Slavery could be contained by the federal government and put on a path to destruction through a "cordon of freedom" about the slave state, in which the District of Columbia, all new territories, and the high seas would all be subject to federal law prohibiting slavery because, after all, the Constitution did not protect property in people!

Progress was so slow, however, and the betrayals so common that some Northerners began to suspect something more sinister at work. A "Slave Power Conspiracy" presumed that the Southerners were the puppet masters, but a Slave Swamp? The fact is that genuine realities had entrenched slavery, including racial, sectional, religious, and of course economic. For some people, though, those factors were not enough. Although the Slave Swamp was deep and dangerous, some still wanted to layer on a good old-fashioned conspiracy on top of the potent roots the institution had sunk into antebellum America. It needed no "slaveocracy" conspiracy. It thrived quite well on its own.

Yet many historians would downplay the existence of the Slave Swamp, or paint it as something that Lincoln and other "Black Republicans" concocted. Historian James G. Randall in his legendary *Civil War and Reconstruction* (1937) had dismissed claims of a "slavocracy" claiming that "responsible statesmen of the South were but slightly interested in the fantastic expansionist schemes" of a slave empire extending from Mexico through Cuba and into Central America.[8] He ridiculed the notion that even the free states would eventually have to open their doors to slavery and that "the magnates of the South would not be satisfied until slavery had been made legal in every state."[9] Were such ideas fanciful? Lincoln was not sure. Writing a friend in the wake of the Kansas-Nebraska Act he asked "Can we, as a nation, continue together *permanently—forever—half slave, and half free? (emphasis his)*" He demurred answering his own question as "too mighty" for him to decide.[10] One of the most fascinating speeches of Lincoln's was his keynote speech at Bloomington, Illinois... which was *not* recorded by anyone present. Whether he used the actual phrase slaveocracy is not known with certainty, but he clearly alluded to it.[11] As a politician in a swing state, Lincoln stayed away from incendiary phrases such as "slave power," but his audiences were quite sympathetic to the concept.

In fact, the Slave Swamp probably was more powerful and insidious than most historians have admitted for quite some time. First, the famous Three-Fifths Compromise in which at the Constitutional Convention, the delegates agreed to count three out of every five slaves toward both representation and taxation, proved a significant advantage to the South over time. Whereas the Southern states had only 38 percent of the seats in the Continental Congress (which was apportioned equally by state), in the first United States Congress their number rose to 45 percent. Northern population growth slowly reduced this, but over time it is estimated that the Southern representation in the House benefited from an average of about six seats due to the Three-Fifths Clause until the Civil War.[12] The *Wooster Republican* of February 2, 1859, posted a chart showing free states with 147 representatives to ninety from slave states.[13]

Then there was the fact that many of the presidents, whether Southern or not, were or had been slaveholders. George Washington, Thomas Jefferson, James Madison, and James Monroe—four of the first six presidents—all came from Virginia. Andrew Jackson, who followed the second Adams, was a former slaveholder from Tennessee, as was James K. Polk, who followed Martin Van Buren. William H. Harrison, a Whig, nonetheless was another Virginian who at one time had held slaves (though not while in office). We will revisit later the non-slaveholders who served as president prior to 1860, but not one of them opposed slavery as a matter of principle. On the other hand, Jefferson and Washington both believed that the Constitution did not protect property in people, but rather the state laws protected slavery.

The "Slave Power" indeed looked mighty. One Philadelphia paper in 1865 noted that the South, "with less than a third of the free population, and less than a third of the wealth…had eleven Presidents out of sixteen; seventeen Judges of the Supreme Court out of twenty-eight; fourteen Attorney Generals out of nineteen; sixty-one Presidents of the Senate out of seventy-seven; twenty-one Speakers of the House of Representatives out of thirty-three; [and] eighty-four foreign minister out of a hundred thirty-four.…"[14] (It might be noted that some of these disparities exist for a variety of reasons: in 2020, there was not a single evangelical Protestant out of nine Justices on the US Supreme Court, despite the fact that evangelicals and black Protestants make up almost 40 percent of all Americans. Catholics, who comprise about 21 percent of Americans, hold over half of the positions.) Still, the preponderance of Southerners in positions of power in the US government was disarming to many. As historian Allan Nevins wrote, "The South, far from groaning under tyranny, had controlled the government almost from the beginning."[15]

It might seem like the slave states had disproportionate control of the levers of government. Eventually a term arose to describe the (to some, mysterious) grip the Southern states seemed to have over the nation: a "slave power conspiracy." First used in 1839 when the Cincinnati *Philanthropist* warned that a "SLAVE POWER is now waging a deliberate and determined war against the liberties of our states," the term was considered by historians to be a propaganda rhetoric of the abolitionists.[16] Historian Russel B. Nye saw the concept as relegated almost entirely to the extremists due to the fact that many of the idea's leading advocates published in abolitionist papers. Nevertheless, in a key article in *Science & Society* in 1946, cited *Five Years' Progress of the Slave Power* (1852) as providing the first real definition of the conspiracy: "That control in and over the government which is exercised by a comparatively small number of persons…bound together [by] being owners of slaves."[17] According to the Slave Power Conspiracy, Northern capitalist had joined the Southern slaveowners to form a "ruling oligarchy," or, in modern terms, a Slave Swamp. Abolitionist Wendell Phillips coined the term "The Lords of the Lash and the Lords of the Loom."[18] Similar phrases were found in the *Anti-Slavery Bugle*: "The wealth of the North and the wealth of the South."[19]

Relegating the "Slave Power" to the backwoods of abolitionism was a historical error. It is true that at no time did abolitionists (those who wanted immediately uncompensated emancipation for all slaves) or abolitionism constitute a majority in the North. It is also true that many, if not most, Northern laborers and free farmers considered abolitionists like Phillips, William Lloyd Garrison, and, of course, Frederick Douglass, to be the mid-1800s version of "Q" whose views were detached from reality. And it is also, finally, true that clever politicians on both sides of the slavery aisle avoided the term while privately believing there may have been something to it. (Before Lincoln's election, Republican papers said slavery was "seated in the President's chair, ruling in the Council chamber, judging on the bench of the Supreme Court, moving to and fro armed among Senators and Representatives.")[20] Only control of the federal government, opponents of slavery felt, kept the institution from collapsing of its own flaws. The suspicion that the South was being propped up by something other than merely cotton sales was troubling to many in the "mainstream."

For example, the Cincinnati *Daily Commercial*, a more mainstream business paper, concluded, "There is such a thing as the SLAVE POWER," in 1857. At times, it was difficult to distinguish between the pressing interests of all slaveholders and those of a group of elitists mysteriously pulling strings behind the stage. Attempts to blame the efforts to reopen the slave trade were routinely assigned to the slave power, when in fact many Southern slaveholders supported the idea. Likewise, calls by Southerners to expand American boundaries to include more slave territory was a widely held goal not requiring a group of secret extremists. When the prospect of acquiring Cuba from Spain briefly surfaced, then-senator from Mississippi, Jefferson Davis, brazenly announced, "Cuba must be ours!"[21] Mississippi's other US senator, Albert Brown, went further, urging the acquisition of Central American states. "I want these Countries," he admitted, "for the spread of slavery. I would spread the blessings of slavery, like a religion of our Divine Master."[22] Such comments convinced Northerners that the South even intended to bring slavery to their own doorsteps. Gamaliel Bailey, writing in 1844, cited "a deliberate plot" to extend slavery "over almost illimitable regions."[23] Brown said as much, declaring he would extend slavery into the North, though not by force. Both Georgia senator Robert Toombs, who promised to one day call the roll of his slaves on Bunker Hill, and New York senator William H. Seward of New York knew that extending slavery across all of America was not just the crackpot notion of a handful of agitators, but a deeply held feeling in the South. Seward, however, did see the hand of the slave power behind the Mexican War, the events in Kansas, and the Compromise of 1850.[24]

Certainly it wasn't the "Slave Power" that led the United States, in 1854, to offer Spain $130 million for Cuba (which Spain rejected). The *New York Herald* was not a Southern paper, but it was part of the Slave Swamp. It proclaimed in March 1854, "Now is the time to get Cuba."[25] Word spread that slave uprisings in Cuba were making the island ungovernable, and a group of American ministers in Ostend, Belgium, drafted a confidential memorandum urging the US government to simply take Cuba in such a situation. This "Ostend Manifesto" leaked out to the public, and President Franklin Pierce had to repudiate it.

Foreign intrigue continued though: in 1850 Mississippi governor John Quitman met with a Venezuelan adventurer named Narciso Lopez to lead an expedition of mercenaries to liberate Cuba from Spain. Quitman did not want to leave the governor's mansion at the time, but assisted Lopez in outfitting the expedition. Charged with violating the Neutrality Act of 1817, Quitman barely escaped jail with three hung juries. Three years later, Tennessean William Walker launched a scheme to conquer several Mexican territories and establish a new "Republic of Lower California." After several months, he had to withdraw due to lack of supplies and Mexican resistance. Walker inspired Quitman to give Cuba another try. Encouraged by President Franklin Pierce, Quitman and Mansfield Lovell began planning a new "filibuster" (as such expeditions were called) into Cuba in mid-1853. They had several thousand men equipped and ready to invade when Pierce's administration abruptly withdrew its support. The Kansas-Nebraska Act had just passed and had stirred up a hornet's nest as both Free Soilers and proslave settlers flooded into the new state to determine its future. Pierce feared that the Democrat Party—which was already reeling from the act—would be fatally damaged if a proslave filibuster to Cuba looked like it, too, would add new slave territory to the Union.

No sooner had Quitman failed than Walker resurfaced, this time invading Nicaragua. He supported one side in a Nicaraguan civil war and in return received a contract from the president of Nicaragua, Francisco Castellon, to bring up to 300 "colonists" into the country. These, of course, were more of Walker's mercenaries. But the man was successful: Walker defeated the "Legitimist" army and was himself recognized as president by Pierce. He immediately repealed Nicaragua's laws prohibiting slavery. Nicaragua's neighbors had had enough. Costa Rica and Honduras, with support from American shipping magnate Cornelius Vanderbilt, sent in forces and defeated Walker. Upon his surrender, he was repatriated to the United States, released, then started yet another expedition; was arrested again, and released yet a second time. One would think Walker would have learned, but he *again* returned to Nicaragua where the British captured him and handed him off to Honduras, who had him shot by firing squad.[26]

Based on the Quitman and Walker expeditions and the Ostend Manifesto, it was neither hyperbole nor fantasy about a slave power to admit that the South had as a sectional goal for over two decades sought footholds in Cuba, Mexico, and even Central America as a means of expanding slave territory. It was not paranoid of the North to think that by the end of the Mexican War, that the South wanted to make New Mexico, Utah, California, and Texas all slave states (and had succeeded already with Texas), or that Nicaragua and Cuba might become part of a "vast slave empire."[27] Historian David Potter, in fact, argued that the South sacrificed the "Cuban substance for a Kansan shadow" in the

1850s, and very easily could have added Cuba to the Union.[28] In short, while the power of a "slaveocracy" may have been exaggerated, certainly its goals seemed to align perfectly with those of the slave South as a whole, again and again.

Depriving any group of rights always risked the possibility that other groups might similarly see their rights infringed. Slavery for some people posed a constant threat to the liberties of all—Lincoln would say so repeatedly. Northern antislavery papers drove to the heart of the matter for new immigrants: "What security have the Germans and Irish that their children will not, within a hundred years, be reduced to slavery….?"[29]

Among abolitionist circles, the "slave power conspiracy" concept was best popularized by Frederick Douglass and Horace Greeley.[30] Admittedly, the numbers at times did not seem to add up. Only about 12 percent of all Southerners owned slaves, and 36 percent of Southern farms in fertile valley regions had no slaves at all, suggesting to some the Slave Swamp was a figment of abolitionists' imagination. Until recently, even some of the most vocal advocates of a "Slave Power conspiracy" had little quantitative data on just how important slavery was to the South. Notions that slavery was not profitable were demolished by many studies between 1950 and 1975, culminating with the controversial book by Robert Fogel and Stanley Engerman, *Time on the Cross*.[31] Farms with slaves were much more productive than those without slaves and, Fogel and Engerman found, gains increased as farm size increased.

For many years—up until the 1950s however—many still believed the myth that slavery was not profitable. This came partly from anecdotal evidence of Free Soil advocates such as Frank Blair, who touted the advantages of free farms ("no one from a slave state could pass through the splendid farms of Sangamon and Morgan, without permitting an envious sigh to escape him at the evident superiority of free labor").[32] Some historians, such as Ulrich Bonnell Phillips and Charles Sydnor, found difficulty rationalizing the immorality of slavery with a free-market system, drew selected evidence from plantation records and owners' own "poor-me" comments. Plantations they concluded, were losing money because the owners said they were.[33] Only later did economists discover that the Bonnell/Sydnor analysis missed something rather important: that slaves *themselves* were property, and as such, had value that needed to be included in profitability calculations. Suddenly, the importance of slavery took on a whole new light.

On the eve of the Civil War, in fact, as Paul Johnson pointed out, "Virginia was living on its slave-capital…it was selling its blacks to the Deep South."[34] Professor Thomas Dew of William & Mary College in 1852 wrote in his book *The Pro-Slavery Argument* that Virginia was a "*negro-raising* state for other states" (emphasis his).[35] Structurally, the slave edifice existed because the slave trade had ended: this, ironically, drove the prices of remaining slaves in America up. It also accounts for the practical—if not theoretical—failure of all efforts at "gradual, compensated emancipation," a catchphrase for any resolution to slavery short of abolition. Under gradual, compensated emancipation (a concept Lincoln embraced for a short time), slaveowners would be compensated for newly freed slaves. Market forces, of course, meant that under such a plan each remaining slave would see his value increased. In theory, the more slaves who were emancipated under such a plan, the higher the cost to free each additional slave until finally the cost would be prohibitive. And, slave breeders could merely add more slaves to the overall pool. Lincoln would eventually realize there was no resolution short of total national emancipation without compensation.

If one moves away from images of cigar-smoke-filled back-room conspiracies, the reality of the Slave Swamp was obvious. According to the 1860 census, slaves accounted for $3 billion in wealth, "an amount exceeding the investments in railroads and manufacturing combined!"[36] Of the eleven wealthiest states by 1860, slave states accounted for ten of them.[37] Thomas Dew calculated that in 1831 Virginia slaves were worth $94 million, while all the houses and land in the state were worth $206 million. Slaves alone, he observed, represented more than one-third of all the wealth in the Commonwealth.[38] It is notable that repeatedly pro-slave voices themselves fixed the value of slavery at extremely dizzying heights: John C. Calhoun put the number at $900 million; James De Bow, in 1850 estimated that slavery constituted over $2 billion in wealth;

Governor James Pettus of Mississippi in 1857 said slave property exceeded $2.6 billion; and Mississippi's J. Curry fixed the number in 1860 at "a property valued at $3,000,000,000."[39] Economic historian James Huston calculated that planters with over 20 slaves were just .5 percent of the US population yet controlled slaves worth over $1.5 billion—more than the entire investment in railroads in 1860.[40]

One implication of this new research has been to show that to a very large degree, the clash over the territories—and the Civil War itself—was largely a conflict over the definition of property rights. Historian James Huston argued, "The property rights argument was the ultimate defense of slavery, and white Southerners and the proslavery radicals knew it [and] the weak point in the protection of slavery by property rights was the federal government."[41] Non-slaveholders participated in the national government and, the Slave Swamp reasoned, since they did not possess the perspective or financial investment in the slave system, they were much more likely to support laws that weakened the property rights in slaves in the South. The fear was that at some point, the federal government could, with a single vote of Congress, change the definition of property—namely state that people could not be property. And this threat was most prominent in the territories where slavery could still be prohibited.

When Southerners spoke of "States' Rights," they really meant "the right to own slaves." Alabama's Franklin Bowdon warned, "If any of these rights can be invaded, then there is no security for the remainder."[42] It went deeper than that, however. As James Oakes shows in *Freedom National*, the presumption among both pro- and antislave advocates prior to the 1830s had been that the Constitution protected *property* in slaves. Instead, rereading the text of the Constitution, abolitionist forces forced a new line of argument: that the Constitution differentiated between servile persons who were put in such a status as state law and chattel slaves. The latter, they argued correctly, did not exist in the Constitution. If slaves were "persons," then, the Constitution was on their side at the federal level. Freedom was national, slavery local. Lincoln approached it from this position, namely that if one group of people could be condemned to slavery for their race, another could suffer the same fate for their religious convictions, or their political affiliations.[43] "Persons" had *natural* rights that superseded the laws of a government.

Lincoln's diametric opposite, Virginia writer George Fitzhugh, agreed with him that free and slave states could not live together.[44] The notion was absurd. Fitzhugh, an ardent reader of Karl Marx and a self-avowed Communist who argued for enslaving white and black alike under the pretense that such an arrangement would address basic needs better than capitalism, answered the question Lincoln once thought "too mighty" to decide. Fitzhugh said, "Two opposite and conflicting forms of society cannot, among civilized men, co-exist and endure."[45]

But the power of the Slave Swamp was even more pronounced due to the fact that small farmers in the South feared free blacks more than they disliked the unequal competition with slaves. It was the large majority of small non-slaveholding farmers who supported the ban on slave marriages; the prohibition in five states against teaching a slave to read or write; and the restrictions on slaves giving testimony in court. Lincoln and the Republicans believed that a "cordon of freedom" around the slave South, with the federal government in the hands of Free Soilers, would enact national laws that states were subject to, including opening the mails to abolitionist literature. This, they held, would open up the South to voices resistant to slavery and, ultimately, bring about the demise of the Slave Swamp.

Quite the opposite of the twenty-first century when critics elevated the "Q" phenomenon to influence it never had in order to paint all conservatives as conspiracy-minded lunatics, in the mid-1800s Fitzhugh's arguments were muffled, lest they paint slaveowners as too extreme. Perhaps even more important, a century later liberal historians sought to characterize the Virginian as outside the fold of proslave defenses, precisely *because* Fitzhugh was entirely accurate in his assessment of slavery and communism as essentially the same in outcome. Were Fitzhugh to be allowed to become the apex of proslavery voices, it would portray modern leftist/liberalism in exceptionally unfavorable light. Better to let Fitzhugh be the 1850s equivalent of Q.

Unfortunately for both slavery advocates of the day and modern leftists, other proslave voices soon picked up Fitzhugh's arguments that slavery was the only system that protected the laborer. T. R. R. Cobb observed that under slavery labor and capital ceased to be at odds and the war of the employer and laborer in the factory system disappeared.[46]

Slaveholders concocted a boogeyman to keep the non-slaveholding farmers in line. The North, they said, was seeking to turn the South into a vassal state with its trade and tariff policies. Only a few questioned why the plantation owners insisted on growing only cotton, rice, sugar, and tobacco—cash crops that all required massive workforces of unfree labor and annual loans. Instead, they shifted the focus to Northern economic policies. At times, Southern spokesmen couldn't decide whether to demonize such policies or ridicule them. "Free society!" exclaimed one Alabama paper. "We sicken of the name! What is it but a conglomeration of greasy mechanics, filthy operatives, small-fisted farmers, and moon-struck theorists?"[47] Similarly, the *Charleston Mercury* warned that a free society consisted of a "servile class of mechanics and laborers, unfit for self-government, and yet clothed with the attributes and powers of citizens."[48] (It is worth noting that similar sneering condescension against lower- and middle-class workers in America characterized much of the Democrat Party's rhetoric in the elections of 2008, 2012, 2016, and 2020.) Nevertheless, the propaganda worked. By the late 1850s, the planters often—though less in reality than they believed—saw themselves as living in the grip of Northern bankers, factors, and "stock-jobbers." These Northern capitalists, as we shall see, became a component themselves of the "slave power conspiracy" at the very time that many Southerners saw them as part of another conspiracy…aimed at them!

Then there were the secession conventions themselves. Born of extremely restricted votes, often derived from state legislatures, secession "conventions" were completely controlled by the Slave Swamp. Georgia's vote was 208-89, meaning that 297 men in the state decided the outcome. In Arkansas, the secession ordinance passed by only 5 votes out of 70. South Carolina's ordinance, of course, was lopsided, with all 169 delegates voting to leave the Union. Overall, the secession conventions totaled 854 men who met to decide the fate of the South, mostly wealthy slaveowners. Of these, 157 voted to stay in the Union. Thus, fewer than 700 mostly wealthy slaveowners decided the future of some nine million Southerners, most of them non-slaveowners. Declarations for secession ranged from "insult[ing] and outrag[ing] citizens" (Mississippi) to simple Lincoln hatred (South Carolina).[49] In January 1861, Jefferson Davis explained to a friend that the South had merely transferred its institutions from hostile to friendly hands. Yet at the very moment secession occurred, the South and Democrats had a majority in both houses of Congress; and the United States Supreme Court had only four years earlier handed the South the most lopsided and poorly reasoned decision in favor of slavery that could be imagined. It was with these levers of power—control over Congress, the Supreme Court, a sharp edge in America's wealth, near-complete censorship within the press and the mails—that the South chose war.

Aside from the four-way presidential election of 1860 in which the Slave Swamp in a hissy fit threw away its greatest single asset, the South controlled all but the truth. Jefferson Davis was doing his level best to ensure that no conflicting opinions were tolerated in the South. Seeking censorship and a "cancel culture" that would mirror that of the modern-day politically correct "woke" movements, Davis wanted education to "indoctrinate [children's] minds with sound impressions and views," and sought to kick out "Yankee schoolteachers."[50] Churches in the South had already exorcised all abolitionist sermons and teaching. It is hard, therefore, to imagine a situation where one section, party, or political perspective wielded such significant advantages. The South not only had a "Slave Power Conspiracy"—it had the Slave Swamp.

Into this maw stepped Abraham Lincoln. At one time in the not-distant past, the details of Lincoln's life would be common knowledge to schoolchildren. Born in Kentucky in 1809 to a poor family, Lincoln moved with his family to Indiana where Lincoln's mother died. He had already learned to read, educating himself with the Bible, *Robinson Crusoe*, Franklin's autobiography, and Gibbon's *Decline and Fall of the Roman Empire*. When his father moved the family again, this time to

Illinois, Lincoln memorized the Illinois statutes. In particular he studied the Bible as much for its literary value as for its theology: he came to appreciate syncopation, rhythm, and techniques such as assonance, consonance, and alliteration.[51]

Standing 6'4", Lincoln was physically strong. He worked hard labor jobs, first on the farms, then on flatboats. (He remains the only US President ever to hold a patent—for a flotation device that could lift a flatboat off a sandbar.) Known for his character, sincerity, and humor, Lincoln suffered from depression, hypochondria—or the "hypos," as he called it. "I never dare carry a penknife," he once joked.[52] After studying law, he learned the sting of business failure firsthand when a partner took off with the store's cash and left Lincoln with obligations exceeding $1,000. To pay those off, he took odd jobs including rail splitting. He served in the Black Hawk War, was a town postmaster, then a Whig state assemblyman in 1834. Two years later, with a law license in hand, Lincoln began taking cases for insurance companies and railroads, earning a reputation as a solid attorney in his partnership with William Herndon. This came despite a personal inclination toward disorganization and even chaos. When he won his seat in Congress in 1847, his entire campaign expenditure was a seventy-five-cent barrel of cider. His opposition to the Mexican War, wherein he introduced the so-called "Spot Resolutions," put him on the national map.

But seemingly as quickly as he rose, he disappeared. Zachary Taylor did not give him a patronage job after winning the 1848 election. He returned to his law practice. His partner, William Herndon, became a friend and advisor. Lincoln was a Whig who said, "I am in favor of the internal improvements system, and a high protective tariff."[53] Then came his run against Stephen Douglas for the US Senate seat from Illinois. His state convention speech at Springfield, considered one of the greatest political speeches in American history, reviewed the perpetual failure of compromises to deal with slavery. "A house divided against itself cannot stand," he said, again quoting the Bible. "I do not expect the house to fall—but I do expect that it will cease to be divided."[54]

Slavery troubled Lincoln on the deepest personal level. Not as incendiary as abolitionists like William Lloyd Garrison, who would burn down the Constitution itself to destroy slavery, Lincoln spoke of "our progress in degeneracy." Slavery put America in a "death-struggle." The "heart is wrung," he said, when he observed slaves in Ohio.[55] Yet he did not chain slavery to religion, either—that would only come later, as he began to see the war as America's atonement for the sin of slavery. This also was classic Lincoln, who hesitated to impose biblical overtones onto what he saw as predominantly political questions. As would Ronald Reagan 120 years later, Lincoln separated the individual from the policy, perhaps holding out hope that enough logic and good will could overcome fundamental disagreements about human nature.

Much attention has been paid to the "House Divided" speech, but little emphasis has been placed on the notion of definitions of property. This lay at the heart of the matter. As the Slave Swamp well knew, if slaves were defined as people in court, then sooner or later the definition of people as property would meet defeat everywhere. It was this aspect of slavery in the territories that Chief Justice Roger Taney had sought to stamp out, once and for all, in the Dred Scott case. Yet that wasn't the tack Lincoln took in dissecting his opponent, Stephen Douglas, who was the Democrat mouthpiece for the Slave Swamp.

Douglas was a politician *par excellence.* He was better than Henry Clay at fence straddling. Often called "The Judge," Douglas was one of those Northerners "personally opposed" to slavery, but who would take no action that would actually prevent it (similar to many politicians today who are "personally opposed" to abortion but always wiggle out of legislating against it). Although he was a politician—like Lincoln—the similarities ended there. Douglas was short and squat, Lincoln tall and lanky. Douglas had a stentorian voice as opposed to Lincoln's high-pitched shrill delivery. He had, like Lincoln, worked with his hands as a younger man, but climbed the ladder quickly as a lawyer, legislator, secretary of state of Illinois, senator; then married a pair of Southern heiresses. But he had money in his own right.[56] (Lincoln, it should be noted, was not poor due to his railroad and bank litigation.) Douglas traveled extensively, met royalty, and arrived in a carriage drawn by six horses. He found Lincoln a hayseed irritant.

Lincoln found Douglas deceptive. He had little respect for him: "He is a man with tens of thousands of blind followers. It is my business to make some of those blind followers see."[57] It was also clear to Lincoln that Douglas was the 1850s equivalent to the modern politician who talked tough, but whose only goal was to protect the status quo. By adopting the principle of "popular sovereignty," a concept first introduced by Lewis Cass of Michigan in which the people of a state can choose whether to accept slavery or not, Douglas sought to foist the burden of deciding a difficult question off to the citizens of the states as opposed to the federal government. At the same time, he sought to maintain solidarity with his "base," the Slave Swamp in the South, by claiming to support the Dred Scott decision.

Dred Scott was a slave of a US Army surgeon, John Emerson. As Emerson moved from base to base, he took Scott, first to Fort Armstrong in Illinois (a free state), then to Fort Snelling in Wisconsin territory (which was free territory under the Northwest Ordinance and prohibited under the Missouri Compromise law). Emerson moved yet again, to Missouri, in 1837, but left Scott in Wisconsin where he leased out his services, thereby bringing slavery into a free state (just as Lincoln predicted). Scott had been married in a civil ceremony to Harriet Robinson, a woman whose master, Major Lawrence Taliaferro, permitted the wedding. He gave the bride away and later claimed he freed Harriet Scott. Even the wedding itself complicated matters as slaves could not marry. When Emerson moved to Fort Jesup in Louisiana, he married Eliza Irene Sanford, then sent for Scott and his wife. On the steamboat journey southward, Scott's wife had a daughter, Eliza, somewhere in free territory. At that point, many scholars think Scott should have filed for his freedom in Louisiana, which tended to observe laws of free states when slaveholders lost their rights to slaves who were brought into free territory for any length of time.[58] After returning to Iowa in 1843, Emerson died and his widow, Irene, inherited the Scotts, whom she continued to hire out. In 1846, Scott tried to purchase his own and his family's freedom, but Irene Emerson refused.

With some abolitionist legal advisors, Scott sued Emerson for his freedom in Missouri in 1846, citing his residence in free territories and a free state. The court ruled against Scott, saying that Mrs. Emerson had not actually enslaved him. (As David Hardy shows, Scott's attorneys committed a significant error by failing to produce a single witness who could confirm Scott was actually a slave—a necessity in a "Freedom Suit.") In a second, delayed trial, Scott won, and Mrs. Emerson appealed to the Missouri Supreme Court. By that time, she transferred ownership of Scott to her brother John Sanford. The Missouri Supreme Court overturned the lower court's decision to free Scott with bizarre reasoning that basically amounted to, "Things have changed since the earlier decision."[59] It concluded that a slave who had gained his freedom and returned to a slave state forfeited his claim to freedom. After losing his lawyers, and acquiring new ones, Scott sued John Sanford, Mrs. Emerson's brother.

This seemed odd. Sanford was a New Yorker who played little role in the matter and technically Irene Emerson was still the owner. But as Hardy pointed out, the answer to the mystery lay in Mrs. Emerson's new husband, Calvin Chaffee, a Massachusetts "Know Nothing" who would soon become a Republican. Not only was he antislave in his views, but he was an aspiring politician. At the same time, John Sanford had married into the St. Louis slaveholding Chouteau family that pressured him to fight the freedom suit. Sanford could protect Chaffee and his sister, and at the same time satisfy his new in-laws, so he acted as a stand-in for Irene Emerson.

The case went before a federal court, which upheld the Missouri ruling, so Scott appealed to the US Supreme Court. On March 6, 1857, the court ruled against Scott 7-2 with Chief Justice Roger Taney writing the majority (and most-cited) opinion in what was the worst Supreme Court decision in American history. Taney said that black African slaves "were not intended to be included, under the word 'citizens' in the Constitution." He could have stopped there, but addressed the constitutionality of the Missouri Compromise claiming that by freeing slaves living north of the 36 degree 30 minute line, that would violate the property rights of the owners. Taney ruled both congressional efforts to address slavery *and* popular sovereignty by territories as unlawful: only a state that had already become a state could then vote to exclude slavery. The default position, then, was always slavery.[60]

Lincoln disagreed: "The right of property in a slave is *not* distinctly and expressly affirmed in the Constitution." Quite the opposite, the natural rights of *personhood* were, and whenever property rights came into conflict with the rights of persons, he favored persons over property. This came from a long-standing tradition in both English and American law that said that a person's right to property *in himself* is the primary natural right of all—the right to life and liberty.[61] James Madison, the primary author of the Constitution, agreed, saying it was "wrong to admit in the Constitution the idea that there could be property in men."[62]

Nothing smelled of Slave Swamp more than the Dred Scott decision. It effectively reversed the rising presumption that freedom was national, slavery local. Taney had gone out of his way to make it all but impossible for any governmental institution to prohibit slavery at any point except after statehood...*with* slavery. He had turned the presumption of "Freedom National," as Republican Isaac Arnold described the presumption that human rights (including to liberty) superseded property rights. Moreover, Taney had attacked the very foundations of the Republican/abolitionist constitutional challenge to slavery, namely that the Constitution referred to "persons," or "unfree persons" and not slaves, and *in no place* did the Constitution support chattel slavery as a national institution. Rather, it was assumed that freedom was national, and slavery a locally protected "peculiar" institution.[63] The decision sent an economic shock wave across the country, putting east–west railroad stocks into a tailspin and instigating the Panic of 1857, although it was not until the end of the twentieth century that scholars finally realized the financial impact of the case.[64] More immediately, the Slave Swamp seemed to have won again. What it could not secure by legislation in the Compromise of 1850 and the Fugitive Slave Law, it now had obtained by judicial activism.

For Douglas, however, the decision was a disaster. How could he reconcile the freedom of people to prohibit slavery in territories when Taney's court clearly said they could not? His logical gymnastics were worthy of a performance by Nadia Comaneci. The people, he insisted, still could prohibit the Peculiar Institution: "Slavery cannot exist a day in the midst of an unfriendly people with unfriendly laws."[65] Again: "It matters not what way the Supreme Court may...decide as to the abstract question of whether slavery may or may not go into a Territory.... The people have the lawful means to introduce it or exclude it as they please."[66] And yet again: "These regulations...must necessarily depend entirely upon the will and wishes of the people of the territory, as they can only be prescribed by the local legislatures."[67]

Lincoln had forced Douglas into giving people in the territories reason to break the national law supporting slavery. Douglas's view, immortalized as the "Freeport Doctrine" (as he outlined it at the Freeport debate), alienated his Southern support and ended his hopes for the presidency, though in the short run he won the Senate contest with Lincoln. On a higher plane, Lincoln had cast the argument of republicanism against democracy in the purest sense of their definitions. A democracy could literally enslave anyone with a majority vote. In their final debate, Lincoln said that the real issue was that one group "looks upon the institution of slavery *as a wrong*.... The Republican Party look[s] upon it as being a moral, social and political wrong." One way to treat it as wrong was to "*make provision that it shall grow no larger*...." (emphasis Lincoln's).[68]

Far from ridiculous modern revisionists such as Howard Zinn who saw Lincoln as little more than a political opportunist—Zinn wrote that Lincoln kept abolition "close enough to the top" of his priorities that it could be used for political advantage—Lincoln held his views for many years and knew they were unpopular.[69] (To damn Lincoln, Zinn had to quote him as little as possible on slavery.) Lincoln, like any politician, said different things to different audiences. He repeatedly rejected full political and social rights for blacks, as he said to voters in Southern Illinois.[70] At the same time, further north, Lincoln urged unity "until we shall once more stand up declaring that all men are created equal."[71] Lincoln always sought a peaceful resolution to slavery, entertaining a number of less-than-desirable half measures that nevertheless would have prevented a war that killed over 650,000. To someone like Zinn (as to all leftists) such bloodshed on behalf of a cause was irrelevant. Of course, it is always with the blood of others.

Yet from an early age, Lincoln knew what was right and eventually what must transpire. He said in 1839, "I standing up boldly and alone and hurling defiance" at the oppressors of American liberty. "Here without contemplating consequences, before High Heaven…I swear eternal fidelity to the just cause, as I deem it, of the land of my life, my liberty, and my love…."[72] Lincoln walked a thin line, constantly stating something few others in his position would, that slavery was "founded on injustice and bad policy," but that a war to eliminate it would be disastrous and could end the only chance to eliminate slavery nationally. Therefore, he likewise denounced abolitionists (who wanted the immediate end of slavery nationally) and slaveholders.[73]

Lincoln was unequivocal and straightforward in all of his statements related to slavery. In spite of efforts by leftists such as Zinn to muddy the waters and portray him as malleable, Lincoln said, for example, "I believe that the right of property in a slave is *not* distinctly and expressly affirmed in the Constitution."[74] Like so many others, Lincoln believed for a time at least in the "natural limits" of slavery; that conditions in the cotton South favored slavery but that strong market forces would drive it out of business regardless of moral views about it. He gave up on this. Nevertheless, a key element of the natural limits argument was that no matter what, slavery could not be permitted to expand beyond the South. Debating Stephen Douglas in 1858, Lincoln said, "God did not place good and evil before man, telling him to make his choice. On the contrary, he did tell him there was one tree, of the fruit of which, he should not eat, upon pain of certain death. I should scarcely wish so strong a prohibition against slavery in Nebraska."[75]

These weren't the words of a political opportunist. Indeed, Lincoln biographer Stephen Oates credits Lincoln with both killing the Whig Party and creating the Republican Party in Illinois in mid-1856 in

Bloomington, where he delivered the "Lost Speech." There is no written record of what he said. Even William Herndon, a perpetual note-taker, was so mesmerized he quit taking notes. When Lincoln finished, "the crowd jumped up and cheered him again and again. On Lincoln's key-note address, the Republican Party was born in Illinois and the Whig Party...was dead."[76] One spectator looked at Lincoln in wonder: "At this moment, he looked to me the handsomest man I had ever seen in my life."[77] Herndon praised the speech as "full of fire and energy and force. It was logic. It was pathos. It was enthusiasm. It was justice, equity, truth and right set alight by the divine fires of a soul maddened by the wrong. It was hard, heavy, knotty, gnarly, backed with wrath."[78]

Arguing against the Slave Swamp, Lincoln arrived at the nub of slavery's immorality: "If A. can prove, however conclusively, that he may of right, enslave B.—why may not B. snatch the argument, and prove equally, that he may enslave A.?" He then attacked the logic by color: "You say A. is white, and B. is black. It is *color*, then: The lighter, having the right to enslave the darker? Take care. By this rule, you are to be a slave to the first man you meet with a fairer skin than your own." Or, was slavery determined by intellect? "Take care again," Lincoln warned. "By this rule you are to be slave to the first man you meet, with an intellect superior to your own."[79] The *Richmond Enquirer* had already made just that argument, declaring that "the laws of the slave states justify the holding of white men in bondage." Its sister publication, the *Richmond Examiner*, agreed, saying that "the principle of slavery is in itself right, and does not depend upon difference in complexion.... Slavery black or white is necessary."[80] Little did Douglas realize that already in the North, ordinary citizens were ignoring the Fugitive Slave Law, which required free Northerners to assist in apprehending runaway slaves in their states.

Defeating the Slave Swamp required, in Lincoln's view, adherence to the laws. He had emphasized in his 1838 Lyceum Address that reverence for the laws should "be breathed by every American mother to the lisping babe that prattles on her lap; let it be taught in schools, in seminaries, and in colleges; let it be written in primers, spelling-books, and in almanacs; let it be preached from the pulpit, proclaimed in the legislative halls, and enforced in courts of justice."[81] Lincoln's admonition would have at that time been just as well served if it were delivered to the Attorney General's office, the FBI, the state legislatures, and the court system during the presidency of Donald Trump, when *every single one* failed to even obliquely enforce or apply the laws.

Because of his reverence for the laws, Lincoln sincerely hoped—possibly even believed—that the South would not secede. He affirmed the laws when he said, "I have no purpose, directly or indirectly, to interfere with the institution of slavery in the States where it exists. I believe I have no lawful right to do so, and I have no inclination to do so."[82] To leftists such as Howard Zinn, these comments meant that Lincoln was a coward. Quite the contrary, he was one of the few courageous men in the nation for *both* opposing slavery and insisting that it be dealt with constitutionally and legally. He did not need to "interfere" with slavery: merely relying on the widespread "spoils system" created by one of his predecessors, Martin Van Buren, Lincoln could sharply tilt the scales against slavery entirely within the context of the law. By denationalizing slavery, Lincoln and others believed, it would weaken it so much it would collapse locally. Southerners readily grasped this: one Louisiana secessionist paper blared, Lincoln and the Republicans "will set fire to all the surrounding buildings in the hope that some spark may catch, and everything will be destroyed in a general conflagration. They will undermine the pillars of the institution, and then wait quietly for the whole edifice to tumble."[83]

Salmon Chase, exulting in Lincoln's victory, wrote that one of the "great objects" of his life, "the overthrow of the Slave Power, is now happily accomplished."[84] A jubilant Henry Ward Beecher announced, "The power of the slave interest is broken."[85] They perceived that indeed the denationalization of slavery would follow. Southern papers, such as the *Daily True Delta*, agreed: the election of Lincoln would be "the death knell of social a political prosperity in the south."[86]

Therefore, even though we will do so at length in the next chapter, it is necessary to review the creation of the "spoils system" in the 1820s. Simply put, the "spoils system" or patronage was a deliberate strategy woven into the creation of the Democrat Party as a means to ensure perpetual power for Democrats and, by extension, protection and perpetuation of the slave system in America. Martin Van Buren, at the time a congressman, feared that the imbalance between free and slave states created by the Missouri Compromise would soon lead to free states voting to eliminate slavery, which in turn would lead to secession and war. He therefore founded a new political party, the Democrats, on the basis of rewarding people for party loyalty with party and government jobs. The more a person "got out the vote" for the party, the bigger his patronage reward. Van Buren believed this promise of jobs or money would cause antislavery Northerners to ignore their views on slavery and impose a legislative gag rule on the institution nationally.

One key element in Van Buren's plan was to ensure that the "right" man was elected president. He knew that no Deep South slaveowner could ever get elected again after James Monroe's term ended in 1824. Likewise, no antislave activist could win the presidency. A president would have to be a westerner (like Andrew Jackson, who, though having been a slaveowner, was considered "pure" because of his western credentials) or a Northerner who was sympathetic to slavery. His plan worked. From 1828–1860, every elected president was either a westerner or a slave-sympathetic Northerner. (The only Deep South president was John Tyler of Virginia, who came into office with William Henry Harrison's death—and Harrison himself was a westerner from Indiana.)

What Van Buren ignored was the fact that even if the Democrats had no opposition, the federal government would slowly grow in size and influence. If it *did* have an opponent, that rate of increase would accelerate. When Abraham Lincoln was elected—a Northern antislavery man—the government had grown dramatically from when Andy Jackson had entered office. Uncle Sam had 36,500 civilian employees (all but 6,500 of them postmasters) plus a standing army and navy of 28,000. With Lincoln's election, many of the patronage jobs that in Van Buren's scheme would have been used to reward Democrat followers now fell into the hands of a "Black Republican." These were not innocuous positions. Whereas county and town positions still commanded most of the power apparent in everyday life, federal appointees included such key posts as

US marshals, federal judges, customs agents, and of course the ubiqui-
tous postmasters. Each of these stood to significantly affect the strength
of local slavery laws and the culture as it related to tolerance of slavery.
Marshals could simply refuse to track down runaways; postmasters could
defy censorship edicts and allow in abolitionist materials (including the
number one bestseller of the age, *Uncle Tom's Cabin*); judges could rule in
favor of slaves if given the opportunity; and customs officials could refuse
to enforce laws keeping free black merchantmen on their vessels while
in port. In other words, President Lincoln could severely damage slavery
without doing a single thing to actually target it, just as he promised.[87]

Lincoln's intuition that the Law (versus "laws") was emblazoned
on the hearts of Americans was evident in another legacy of Van Buren
and Jacksonianism, namely the concept of rotation in office. While it
was flawed in the sense that virtually any man could *not* do any job in
government—there were skills required for certain positions—it was
nevertheless a widespread judgment until the late 1800s and the rise of
"professionals" in government that usually even the poorest performing
ordinary citizen could govern almost as well as a trained lawyer or judge.
And elections were decided, by and large, not by uneducated hicks but
by voters who were informed on issues: turnout was exceptionally high
(averaging over 75 percent for much of the nineteenth century, and if the
South is removed from the equation, turnout often was over 80 percent).[88]

Why is this important? Because it shows that Americans internalized
"the Law" in local and state elections, that they were well informed, and
that Americans were a political people. It also means that a threat to
order, that is, demonstrations of *disorder*, were deeply troubling to the
American psyche in both sections of the country. (It should be noted that
even William Seward's "Higher Law" speech did not, in fact, deny the
authority of the Constitution because the principles of the "higher law"
were already embedded in the Constitution.)

In the South, this concern (even paranoia) was funneled almost
exclusively at the possibility of slave revolts. Even in the North though,
"mobbing," which overwhelmingly involved one aspect of slavery or another—from free blacks "taking" white jobs to whipped up abolitionist

hordes who targeted unfortunate Southerners—were clear expressions of disorder. That deeply concerned the public. As Americans had advanced all the way to California, each step from cattle towns to mining camps had featured a rapid and decisive effort to bring "law and order." Often this came first from private groups (the cattlemen's organizations, mining claims clubs), then to official law enforcement agents authorized by towns to keep the peace.

In sum, the advance of slavery, and the chaos it was bringing, threatened both local government and, more important, *self-government*, for if the Slave Swamp meant what it often said, free men in the North would soon be enslaved. Lincoln's arguments then constituted a subtle cloth woven of fears that destruction of the Union meant destruction of all government, at all levels. Douglas's arguments were over a century too early. He implored, through popular sovereignty, "If it feels good, do it." Lincoln was the parent, warning that something that feels good at the moment might kill you. In the 1850s, Americans still listened to their parents.

As sectional tensions rose, slavery—in direct contravention of the purposes of the Democrat Party—emerged at the heart of every debate. First, in a debate in the Senate over land in 1830, the "Webster-Hayne Debate," although superficially the discussions centered on the South Carolina nullification crisis, references to slavery and Southern expansion lay at the heart of the issue. Then, during the war with Mexico, a Democrat Pennsylvania congressman David Wilmot had introduced an amendment to an appropriations bill that came to be known as the "Wilmot Proviso," prohibiting slavery in any territory taken in the Mexican War. (Because of the 1836 "gag rule," no legislation dealing with slavery was allowed to even be submitted in the House, but that rule had finally been lifted in 1844: however, Democrat power brokers in both the House and Senate still endeavored to prevent any antislavery legislation from even being discussed.) The appropriation bill died and was not picked up again until 1847, when the House passed the Proviso but the Senate did not. Next followed the Compromise of 1850, where, again, disposition of territory taken in the Mexican War was drenched in concerns about whether the lands would be Free Soil or permit slavery. The Compromise established that California would be free, the Utah-New Mexico Territories would decide their status on the basis of popular sovereignty, and most importantly for the South, a national Fugitive Slave Act required citizens (including Northerners) to assist in catching and returning runaway slaves.

Slavery, thus, emerged as the *key* issue, regardless of what other issues were being discussed. With the Kansas-Nebraska Act of 1854, slavery no longer hid in the shadows but rather emerged as the obvious focus of the legislation that sought to bring in two new states on the basis of popular sovereignty. The result was predictable. In Kansas, proslave and Free Soil settlers and agitators moved in to be the first to establish a government. Although Southerners had the lead and created a capital at Lecompton, Kansas, Free Soilers soon arrived in such numbers that they formed their own government at Topeka. Slavery (and popular sovereignty) had put Kansas in the predicament of having two legislatures and two capitals. Literally, where a person paid his taxes made him an ally or an enemy of one government or the other. The Charleston *Evening News* called the bill a "skillful specimen of...political non-commitalism."[89] Despite a significant bribe by Congress in the form of the "English Bill" that would have added 23.5 million more acres to Kansas if the public would accept the Lecompton government, the voters of Kansas rejected the offer by a 10:1 margin.[90]

America's great historian Allan Nevins summarized the impact of the Kansas-Nebraska Act as follows:

> Northern anger, widespread Southern dissatisfaction, a fierce contest on the Kansas plains, a nascent schism between two schools of the Democratic Party, an embitterment of sectional relations—these were among the direct consequences of the Kansas-Nebraska Act.[91]

Put another way, the Slave Swamp was about far more than plantation owners and a few Southern politicians "controlling" the nation. As

Lincoln well knew, the Slave Swamp *was the status quo* that protected and preserved slavery through inertia, compromise, and willful ignorance.

Kansas devolved into a series of conflicts, culminating with John Brown's murder of five supporters of slavery at the "Pottawatomie Massacre" in May 1856.[92] What is less relevant than how many were actually killed in Kansas is how it was perceived nationally. And the answer to that is, Kansas was seen as the future of America if something wasn't done about slavery. Taney's Dred Scott decision, far from ending the debate, only magnified it. One immediate result was that it triggered the Panic of 1857 as investors worried that "Bleeding Kansas" would soon become "Bleeding [fill in the next territory to apply for statehood]."[93] The peaceful process for admitting states had been destroyed. With it went the law itself. As the first votes for the territorial government of Kansas proceeded, illegality and fraud were rampant. Out of 2,871 votes cast, later it was found that only 1,114 had been legal, and in one county, only 20 legal votes were cast out of 604 total.[94] Even determining what was legal stumped judges observing the process, for no term of residence at all was prescribed.

It was in the wake of Kansas-Nebraska that Lincoln first made clear he intended to re-enter politics, beginning with his "Peoria Speech" in which he said "no man is good enough to govern another man without that other man's consent. I say this is the leading principle—the sheet-anchor of American Republicanism." Americans have been "giving up the old for the new faith," that "for some men to enslave others is a 'sacred right of self-government,' These principles cannot stand together."[95]

By 1859, then, the American river of liberty had split into two main tributaries. Southerners, increasingly disenchanted with federal efforts to protect slavery, spoke with ever-growing conviction and certainty about secession. Northerners, at an equally growing rate, were certain that slavery had been put on the road to extinction and that Southerners would have to just live with that reality. Swimming in these waters, two other realities were clear to those who had eyes: Lincoln was a rising star, not only because of his positions—which were on the side of history and God—but also because of his utter dominance in the media of the day, the public speech, and the newspaper. At a time when a typical speech would easily go an hour and up to three, Lincoln's alliterations, his logic, his ability to tell stories was unmatched in America. He was a political Mark Twain, a Will Rogers endowed with a deep understanding of government.

The other reality was that treading water in this same channel was Stephen Douglas, slowly being dragged down by his own political incompatibilities. While the North stood ready to elevate Lincoln, the South was poised to discard Douglas. Of the two, only the Judge could have carried any votes from Dixie. As Douglas sank into the silt, only Lincoln could ride the current—sectional though it was—to the presidency.

But there was a second, equally important theme the Republicans had developed to their argument via personhood for making freedom national, and it was that if violence occurred, and if the South should secede, then the federal government would have both the authority and the power to emancipate slaves by military force. In fact, this had already happened in the Second Seminole War when the US military had offered freedom to any slaves who ran away from the Seminoles. Following the war, the government honored the military emancipations. If the South engaged in insurrection, and military forces were needed to suppress it, then in wartime the restraint normally in place during peacetime was forfeited. Emancipation was fully accepted under the laws of war. As Salmon Chase said, "Disunion…is abolition."[96]

Meanwhile, John Brown, who had left Kansas, reappeared in Harpers Ferry, Virginia in 1859 with a raid designed to provide weapons for a slave revolt Brown imagined would follow. His band of twenty-two followers was defeated by Marines. Overall command of the operation to seize the arsenal back from Brown was under Col. Robert E. Lee. Brown's raid failed: he was arrested by troops that included Thomas "Stonewall" Jackson and J. E. B. Stuart. The raid sent shockwaves throughout the South, which now more than ever believed that slave uprisings were around the corner.

More important, John Brown's Raid accelerated the lawlessness enveloping the country. From gun battles in Kansas to lynchings to the caning of Charles Sumner by Preston Brooks, the "reverence" for the law that Lincoln aspired to was disappearing rapidly.[97] Historian Phillip Paludan referred to the Civil War itself as a "Crisis of Law and Order," as indeed it was.[98] Specifically, Paludan posed the critical question of the war as: "What was there in the daily experience of most Northerners that made them sensitive and responsive to the images the Union evoked?" Paludan's answer was chaos, disorder, and lawlessness. Phrases such as "contempt for order," "resistance to law," "organized anarchy," "suicide of government," and words such as "despotism," "treason."

Both the Fugitive Slave Law and the Dred Scott decision struck at the apparent contempt for local traditions and elites telling ordinary citizens how to live. In reality, it was an ironic inversion of the Slave Swamp's constant complaints that Northerners were trying to tell *them* how to live.

As if to compound the breakdown of law and order, in 1859, the newly elected Congress found itself so divided it could not even elect a Speaker. The structure collapsed entirely the following November when the presidential race shattered into four parts. Douglas had entered the Democrat Convention as the clear favorite of the majority—but completely unacceptable to the South due to his "Freeport Doctrine." The Alabama State Democrat Convention in January 1860 had already adopted a resolution that committed them to withdrawing if they did not get their program plank opposing popular sovereignty. Mississippi was ready to follow.[99] With Douglas as the candidate of the Democrat Party (but really, only the Northern Democrats), Southerners met in Baltimore to nominate John Breckinridge of Kentucky. Then the newly formed Constitutional Union Party nominated John Bell of Tennessee. Lincoln carried almost 40 percent of the vote to Douglas's 29 percent, but won 180 electoral votes to Breckinridge's 72 and Douglas and Bell's 51 combined. Thus, Lincoln still beat all of his challengers combined in the Electoral College, although their popular votes combined exceeded his by a million votes.

Once Lincoln's election was ensured, the Slave Swamp exerted its power for secession. Opponents, Unionists, and even so-called "moderates" were isolated, scattered, shouted down by the Swamp media of the day. Southerners had been fed a diet of secessionism since the "Tariff of Abominations," to which was added "an ever-deepening hatred for the Free Soil movement in the North."[100] Indeed, just as Northern citizens saw the impending secession as a challenge to social order, the Southerners increasingly saw their future as laying in the disorder caused by "States' Rights" and secession. It didn't matter what Lincoln said, bellowed the Slave Swamp representatives such as James Bayard: a "war which has been carried on for four years by all manner of devices by the antislavery fanatical sentiment" was the "sole cause of the existing disunion excitement."[101] Governor Andrew Moore of Alabama warned that the Republicans had elected a president and would soon have majorities in both houses, and "Slavery will be abolished in the District of Columbia, in the dockyards and arsenals, and wherever the Federal Government has jurisdiction. It will be excluded from the Territories, and other free states...[will be] admitted to the Union, until they have a majority to alter the Constitution. Then slavery will be abolished by law in the States."[102]

It bears repeating that the Slave Swamp understood that while Lincoln may not have been inclined to do anything specifically about slavery, the power of government and the momentum was against the South regardless. Lincoln, though, was not standing still. Later, in 1862, he put it this way in a story he told to Wendell Phillips:

> An Irishman walks into a drugstore in Maine, where liquor can only be sold for medicinal purposes, and orders a shot of whiskey. The druggist sees that the man is clearly healthy and will sell him only soda. "Well, asks the Irishman, can't you 'slip' a little of the stuff into my soda 'unbeknownst to yourself?'"
>
> "That's what I'm doing.... I have 'put a good deal of Anti-slavery' into my policies, 'unbeknownst' to most people."[103]

Swampers therefore repeated and recast Lincoln's "House Divided" prophecies. Lincoln had promised, however, that he would not act against even the seceded states—but he would "hold, occupy, and possess" federal territory, including forts, in the new so-called Confederacy. To the South, there was only one answer. Ex-senator from Texas Louis Wigfall cabled to Charleston, "Inaugural means war."[104] War drums beat an ever-deafening warning that Lincoln could not ignore.

He had observed for years that far from moving toward emancipation, the South was moving further from it. This realization caused him to abandon his "natural limits of slavery" position. He also assessed that one of the main stumbling blocks of emancipation at all was race, and that free blacks both North and South would pose an obstacle to freeing slaves. Consequently, he supported various programs of colonization in Africa—which, of course, few freed slaves in America ever wanted. One problem, from which Lincoln himself did not suffer, was that abolitionists tended to view blacks in antebellum America as white men with dark skins, ignoring the wide cultural and social (not to mention economic) divide.

Yet the South also realized that every measure it took to buttress the Slave Swamp below the Mason-Dixon line was in large part caused by the internal weakness of the slave position. Intellectually and practically, the periphery of the South was drifting toward freedom. Slavery was decaying in western Virginia and parts of Kentucky. It was also dying slowly in Maryland and Missouri, and people with foresight could see a day in the not-distant future when some of those states would join the ranks of the Free Soil states. It was a choice of a slow death or war, in which case if the South lost, slavery would die a very quick death.

Secession settled the matter. Virginia did not go out with the Deep South, but held its secession convention as Sumter was besieged. Lincoln toyed with the idea of trading a fort for a state, according to some accounts promising to withdraw troops from Ft. Sumter if the Virginians broke up their convention. They would not. He sent commissioners to South Carolina to determine whether peace was still possible. Stephen Hurlbut returned and, after meeting with a group of prominent Charlestonians, told the president, "I have no hesitation in reporting as unquestionable—that a separate nationality is a fixed fact [there]."[105] Confederate bombardment of Ft. Sumter on April 11 confirmed that fact.

Lincoln had already asked his War Department for the specifics on defending or relieving Ft. Sumter, and realized it really couldn't be done. Lincoln put out a call for 75,000 ninety-day volunteers, still clinging to the hope that the Confederates would come to their senses. A practical issue—that the Union government had not made war plans at all, and that the volunteers who had already arrived in DC to protect it were insufficiently fed and clothed—limited Lincoln in calling for an even larger force. Simply put, the buildup would be slow.

It is not the purpose of this chapter to review the war battle by battle. Instead, what is necessary is to review the war *aims*, which at first were to bring the rebellious states back into the Union but into the "cordon of freedom." As such, Lincoln had no plans to deal with slavery other than to return the institution to its pre-war status. Yet he knew his battlefield commanders would soon solve the problem for him. In the Yorktown peninsula, General Benjamin "Beast" Butler took Fort Monroe and immediately was swarmed by fugitive slaves. Rebels demanded the army give their slaves back—citing the very legal authority (the US government) that they had just seceded from. Butler refused, calling the blacks "contraband of war." Lincoln feared this would be viewed as emancipation, lose him northern Democrat support, and cost him the border states that still had slavery. Nevertheless, he approved Butler's policy by saying it related to the Fugitive Slave Act, which no longer applied in states that were in rebellion. It was an ingenious way of using secession against the South. The word went out, and every slave even close to Union lines ran to safety claiming "contraband" status.[106] There were no widespread slave revolts, however, which some in the North had predicted.

During the summer of 1861, Lincoln came under increased pressure from Senators Zachariah Chandler, Charles Sumner, "Bluff" Ben Wade, and others. They argued that war changed things, and now ending slavery could—and should—be a war aim. Lincoln resisted, not because he had an elevated view of blacks, whom he thought were not ready to coexist in white society, but because he was still, as he saw it, the caretaker of the nation as a whole. That required him to move carefully. Then there was his pledge not to attack slavery. Such a move, he thought, would cost him the Union that was his first priority to preserve. So he hewed to a course of restoring the Union with slavery still entrenched in the South, yet its commercial lifelines cut and surrounded by free states that would not support it.

Sumner, however, who had become a friend of Lincoln's, thought it was only a matter of time that the pressure of the war would force him toward emancipation. Congress, using Butler's "contraband" concept, pushed through a confiscation bill as a "war measure" that allowed seizure of any Rebel slaves used in the war effort, which, of course, was all of them. Individually, though, commanders continued to push toward emancipation. John C. Fremont, "The Pathfinder," in charge of the Western command, reacted to information that a Rebel force was moving northward in Missouri, placed the state under martial law and ordered that the slaves of all Confederates in the state be seized and declared free men. Word reached Lincoln, who certainly had not authorized such emancipation, and on September 11, 1861, ordered Fremont to comply with the confiscation act's provisions. The president also made his response to Fremont public. Every mile further south the Union army moved, it emancipated more "contraband" and weakened the Confederacy even more.

Lincoln called Congress into special session on the Fourth of July, 1861, to consider war measures. Congress met amidst reports of chaos and confusion from military commanders as to whether they were required to return runaway slaves or employ the "contraband" terminology. As in our own time, generals with different ideas than the president or Congress issued their own orders, as did General George McClellan urging Virginians to disregard stories that their runaway slaves would be freed. Not only would the Union "abstain from all interference" with slaves, but "we will on the contrary with an iron hand, crush any attempt at [a slave] insurrection on their part."[107] McClellan's views were largely irrelevant. Lincoln had already told Illinois Senator Orville Browning that the Union government would not be sending slaves back into bondage.

In May Lincoln told his secretary that despite his original objective of simply reuniting the Union, he could not disregard slavery, the "vast and far reaching disturbing element" that caused the war in the first place.[108] Senator James Dixon of Connecticut insisted that while abolition was not the purpose of the war, "in the course of events, it shall appear that either slavery or the Government must perish."[109]

Like Donald Trump in 2017–2020, Lincoln felt undercut by his subordinates yet did little to address the situation: he did not immediately fire Fremont, or Simon Cameron, the secretary of war who was a thorn in his side, or demote the mutinous McClellan. Only after he received a report of Fremont's corruption with his California friends did Lincoln sack him. Similarly, like many politicians today, some Republicans hid behind the assertion they were being forced to confront slavery—now that removing it was actually going to involve blood. He was also acutely sensitive to language (being a lawyer) and wanted to make sure that any of the several bills discussed or actually passing in Congress *not* imply that either slaves were property *or* that the federal government could free slaves as persons in service within a state.

As the war dragged on through the end of 1861, Lincoln felt pressure from many of the Republicans to act on slavery: how could he fight a war without acting on its cause, they asked. He still clung to "gradual, compensated emancipation," with the federal government buying the slaves and granting their freedom. Lincoln gave thought to such a plan beginning with Delaware, to take place over thirty years. This would be tied to colonization, which Lincoln thought essential to gain support of the Northern states. Congressional Republicans were also pressing Lincoln to recruit black soldiers. He rejected the notion out of concern that, again, border states would not tolerate such a position. His disloyal secretary of war, Cameron, put out his own statement that slaves should be freed and enlisted in an all-Negro army. Lincoln, aghast, ordered Cameron to retrieve the statement, but even in the slow communications of the 1860s, it nevertheless leaked out.

In July 1861, Illinois senator Lyman Trumbull introduced a confiscation bill to the floor, whose final section did not refer to property at all but to "persons." Any person engaged in supporting the rebellion would "forfeit all right to such *service or labor*, and the person whose labor or service is thus claimed shall be henceforth discharged therefrom; any law to the contrary notwithstanding" (emphasis mine).[110] This was flat-out emancipation. And the Republicans hammered at the slave issue in a tax bill, where new taxes would be imposed on various forms of property including slaves as "taxable persons."[111]

Events on the battlefield did little to dampen the abolitionist fires now rising in the North. Reports that the Confederates had "thousand of slaves" supporting the combat troops at the battle of Bull Run led one Rhode Island congressman to state that after two battles, "We shall not only not restore any more slaves, but shall proclaim freedom wherever we go."[112] Only Confederate victories could stave off the inevitable military emancipation of slaves as the Union Army controlled territory. In the meantime, Lincoln had to caution his generals that in the border states, which were still loyal, the Fugitive Slave Law was still in place but under enforcement from the federal government.

Congress pushed him again in July 1862 with the Second Confiscation Act, which he signed. Generals now could assume that certain classes of slaves defined in the act could be immediately emancipated, and whereas court orders were needed to seize other property, such orders were not needed to free slaves. This act in principle shifted federal policy from limited emancipation to universal emancipation in the Confederacy. It is important to note, however, that Lincoln had already come to the conclusion he would issue an "emancipation." Intellectually, Lincoln had arrived at the moment he knew that "this [war] was a great movement of God to end slavery."[113] Still, Lincoln appreciated what Charles Sumner and other abolitionists did not: Union troops, not God, had to fight and die on the battlefield. The president needed a substantial victory in the East before he could issue any edict on emancipation. He had victories, courtesy of Ulysses Grant, in the West, and the Union Navy had done its job: the South was isolated from munitions from Europe. But the papers focused almost entirely on the Army of Northern Virginia, which had whipped the federal forces at Bull Run, then (despite heavy casualties) at the Seven Days' battles, then again at Bull Run again. Ironically, it was the Confederates that handed Lincoln exactly what he needed.

General Robert E. Lee, leading the Army of Northern Virginia, went for a knockout punch by invading Maryland. He was misled into thinking Marylanders would rally to the Confederate cause and help him surround Washington, DC. Lee also thought Union general George B. McClellan too slow to counter his invasion. But the "Napoleon of the West," as McClellan was called, obtained Lee's orders that a courier had dropped, and uncharacteristically moved rapidly to meet the Confederates at Antietam. On September 17, 1862, McClellan advanced across two broad fronts. Despite high casualties, the Yankees finally outflanked the Rebels on one side and threatened to envelop the entire army. Lee withdrew, technically handing the Union its first major victory in the East.

Frederick Douglass, the former slave who had used his newspaper to champion abolitionism, had gently nudged Lincoln toward action. But for the better part of a year at war, Douglass grew frustrated that Lincoln had not seen the light and admitted abolition had to be the central war aim. "From the genuine abolition view," Douglas wrote, "Mr. Lincoln seemed tardy, cold, dull, and indifferent, but measuring him by the sentiment of his country—a sentiment he was bound as a statesman to consult—he was swift, zealous, radical, and determined."[114] Over the summer of 1862, Lincoln had let his feelings be known, telling border state representatives, "The war has doomed slavery and if any of them rejected compensation at that time, they would never have another chance. He received a chilly reception, which proved to Lincoln that the Slave Swamp was indeed real, and that even loyal slaveowners were too immersed in the system to free their own slaves and voluntarily transform their culture. In addition, though, border state representatives wondered why they should free their slaves if the Rebels came back into the Union *with* theirs. Lincoln couldn't disagree, and concluded that "if abolition was to come, it must commence in the Rebel South, and then be expanded into the loyal border states."[115]

As Michael Allen and I wrote in *A Patriot's History of the United States*

Truly, it was a "Damascus Road" experience for the
president. The following day, in a carriage ride with
Williams Seward and Navy Secretary Gideon Welles,
Lincoln stunned the two cabinet officials by stating that
given the resistance and persistence of the Confederates,
it was a necessity and a duty to liberate the slaves.[116]

But that was when he told them: he had steadily marched toward
that position. He did so—reluctantly, as some historians claim—because
military necessity demanded it. This is key: it was *not* the military necessity of needing black soldiers, but the military necessity of somehow
handling the battlefield contingencies of runaway slaves and establishing
a formal policy.

He stated flatly that the time for an amicable return to the Union was
over; that he would rip out the "heart of the rebellion" and end slavery.
His journey had led him to the final reality that the issue was not merely
slaveholders who had rebelled, but the very institution of slavery that
had bred rebellion among an entire slaveholding class—the dominant
and powerful Slave Swamp. Lincoln's great Proclamation, though, has
through the ages concealed a larger truth about the Slave Swamp: one
man alone, with no help, had no chance of draining it. Rather, Lincoln
led a movement that had been building for decades and had the complete
support of the majority of the press at the time. Unlike Donald Trump
and the Deep State Swamp, where *all* those forces were aligned against
him, Lincoln had the antislave equivalent of an offensive line plowing
the way for him.

While, to Lincoln, emancipation was always first and foremost a
moral and legal issue, he nevertheless also came to realize that there
were powerful military and strategic aspects to it as well. None of these,
by the way, involved the reason leftists such as Howard Zinn have given
for emancipation, namely that the Union needed more troops—black
troops. Zinn claimed that the Emancipation Proclamation was "a military move...threatening to emancipate [the South's] slaves if they continued to fight, promising to leave slavery untouched in states that came

over to the North," and also, "With the Proclamation, the Union army was open to blacks...."[117] More recently, the notion that the North was running out of troops and could "tap this human reservoir [to] offset the immense losses on the battlefields and the declining zeal of white volunteers."[118] As I pointed out in *48 Liberal Lies About American History*, "Never in discussions with any of the border state representatives or with Lincoln's own cabinet were conditions of black soldiers raised," and as shown above, Lincoln made up his mind on emancipation *before* the costly battles of Antietam (September 1862) or Fredericksburg (December 1862) or Gettysburg (July 1863).[119] It was a strange motivator indeed that it came after the purported need.

Quite the opposite of the Emancipation Proclamation serving as a troop magnet, it threatened to undermine the strength of existing federal units, who scarcely approved of the objective. One regiment, the Illinois 109th, had to be disbanded for disloyalty after the Proclamation was issued. It is critical to understand that very few in either army thought blacks could make effective troops or belonged in the army. That, after all, was the message of the movie *Glory*. Only in October 1862 (not, as depicted in *Glory*, the 54th Massachusetts in South Carolina in July 1863), did the 1st Kansas Colored Volunteers beat back Rebel attacks at the Battle of Island Mound, Missouri. Again, this was after Antietam and the Proclamation but before the six months of heavy Union casualties. And it was Mainers and New Yorkers who smashed "Bobbie Lee" at Gettysburg, not black troops.

What emancipation did do, militarily, was threaten the South's labor support system that allowed the Confederacy to put more white soldiers at the front; throw what was left of the Confederate financial system into chaos, for slaves constituted the majority of collateral backing all plantation loans; end any hope the Rebels had of getting support from England or France (who would not ally with a slave country); and, yes, down the line also add new regiments to the Union Army. Economic aspects of the Proclamation should not be minimized: Lincoln pulled the rug out from under the entire slave economy, in a single decree wiping off the books millions of dollars of plantation assets which "suddenly disappeared as mysteriously as the Roanoke colony!"[120] Almost regardless of what happened after that on the battlefield, the Southern economy turned to mush and the future instability of slave plantations as banks denied them loans would make slave-based plantations unsustainable.

On September 22, having as he said made a promise to himself "and my Maker," Lincoln issued the "preliminary Emancipation Proclamation." He not only smiled as he did so—unusual for Lincoln—but said, "I never, in my life, felt more certain that I was doing the right thing than I do in signing these papers."[121] In the Proclamation, he quoted verbatim Section 9 of the Second Confiscation Act as it dealt with captives of war. Much has been made of the details of the Emancipation Proclamation, namely that it only freed slaves in those states "still in rebellion," which meant no substantial number of slaves in the South were freed (because the Union had yet to defeat the Confederacy), but neither were slaves in the border states freed. But in the context of what had *already happened* and the direction of all Union policy by that time, the Proclamation virtually was the death knell to the Peculiar Institution.

Even with the Proclamation, there was a chance that courts could used the Dred Scott decision to order blacks re-enslaved after the war. Republicans perceived that and found a solution: citizens could not be enslaved, therefore emancipation meant citizenship. It was the first major institution, however fragile, of national color-blind citizenship. Lincoln hinted at this likelihood in his second inaugural. Quickly antislave congressmen argued that once free, no former slave as a citizen could ever be put in bondage again. Lincoln's attorney general Edward Bates so stated in a ruling immediately after the Proclamation. (Again, note that Lincoln was supported in his Swamp Draining by his own attorney general, not obstructed by him.) Congress had already provided the foundation for this in the Militia Act of July 17, 1862, that eliminated the words "free" and "white" from enrollment in militias, thereby conferring citizenship on any enlistees. In a March 1863 Enrollment Act, however, Congress made all able-bodied males eligible for the draft, flipping the order: now citizenship was not a reward for blacks to obtain freedom but confirmed a citizenship obligation already existing.

In Lincoln's last days, the citizenship and the possibility of re-en-slavement rose to the forefront of debate, as clearly the South and border states intended whenever possible to re-enslave any emancipated for-mer slaves. Senator James F. Wilson warned slavery was a "condemned" but "unexecuted culprit" and "not dead."[122] Practically speaking that meant that during Reconstruction the seceded states had to be reduced to the status of territories seeking reentry into the Union. And since Congress could not abolish slavery, constitutional amendments made permanent both abolition and citizenship. The Thirteenth Amendment to the Constitution provided that neither slavery nor involuntary servi-tude, except as punishment for a crime, would exist in the United States or any place subject to its jurisdiction. After Lincoln's death, the 14th Amendment would provide that no state could make any law abridg-ing the "privileges and immunities" of life, liberty, or property without due process of law and ensconced political rights in both Section 1 and Section 2 of the Amendment.

Lincoln, who had prophesied a house divided over slavery, now for a short time presided over one reunited without it. In his second inaugural Lincoln had urged that the nation again be one, "With malice toward none; with charity for all...let us strive to finish the work we are in; to bind up the nation's wounds...."

Lincoln had defeated the Slave Swamp. That was a wholly different animal than defeating racism or prejudice, or from ensuring that all Americans were secure in their civil rights. This would be the "new birth of freedom" Lincoln referred to at Gettysburg. No one can do it all; Lincoln had done more than his share. In beating the Slave Swamp, he was the only one of our six presidents to achieve a knockout over a swamp foe. Slavery would never again exist in America. Freedom was national.

Scorecard: Lincoln and the Slave Swamp

- Overall extremely successful in defeating the Slave Swamp
- Meticulously followed the wording of the Constitution in emancipation.
- Had overwhelming support from Congress
- Had extremely good support from the Northern newspapers/press

CHAPTER 2

Grover Cleveland and the Spoils Swamp

braham Lincoln's task was both brutally difficult and ultimately clear-cut: end slavery. Although it would be bloody, abolition was something that could be (and was) done universally and permanently in the United States. No one could doubt whether his solution had worked: by 1865, slavery had ended in the United States. Lincoln had beaten the Slave Swamp and confirming his victory was relatively obvious.

The Spoils Swamp that Grover Cleveland would grapple with proved much different. It was far less bloody, but much more difficult to control and terminate. While Lincoln proved far more successful with his Swamp than did Cleveland, it was not for lack of effort on the part of the 22nd (and 24th) President. Unlike the Slave Swamp, the Spoils Swamp changed shape, effectively dodging efforts at complete reform. And worse, unlike the Slave Swamp, the Spoils Swamp in some ways proved worse after its "defeat" than before.

Few people know who Grover Cleveland was. A truly remarkable man—and president—Cleveland had a number of firsts. He was the first US president (and only US president to the present, though some speculate in 2024 Donald Trump may be the second) to win an election, lose an election, then come back and win election again. He was the first president (followed by Franklin Roosevelt in the 1930s) to win the popular vote three times. He was the only US president to undergo secret surgery on a yacht—and the mouth surgery for cancer was so successful and the prosthesis so good that very few even in his inner circle even noticed. And he was the last national Democrat to run on a standard of "hard money" or opposition to inflation.

But our interest in Grover Cleveland is as a Swamp Fighter, and before we can assess him, we need to start at the beginning…with the origins of the "Spoils Swamp." In the beginning, as it were, the "Slave Swamp" and the "Spoils Swamp" were interconnected. Indeed, the latter was largely founded to prevent a war over the former.

Our journey through the Spoils Swamp begins with the most unlikely event, a compromise in American politics. The Missouri Compromise of 1820 was intended to prevent a civil war over slavery.[123] In 1820, there were the thirteen free and thirteen slave states in the Union. Admitting Missouri, which had applied for statehood in 1818, threatened to disrupt the balance. New Yorker James Tallmadge attached amendments to the statehood resolution in Congress that would have prohibited any further introduction of slaves into the state and included an emancipation of all slaves already in the state by 1825. What became called the "Missouri Crisis" was handled by (at the time) a well-honored tradition of compromising with slave states to prevent secession or war. In this case, Maine was also admitted as a free state to keep the balance and a line was drawn at the 36°30' mark at the bottom of Missouri, below which any new territories wishing to become states could choose to permit slavery, but above the line all new states would have to be Free Soil.

Former president Thomas Jefferson said the news of the Missouri Compromise alarmed him like a "fire bell in the night."[124] New York congressman Martin Van Buren was likewise deeply concerned that the long-term implications of the Compromise meant that before long, free states would greatly outnumber slave states and would be able to force antislave legislation through Congress. At that point, both men thought, the South would react with secession and/or war.

Van Buren, who was a supporter of Georgian William Crawford in the 1824 election, had already developed into a potent political operator. Known as "the Little Magician" (or, the "Red Fox of Kinderhook"), Van Buren came from a politically active area of New York. He belonged to a men's club called "Old Kinderhook," and if you were in the club, you were "O.K." In trying to get Crawford elected, Van Buren had met with his political idol, Thomas Jefferson, in 1824 just a year before the Sage of Monticello died. In the election, no presidential candidate among the four frontrunners—Crawford, the incumbent president John Quincy Adams, Andrew Jackson, or Kentuckian Henry Clay—won enough electoral votes to become president. The race was tossed, as per the Constitution, into the House of Representatives. There, Henry Clay threw his support behind Adams and deprived Jackson of the presidency in what was later called the "Corrupt Bargain," as Adams conveniently named Clay as his secretary of state. (At the time, secretary of state was the stepping-stone to the presidency.)

America's "two-party system" had disappeared when the Federalist Party committed suicide with its opposition to the War of 1812. After the war, only the Jeffersonian Republicans remained and the United States truly had a one-party system. This was known as the "Era of Good Feelings." In truth, though, the first party system with Federalists and Republicans was nothing like what a genuine two-party system should be: it was still largely run by caucuses, there was no national campaigning, and there was nothing in either party to ensure discipline. In its place, Van Buren sought to create a new structure that would guarantee party discipline for a specific purpose, namely to prevent discussion and debate of slavery in Congress or the presidency so as to eliminate the possibility of secession or war. From good intentions...

Neither of the pre-Compromise parties had ever used patronage, or the promise of government and/or party jobs, as a major political tool. Of course both parties rewarded their friends and punished their enemies. But the early nature of parties was such that they were largely "gentlemen's clubs" that settled things in the infamous "smoke-filled rooms." This is why government stayed relatively small. A new election did not mean thousands of existing government employees would be removed and thousands of new ones installed. In the first place, there weren't that many government jobs to give away. The largest bureaucracy in the entire government was the postal system. Postmaster general was in fact a desired position, because by 1830 it had direct control of some 8,700 jobs. The mostly private Bank of the United States was also, for the time, a fairly large political plum with its eight branches in various states and the jobs that accompanied each branch.

Van Buren, however, saw a way to expand patronage at both the party and government levels, creating paid party positions and starting partisan newspapers in many cities. Loyal party members would be moved up the party ranks based on their ability to secure the vote for their assigned area. At some point, the party jobs began to come with a salary. As one moved up in the party, he could be considered for government positions, including (as mentioned) postmaster, customs official, land agent, judge, US marshal, or any other of dozens of government jobs that included a salary. In short, Van Buren relied on the promise of money in the form of jobs as a bribe to maintain political discipline. But discipline for what? *To prevent members of the party—regardless of their personal preferences—from all discussion of slavery in any official capacity.* That is, his party's members would stifle all discussion of slavery so that it could never become an issue that would produce such laws that might trigger secession.

So-called "newspapers" were nothing like the old "broadsides" and were overwhelmingly partisan rags. One study suggested more than 85 percent of all newspapers were completely partisan.[125] Van Buren hired editors, used party funds to support the papers, and the party dictated content.

The new party, called the Jacksonian Democrats or just the "Democratic Party," was born. It was fundamentally different from the Federalists, the Republicans, and in many ways even from its yet-to-be-born rival, the Whigs, in that the Democratic Party was a mass party aimed at getting out the vote of the common man. This stood in sharp contrast to running things through caucuses, with minimal input from only the most wealthy and landed ordinary citizens. Slowly, at the state level, requirements that a voter must own property disappeared, as did, over time, the caucus system for nominating presidential candidates. Those caucuses were replaced by national nominating conventions. Or, the Democratic Party became "democratized."

It is unimportant that over time Van Buren's new party failed to stop a civil war—and indeed in many ways contributed to it. What is important is that by creating the playing field of patronage and the "Spoils System," no one could challenge the Democrats unless the rival party engaged in giving away jobs itself. Thus, a competition arose between (at first) the Democrats and the Whigs in giving away party and government employment and later between the Democrats and the Republicans. However radical the Republican Party (formed 1854) was in its stance toward slavery (i.e., no slavery would be allowed in the territories), it nevertheless in *practical* political terms had to fight on the battlefield of spoils. There was, therefore, no change in the steady escalation of the Spoils System or in the size of government, even under the stewardship of supposedly "small government" presidents such as Jackson and Van Buren. Government at the local, state, and federal level continued to grow because that was how people got elected to government—by promising jobs. And since getting out the vote was utterly essential, cheating and bribery formed central components of elections. For example, in the campaign of 1888, Indiana Republicans "paid $15 per vote (not in silver or greenbacks, but in gold)."[126]

Quickly the opposing parties learned the game. In 1849, a young Abraham Lincoln wrote to Secretary of the Navy William Preston about a "fierce and laborious battle" he and his allies fought for a year for the appointment of "a set of drones," one of whom received the position of district attorney only to defect in the general election and support Henry Clay over the Whig candidate Zachary Taylor.[127] Lincoln decried "almost sweating blood" to elect Taylor, yet after the election "by other men's labor," this candidate was "the first man on hand for the best office that our state lays claim to." Lincoln came face to face with political influence of the Spoils System. He saw it again in 1860 after his election, when, as historian Allan Nevins noted,

> Every Republican in Congress wished to strengthen his
> political organization; every editor coveted a post-office
> connection to swell his subscription list; every jobless
> politician wanted a salary. The Illinois members, for
> example, met in conclave to draw up a slate of appoint-
> ments to be requested of Lincoln. After dividing marshal-
> ships, district attorneyships, and territorial posts, they
> demanded a slice of foreign-service pie. Senator Lyman
> Trumbull wanted two consulships, Representative Elihu
> Washburne one, and Representative W. P. Kellogg one....
> And Illinois was but one State![128]

Nevins noted that three-quarters of the correspondence of a senator, representative, or even a cabinet member pertained to patronage.

The situation in Washington was stunning, and downright dangerous. Hotels overflowed with job seekers. Some 300 men slept in the White House (it was not so named until the administration of Theodore Roosevelt) dining room at a time when almost anyone could just walk into the presidential residence. It took almost the entire month of March 1861 for Lincoln to give out all the jobs that were expected. Indeed, Lincoln wielded patronage like he was born with the spoils scepter in his hand: he removed 1,195 federal officeholders out of 1,520 total positions (and this included the Southern jobs that mostly went unfilled). He had learned well from the Little Magician, naming Republicans to almost all of those jobs. He flatly stated he "distributed to [his] party friends as nearly all the civil patronage as any administration ever did."[129] Over a period of four years, Lincoln removed 1,457 of 1,639 appointed office holders not counting postmasters (new offices had become vacant since 1861).[130] By 1860 as we have seen in the previous chapter, the entire government employed about 36,000, not counting the military, of which about 28,000 were postmasters. In fact, as Lincoln told Carl Schurz who visited him in July 1860—before he was even elected—he was already receiving correspondence and personal visits about pending jobs should he be victorious.

Little did Lincoln dream of what awaited him. William O. Stoddard, one of Lincoln's earliest appointees (in the Interior Department) soon worked so closely with Lincoln that he was appointed as a private secretary. He watched the president as he was deluged with job seekers.

> There was something almost phenomenal in the crowd of hungry office-seekers. They filled the hotels and boardinghouses. They thronged the passages and anterooms of public buildings. Hundreds of anxious politicians, large and small, came pouring in by every train, so ignorant of public affairs that they hardly knew what to apply for, and still less for what duties they were prepared.... They came from every nook and cranny of the country.[131]

Robert Wilson, an Illinois friend who visited Lincoln later recalled the president "was so badgered with applications for appointments that he thought sometimes...the only way that he could escape from them would be take a rope and hang himself on one of the trees in the lawn of the [White House]...."[132]

Of course, in some of the positions there were significant ramifications if the wrong man was put in place. Lincoln had to staff cabinet positions, including state, treasury, and war. Each one not only required someone competent but someone loyal to the president. Finding such people was tricky. Most of Lincoln's cabinet had their own ambitions and saw him—much the way some in Donald Trump's cabinet would view him in 2017—as an untalented executive who came into the office by fortune rather than by his own skills. Some appointees were problematic given their personalities. He noted that Wait Talcott, the collector for the Treasury Department, tended to make enemies and urged him to "make no war" upon Congressman Elihu Washburne, one of Lincoln's friends.[133] A White House employee, William Stoddard, observed "Mr. Lincoln regarded the federal appointments at his disposal as in the nature of a public trust, and not at all as his private property or to be apportioned among his friends, relatives, or personal adherents...."[134] Many were totally unfit for the jobs they sought. In one instance Lincoln was shocked by the lack of qualifications of an applicant, recalling that he had known the man for years and never thought he had "anything more than average ability… and he wants to be superintendent of the mint?…. But then, I suppose he thought the same thing about me, and—here I am!"[135]

Nevertheless, Lincoln stood unique among his presidential peers, in that as he often boasted, he was coming into office "unembarrassed by promises." He said, "I have not…promised an office to any man, nor have I, but in a single instance, mentally committed myself to an appointment…."[136] That was not entirely true, as before he left Illinois he sought suggestions from various people, including his law partner William Herndon. He also took into account the personal circumstances of several potential jobholders. And perhaps worst were the phenomenal numbers of people who just wandered into Lincoln's office, many of whom he befriended because they had something in common. John Hay, Lincoln's personal assistant, found the experience repeated a "hundred times"—"a man whose disposition and talk were agreeable would be introduced to the President; he took pleasure in his conversation for two or three interviews, and then this congenial person would ask some favor impossible to grant and go away in bitterness of spirit."[137] Lincoln's fairness, attention to detail, and sheer time devoted to patronage—not to mention his refusal to be bullied by senators and congressmen—created a well of debts others owed him. This, of course, was the essence of the Spoils System. Political favors begot political indebtedness. That Lincoln successfully navigated those treacherous waters was yet another feather in his political cap.

His successors, though, faced an even greater challenge as the government virtually exploded with growth during the Civil War years. President Ulysses Grant paid a high price for insufficient oversight of his numerous underlings, and suffered a major scandal when his brother-in-law, Abel Corbin, became involved in the infamous "Gold Corner." Samuel Tilden, the Democratic candidate for the presidency in 1876—who may have actually won the office, but was denied by Republican claims of fraud—observed that the opposition party by then (i.e., the

Democrats) would have to win the support of two-thirds of the voters to overcome the reach of patronage. This was even more true after the war, when entirely new pools of job seekers and recipients of government support had appeared as a result of the war, most notably in the Veterans Administration and in pensions provided to veterans.

By the time James Garfield ran for the presidency in 1880, the Spoils System had not only gotten out of control, but it had become a major issue within the Republican Party itself. It was a hotbed of corruption. Garfield, an Ohioan like Ulysses Grant, had known poverty like Lincoln. A Republican state senator when war broke out, Garfield served as a major general in the Union Army, seeing action at Shiloh under Grant. He then was elected to Congress. Garfield's career was such that he took the right steps and supported the right policies at the right time. In 1880, the Republicans were split over the issue of patronage reform, with the "Stalwarts" under Roscoe Conkling of New York supporting the continuation of the system and the reformers, known as "Half Breeds," led by James G. Blaine of Maine, wanting civil service reform. Garfield had to unite the two groups, and did so with a decidedly mushy letter published on July 12, 1880, in which he would not endorse his predecessor's reform measures and refused to ban all federal office holders from participating in politics, yet at the same time he pledged to consult Congress in filling federal positions.[138] Reformers were chagrined, thinking he had reverted back to a Stalwart position on spoils.

Garfield smoothed ruffled feathers with a meeting with Roscoe Conkling's supporters, including his new vice presidential nominee, Chester A. Arthur. The candidate promised to consult with the Stalwarts and abide by their decisions. It was a meeting that proved one of those in which each side came out with an entirely different understanding of what transpired. Stalwarts thought Garfield was in the bag for them; Garfield thought he had agreed to "no trades, no shackle...."[139] As soon as Garfield won, the lines of job seekers appeared. Levi Morton, in particular, thought Garfield had promised him the treasury job, but Garfield, in a private meeting with Morton, told him that treasury was out of the question due to his ties to Wall Street and instead offered him the navy secretaryship. Then, Garfield shocked the Stalwarts by putting in "Half Breed" chieftain James Blaine as secretary of state.

Conkling and the Stalwarts were stunned and outraged. After still other Garfield nominations that offended them, Senator Conkling and his ally, Senator Thomas Platt, staged a theatrical resignation from the Senate…which backfired. Far from uniting all the Stalwarts behind them and holding up all further nominations, their erstwhile allies decided that Conkling and Platt had abandoned them and that they could get along just fine without the two. Stalwarts proceeded to vote for Garfield's nominees. Both senators expected that their New York state legislature would immediately return them to power. Instead, they failed to win the first vote, then a long war ensued lasting over a month. Platt withdrew. Conkling did not regain his seat after Garfield's assassination.

Garfield had first appeared to be a reformer by refusing Morton the Treasury job, then he ordered the resignation of Second Assistant Postmaster General Thomas Brady, the alleged ringleader of the star routes ring. Under that cabal, postal officials received bribes in return for awarding certain "star" postal delivery contracts.[140] The president instructed his attorney general, Isaac MacVeagh, to cut out the corruption in the Post Office "to the bone," even if it led back to his own office.[141]

Like Lincoln and other presidents before him, Garfield was deluged with job applicants. One of those, Charles Guiteau, had supported Garfield in the campaign with the expectation it would guarantee him a position in Garfield's administration. Guiteau met with Garfield once, and was dispatched to Blaine with his request. Blaine, on the other hand, had no intention of giving Guiteau a job and begged off using a deadlocked Senate as an excuse. Guiteau was undeterred. Once the standoff in the Senate was resolved, he again sought out Blaine, who this time told him flatly he would not get the position. Guiteau, convinced he had been discriminated against because of his Stalwart leanings, determined he would eliminate Garfield and put the supposed Stalwart, Chester A. Arthur, the vice president, in office. He approached the relatively unguarded president at a railway station and shot him, proclaiming, "I am a Stalwart and Arthur will be President."[142]

Guiteau's heinous action would prove one of the greatest miscalculations in American history. While Arthur did become president, he hardly became the Stalwart Guiteau intended.

Although Chester Alan Arthur had only a single political miscue in 1881 before becoming president, he possessed a rather stellar reputation. His one error came in March of that year, submitting to Blaine's request to arbitrarily remove the customs collector of New York and replace him with another Half Breed, William Robertson.[143] Conkling, the king of spoils, lambasted Arthur for breaking his word and Grant (of all people) claimed that Blaine had played Garfield, who, in Grant's opinion, "Lacked the backbone of an angle-worm."[144] Grant was wrong. Garfield was, as one biographer put it, "remarkably equitable and nonpartisan." He appreciated that patronage needed to be used to cement a few alliances, but otherwise let the party bosses know who was who. When a group of delegates came into his office to lobby for some of their clients, they put their feet up on the White House desk. Arthur told them to remove their feet or be removed from the office, and they would address him not as "Chet" but as "Mr. President."

Upon ascending to the presidency, Arthur was deluged by newspaper opinion pieces that rushed to remind him of his earlier spoils misstep. The *New York Times* wrote, "He can earn for himself everlasting odium and for his party disunion and defeat by repeating as President [the] blunder which he has already made in a lower office."[145] Instead, the paper argued, "He can disarm the public distrust…by walking steadily in the path of reform…." Arthur, in fact, had already moved far away from the Stalwarts in his appointments. One of his first visitors as president was his old spoilsman friend, Conkling, who revisited the Robertson appointment. Conkling was shocked and disappointed when Arthur said he was "morally bound" to continue Garfield's policies.[146] The way Arthur later described it, he was beholden to Conkling for making him vice president, but when it came to the presidency, "My debt is to the Almighty."[147]

Most were skeptical he could change, let alone reform others. Henry Adams, observing the early days of Arthur's administration, wrote that attempts to "drag President Arthur into the assertion of reform principles,

[have] utterly and hopelessly failed."[148] One could almost hear Adams sighing through the pages as he concluded, "The new administration will be the center for every element of corruption, south and north." Later Adams wrote, "You certainly will not find many reformers [in Washington]: all that swarm have vanished like smoke...."[149] Then, in 1882 a Rivers and Harbors Bill, in modern terms a "porkulus" bill with goodies for everyone, came before the president and Arthur vetoed it as "scandalous and outrageous" spending.[150]

Arthur, after only a few months, was showing signs of depression over the magnitude of his office and the demands upon him. "When you go into his office," said one member of his administration, "you see a man oppressed with either duties or...staggering under a sense of responsibility which he does not like."[151] Unable to delegate much, Arthur was described as "stunned, uncertain, and in any event moody, possibly unhappy." A doctor who visited him thought the president "sick in body and soul."[152] What most did not know was that Arthur was genuinely ill. He started to show signs publicly in the spring of 1883, after signing the first civil service reform bill—an early version of the Pendleton Act.

Over the next few months, Arthur vigorously enforced the new anti-spoils law. As the 1884 convention rolled around, Arthur told his campaign managers to stay away from the convention. "I do not want to be nominated as the result of any political manipulation," he explained. In fact, he was dying of Bright's disease, an inflammation of blood vessels in the kidneys and at the time almost always fatal. In public, he kept up the facade (in the Victorian era it was unseemly to suffer in public), but he also thought simply withdrawing from the race would be seen as weak. So he soldiered on, while privately tamping down any discussion of his reelection.

The Republican reformer James Blaine would take the GOP nomination. But it would fall to a Democrat, Grover Cleveland, to pick up the mantle. And Cleveland would have more success.

Grover Cleveland, the only president to win an election, lose reelection, then win election again, was the first Democrat president elected since the Civil War. He won an at the time unprecedented three popular vote victories in a row. As Buffalo mayor, then governor of New York, he had remained aloof from campaigning for the presidency. In what historian Allan Nevins called his "usual moral courage," Cleveland refused to attend a rally at Tammany Hall—a site notorious for the corruption of the infamous Tweed Ring more three decades earlier.[153] Much like Gerald Ford in 1974, Cleveland was hoisted largely on the basis of his honesty. Even many of his supporters expected little else from him. His integrity impressed everyone, and Cleveland particularly detested corruption, or what he called "boss-ism." Indeed, in the 1884 election his position against the Spoils System led a group of Republicans, known as "Mugwumps," to support his ticket.

As Nevins explained, Cleveland was always driven by two factors: "resentment for the vilification which he had endured, and a sense of dedication to the office before him."[154] This integrity Cleveland applied to himself. He was "appalled to see how unprepared he was for the magnitude of the duties he had obligated himself to assume."[155]

His inaugural address included a pledge to restrain the impulses of patronage.

> The people demand reform in the administration of the Government and the application of business principles to public affairs. As a means to this end, civil-service reform should be in good faith enforced. Our citizens have the right to protection from the incompetency of public employees who hold their places solely as the reward of partisan service, and from the corrupting influence of those who promise and the vicious methods of those who expect such rewards....[156]

To that end he ordered that office holders from the previous administration be examined and divided into competent and efficient employees to be retained or incompetent workers to be fired and replaced with Democrat appointees. As expected, having just campaigned on reform, some in Congress nevertheless turned around and fought actual removals claiming violation of the Tenure of Office Act (violation of which had gotten Andrew Johnson impeached). This was resolved by reformers passing a bill to repeal the Tenure of Office Act, which Cleveland signed in 1887.

No sooner did Cleveland settle into the Oval Office than he was personally engulfed in armies of job seekers. The task left him feeling alone—he only had a handful of assistants, not a giant staff—and unable to trust even one-time friends who now were after appointments. He spent an average of two to three hours a day on appointments. By then there were 126,000 government employees—not counting the military—of whom 110,000 received their jobs courtesy of the president. Moreover, it dawned on everyone that a *Democrat* would be making these appointments for the first time since James Buchanan! The feeling surrounding Washington's Republican circles must have been eerily similar to that among the 1860 Democrats who woke up to find a hated Republican in charge of everything.

Despite Cleveland's reputation for integrity, no one took any chances. The influential newspaper the *New York World* reminded Cleveland of "the obligations which an Administration elected by a great historical party owes to that party."[157] (Note that the paper did not say the president was elected by the people, but by the *party*.) He received a letter from the National Civil Service Reform League seeking assurances that he would remain an advocate for reform, to which the president said there would be no hesitation to enforce all the laws relating to spoils. He even promised not to remove anyone currently in the government who was doing an effective job. But "inefficient employees, offensive partisans, and unscrupulous manipulators" would be sacked.[158] Nevertheless, he couldn't escape the job seekers even in East Room handshaking events. Looking over a mountain of letters from people begging for a position, Cleveland asked in exasperation "My God, what is there in this office that any man should want to get into it?"[159] On another occasion when approached by a leading Democrat politician seeking to snag an appointment for a friend, Cleveland said "Well, do you want me to hire another horse thief for you?"[160] "Those office-seekers," he complained. "They haunt me in my dreams."[161]

Some have criticized Cleveland for not being brutal enough in his appointments, but Postmaster General Adlai E. Stevenson complained that "it is daily asserted that hundreds of postmasters are being appointed, yet the six months which have elapsed since Mr. Cleveland's accession finds only between ten and twelve percent of the offices occupied by Democrats."[162] Historian Nevins claimed that the level of pressure put on Cleveland by spoilsmen was "exaggerated," perhaps less than Garfield had faced.[163] That did not prevent newspapers from running cartoons showing him as an Arab Sheikh, sitting under a tree listening to lines of supplicants.

Cleveland, himself, thought the situation was overwhelming. Writing to a friend who had tried to discourage some of the job seekers outside the presidential mansion, he lamented, "The clock has just struck ten, and the doors must be opened to the waiting throng. The question with me is When (if ever) will this thing stop?"[164] He observed that men came to Washington on other business, with no thought of office, but within a couple of weeks they "caught it," meaning patronage fever. "They seemed to get a mania," he noted.[165] Again and again, well into November of 1885, Cleveland lamented "the d—d everlasting clatter for office continues…and makes me feel like resigning, and Hell is to pay generally."[166]

Soon his appointments began to infringe on relationships with people he thought his friends. "I have been here five months now," he wrote, "and have met many people who had no friendship for me, and were intent on selfishly grabbing all they could get…but I managed to get along with them." He added, "I don't want to let these friends go; but I am tired of this beating about the bush and all this talk about 'second-handed invitation'…" which was Cleveland's reference to job requests via these "friends."[167] Cleveland wrote to the resigning Federal Civil Service Commission chairman Dorman Eaton a letter in which he hoped "the time is at hand when all our people will see the advantage of a reliance…upon merit and fitness, instead of a dependence upon the caprice or selfish interest of those who impudently stand between the people and the machinery of their government."[168] Donald Trump would harbor similar sentiments a century later, and Cleveland experienced the same

Swamp rebuff that Trump would. Bourke Cockran, a proponent of spoils, quickly published a letter attacking civil service reform. As Trump would be later, Cleveland was partially neutered by the Swamp: after Eaton—a solid reformer—resigned, Cleveland sought the resignation of two other members of the Civil Service Commission to replace them with Swamp drainers. In both cases, he failed.

Unlike Lincoln, who, with the exodus of Southern congressmen, inherited a much more supportive (and like-minded) legislature, Cleveland—like Donald Trump—got minimal support from his own party in the Senate. Reformers talked a good game, but when it came time to actually fixing the problem, they were nowhere to be found. Applying the Tenure of Office Act that had resulted in Andrew Johnson's impeachment, Congress obstructed Cleveland's removal of corrupt employees and his bid to replace them with honest ones. In one instance, the president found a Republican postmaster in Rome, New York, described as "a drunken scamp," who had failed to even make monthly required reports to the postmaster general. Yet Cleveland could not dismiss the man. After presenting his case to the Senate in March 1885 requesting it confirm a new appointee, the Senate adjourned without acting.[169] Just as in 2017–2020, the Senate dallied, held hearings, requested endless more information on Cleveland's new appointees. Cleveland played hardball. He instructed his department heads to refuse such requests and to render only official documents already available to the senators. By mid-1886, the president and the Senate were in open battle over appointees. Ultimately, the Republicans, anxious to embarrass Cleveland, announced they would block all appointees unless the president gave in.

Cleveland used a threat that Donald Trump would not later possess in this battle: Congress actually took a recess in the nineteenth century and the president could—and would—make recess appointments. (At the time, it was a common tactic to get offices filled.) In March 1886, Cleveland addressed the nation and enlisted the public on his side. Already the Tenure of Office Act had a poor reputation from the Johnson impeachment. Republicans surrendered, as signified by confirmation of one of Cleveland's appointees, the surveyor general of Utah, on March

12, 1886. Within two weeks, papers quoted senators as saying there would be no more calls for information about other appointees. Cleveland had won a key battle with the Swamp. Others loomed.

The president personally would spend hours every night going over stacks of recommendations. He went deeper into the lists than most presidents, for example, examining the fourth-class Post Office appointees who made less than $2,000 a year when most presidents stopped at third class. Customs commissioners and postmasters were the most sought-after jobs below that of cabinet level. When cautioned by an advisor that the postmaster of Indianapolis was corrupt, he was assured that the people would support his decision against the spoils bosses. "That has nothing to do with it," Cleveland replied. "We must find out what is right and do it regardless of the result."[170]

That is not to say Cleveland was heartless, even in removing people. With E. L. Hedden, the collector of the port of New York, who demonstrated his incompetence in short order, Cleveland sent numerous letters urging him to get on track. Only after those failed did he conclude he had to fire Hedden (who was, in fact, forced to resign). Cleveland replaced him with Daniel Magone, who was superb. And even Cleveland found he had to relent under pressure from his own party to be more flexible. He also was sensitive to accusations of potential corruption, even before the fact. William Whitney, for example, a major fundraiser, expected to be named interior secretary. But when the press labeled him "Coal Oil Billy" suggesting he would allow Standard Oil Company free rein on public lands, Cleveland installed him as secretary of the navy. As such, Whitney had little to do with Standard Oil and spent his time building the new steel navy.[171]

The most obvious point to confront the Spoils System was with the new Pendleton Civil Service Reform Act passed by the Republicans in 1883. It removed 10 percent of the civilian jobs in government from political patronage and subjected them to a series of examinations administered by the United States Civil Service Commission. While Pendleton still left 90 percent of the federal employees not covered by the act, a president could expand the number under the Commission later. It also prohibited the use of "assessments" that were political contributions to the party in return for receiving the job—a "finder's fee," if you will. Cleveland enthusiastically worked to reclassify patronage jobs under the Pendleton rules, adding 13,000 to the classified list and in a single order moving 5,000 of the railway mail service under Civil Service.

Like almost all reforms, Pendleton may have solved one problem while creating a larger one. In essence, for a candidate to get elected, he only had to promise more jobs than his opponent. Before Pendleton, the numbers were in the hundreds or low thousands. But as more and more jobs were removed from a candidate's immediate control a different phenomena evolved. Rather than promise individual jobs, say, a postmaster here and a customs commissioner there, candidates had to appeal to broader forms of spoils. This involved in the twentieth century, for example, catering to the unions, the environmental lobby, the military-industrial complex, and so on. In short, Pendleton took a small problem and made it a massive problem, although one that indeed wrested some of the headaches from presidents who had to specifically allocate appointments to thousands of job seekers. It enabled, however, the "interest group" political favoritism that would appear in malevolent form in the twentieth century.

Cleveland approved of the Pendleton Act, saying, "Good government is the main thing to be aimed at. Civil service reform is but a means to that end."[172] Historian Allan Nevins has argued that this distinction separated Cleveland, whom Nevins called a "reformer," from Theodore Roosevelt, who embraced the term Progressive. To Nevins, the former was intent on purifying the existing processes of government, the latter, on creating entirely new processes to achieve novel aims.

One source of spoils decay was the navy under Zachariah Chandler, which Nevins described as a "scene of hopeless waste."[173] Over a period of nearly twenty years, the nation had poured $75 million into construction, repair, equipment, and maintenance of the wooden fleet to no avail. Not all the ships were bad: the *Wampanoag* was in many ways one of the more advanced ships in the world in terms, able to make over seventeen knots on a trial run (a record that stood for twenty-one years) with its steam power and screw design. It was put into a pier to rot, partly for its unconventional design but also because it burned a whopping 136 tons of coal a day. The navy had a wide assortment of unserviceable ships such as the *Mohican*, a small vessel that cost over $900,000 for repairs in a decade when a new steel cruiser such as the *Atlanta* could have been obtained for two-thirds of that outlay. Another seagoing waste was the *Omaha*, with no apparent use, rebuilt at a cost over $570,000. Major shipyards, managed loosely under the Spoils System, would transform from somnambulant zones where lavishly paid campaign workers "managed" no work at all to bustling hotbeds of activity just before election time when "hundreds of laborers, hastily hired, were marched to the polls" to vote for their political benefactor.[174] The navy experience could be applied to virtually every government fiefdom.

Though not an expansionist, Cleveland knew the growing nation with gigantic coastlines needed a reliable navy. To that end he supported new appropriations that resulted in contracts soon being let for the new "protected cruisers," the *Charleston, Baltimore, Newark, Philadelphia*, and *San Francisco*. Although the contracts were spread out geographically to shipyards around the country (always a good patronage tactic), nevertheless Cleveland and his navy secretary, William Whitney, cleaned up the waste and applied stringent business principles that seemed missing under Chandler.

Yet even those actual federal appointments that fell under the rubric of patronage were now being surpassed by another form of spoils, the massive new army pension rolls. Bolstered by the 400,000-member Grand Army of the Republic (GAR) lobbying organization, the pensioners supported increasingly generous payouts, not just to themselves, but to widows, orphans, and dependent parents who also became eligible for assistance. As Nevins described the patronage situation

> A formidable host had arisen to support even bolder demands on the national purse. It comprised the veterans, armed with their own and their relatives' votes; many Republican politicians who sought these votes; a swarm

of claim agents and pension attorneys; and the local shopkeepers who knew that the pension money would ultimately reach their tills.[175]

Cleveland embraced the presidential veto, using it 414 times in his first term, more than double the number of all presidential vetoes before him combined. Of those, 347 were aimed at Army pension bills. Although Cleveland signed more pension bills than he vetoed, he was the first to insist that every claimant was not necessarily worthy. Making matters more sticky, Cleveland himself had never served. In his first term, the pension issue of the Spoils Swamp would remain mostly submerged with one exception.

When Cleveland took office, there were 345,125 veterans or eligible family member who received pensions totaling more than $65 million (or close to $2 billion in 2020 dollars). This was an amount equal to one-fourth of all federal spending, and while the number of Civil War veterans should have been declining over the years as they died off, in fact the amount of money spent on pensions increased by more than 500 percent since 1865. A veteran denied a pension could petition his local congressman to propose legislation to fund his pension, thereby circumventing the Pension Bureau and defeating the purpose of reform.[176] Biographer Alyn Brodsky noted that "claims came in quicker than they could be scheduled for debate.... Congress set aside Friday evenings exclusively for acting on [pension claims]."[177] In a single day, the Senate passed 400 pension claims and in a six-month period more than 4,000 were introduced in the House...and even more in the Senate! If only allotted ten minutes' debate on each, the pensions alone would consume four months of Congress's time.[178]

These bills eventually settled on Cleveland's desk. In a single day, he received 240 special bills, out of which 198 had already been rejected by the Pension Bureau. He specifically vetoed many of these. Yet Congress, unchastened, increased its efforts at passing pensions, introducing 4,127 in the House in a single six-month period!

Cleveland personally reviewed this blizzard of bills and vetoed hundreds of fraudulent claims, including one from a man whose son died crossing a river—to desert! Another veteran wanted support for injuries he received falling off his horse on his way to enlist, and yet another who was injured twenty years before the war by an explosion of a cannon celebrating the Fourth of July. He even received one from a widow whose husband died after falling off a ladder. At home.

Overall, he found the entire process of overturning the Pension Bureau's decisions by resorting to legislation "exceedingly questionable." Occasionally the circumstances might warrant a special consideration, but "I am convinced that the interposition by special enactment in the granting of pensions should be rare and exceptional."[179] Americans began to agree with Cleveland, and his vetoes gained popular support.

Henry Blair had introduced a pension disability bill in 1887 that granted a twelve-dollar-per-month pension to all Union veterans who had served at least ninety days in any American war. It was exceptionally expensive. Cleveland vetoed it. He argued that "the bounty it affords them is given thirteen years earlier than it has been furnished the soldiers of any other war, and before a large majority of its beneficiaries have advanced in age beyond the strength and vigor of the prime of life."[180] Cleveland also rightly claimed the system would be abused. Already "disabled" pensioners were applying for injuries that occurred after the war. He also envisioned exactly the kinds of Big Government/Big Brotherism that would occur in the twentieth century when, to determine a claimant's condition, the state began to intrude on a person's most intimate privacy. For example, he asked, "Shall the Government say to one man that his manner of subsistence by his earnings is a support and to another that the things his earnings furnish are not a support?"[181] He concluded: "The effect of new invitations to apply for pensions or of new advantages added to causes for pensions already existing is sometimes startling."[182] His message was a shot across the bow not only of the entire increasingly fraudulent system but directly at the Grand Army of the Republic.

Cleveland's veto was sustained. Almost concurrently, Cleveland got another opportunity to show his staunch strict constructionist approach to government and to strike spoils. In 1887, Congress passed a bill that would provide $10,000 for the purchase of seed grain for farmers in Texas communities who had suffered from a drought. The Texas Seed Bill, as it was called, was typical Washington do-gooder-ism: who couldn't be sympathetic to the poor farmers who through no fault of their own suffered from the forces of nature? Cleveland saw it differently. He could "find no warrant for such an appropriation in the Constitution" (he was right) and did not think that "the power and duty of the General Government ought to be extended to the relief of individual suffering which is in no manner properly related to the public service or benefit."[183] While not strictly a patronage issue, the fundamental message was that the federal government was not to be used as a trough of favors to reward constituents, either directly or indirectly.

Toward the end of his term, Cleveland admitted—much as Trump would over 130 years later—that he had underestimated the depth of the Swamp. "I knew," Cleveland said in 1888, "that abuses and extravagance had crept into the management of public affairs; but I did not know their enormous power, nor the tenacity of their grip."[184]

As reelection rolled around, Cleveland got an intimate look at the shift that Pendleton was bringing about. His reelection essentially hinged on his home state of New York, where the president was hurt by favoring a lower tariff. Benjamin Harrison and the Republicans had warned that abandoning tariffs would raise taxes and lower wages. But they also reminded voters that Cleveland had been, in their view, tight-fisted with the pensions. These shifts were not new in 1888, but as political strategies their impact had grown significantly since the Civil War. It was a reminder that in the late nineteenth century, *both* forms of patronage—individual and general—were powerful political weapons.

The president was a rarity among Democrats, as he favored a gold standard. Most Democrats after the war had advocated expansion of the Greenbacks (the unbacked Civil War currency) or favored "free silver" (a phrase that meant the government would purchase *all* available silver and mint it at a fixed rate of sixteen silver dollars to one gold dollar). This was inherently inflationary, as silver was coming out of the mines at a ratio of up to seventeen-to-one. That meant, in theory, that a speculator could take seventeen ounces of silver into a government assay office and exchange it for an ounce of gold and still have an ounce left over. After fifteen more transactions, he'd have a whole extra dollar's worth of gold. Of course, in reality, few farmers or miners could actually *do* this, and as always, it would benefit the very speculators and bankers they hated (such as J. P. Morgan, Brown Bros., Goldman Sachs, or J. & W. Seligman).[185]

Much of the unrest related to the tariff and a growing concern, the international deflation that had set in since 1870, was felt among rural groups. They soon formed third-party responses, first in the Farmers' Alliances led by Mary Lease ("raise less corn and more hell") and soon the Populists. Seeking to mollify the farmers, Congress created the Department of Agriculture and Cleveland signed the bill almost on his way out the door in February 1889. Washington DC had thrown a bone to the agricultural interests, but they and the silverites were a fixture among lobbying groups over the next eight years. Those forces would erupt during Cleveland's second term.

When the new campaign came, it only slowly dawned on Cleveland and his advisors that the usefulness of individual patronage had given way to the more broad-based appeals to group interests. He realized the Republicans had gotten a head start on this new approach and across the country employers were directly threatening their workforces with layoffs if Benjamin Harrison was not elected. Perhaps worse, Cleveland had made an enemy of New York governor David Hill, who was a spoilsman. Hill likely cost Cleveland New York and with it, the election.

Issues such as patronage, the tariff, and silver, however, would not go away. After four years of Benjamin Harrison, they were as hot as ever. Cleveland won the Democrat nomination and then the election. It was the third time Cleveland had won the most popular votes, despite losing the Electoral College to Harrison in 1884.

Patronage was a three-headed hydra: individual job appointments, which had been somewhat restricted by the Pendleton Act; larger scale patronage via promises to interest groups such as farmers or naval building; and the large government spoils systems such as pensions. Although

Pendleton limited some of the specific spoils positions, by Cleveland's second term, he still faced armies of office-seekers. (One of these was future presidential candidate William Jennings Bryan.) Cleveland tried issuing a series of rules that could winnow out the numbers of applicants he dealt with. First, he established a rule to refuse to appoint anyone who had held office in his first administration. As Nevins noted, "unusual crowds began to be observed on outgoing trains."[186] Then he created a rule to exclude newspapermen from appointments. Finally, he had a general rule that anyone who engaged in extreme partisan activity would not be considered.[187]

Still, none of these worked, forcing Cleveland to issue an executive order:

> The time which was set apart for the reception of Senators and Representatives had been almost entirely spent on listening to applications for office, which have been bewildering in volume, perplexing and exhausting in their iterations, and impossible of remembrance. A due regard for public duty obliges me to decline, from and after this date, all personal interviews with those seeking appointments to office, except as I on my own motion may especially invite them.[188]

Anyone paying attention to the impact of the Pendleton Act would have foreseen what awaited Cleveland. Pressure for jobs shifted from individuals to groups. Congressional delegations organized in clumps to approach the president for job seekers; the Senate set up its own "Board of Patronage" to divide the offices before meeting with Cleveland; and state politicians organized into patronage caucuses. The president publicly stated he would not meet with such groups. Even with all of Cleveland's resistance, critics claimed he was giving in too often. A frustrated Cleveland partially solved the problem...with an appointment! He named Josiah Quincy, a noted reformer, as an assistant secretary solely for the purpose of handling the spoils seekers.

The unfortunate Quincy found that his most immediate problem was sorting out a raft of ambassadors and consuls, and even his most modest requirements were met with howls of outrage. For example, he insisted on the ability to speak the language of the country to which a man was sent. Even Cleveland wrote that "Joe Quincy has out-heroded Herod as a spoilsman among the consuls...."[189] When the complaints mounted Quincy decided to do no more direct appointments without specific instructions from Cleveland. This, of course, defeated Quincy's very reason for being.

At wit's end, Cleveland issued a stream of orders expanding the classification of jobs eligible for the Civil Service. By 1896, he had included 85,000 federal employees out of the 205,000 (or 41 percent, up from just 10 percent when Cleveland took office in 1885). It constituted a major victory against the Spoils Swamp.

Yet as Cleveland managed to unload one layer of patronage, another fell upon him. The economy had collapsed when in 1890 Congress passed the Sherman Silver Purchase Act, artificially setting the price of silver to gold at 16.5:1, meaning that silver was over-valued by about fifty cents per ounce. Speculators immediately swarmed the trading houses, sending silver in and taking gold out. Pressure from silver, combined with the failure of a number of large railroads or banking firms—including the Northern Pacific Railway, the Union Pacific, the Atchison, Topeka and Santa Fe Railroad—followed. Some 15,000 companies and 500 banks went under, mostly in the West where the pro-silver Populist energy was exploding. In 1892, the Populist "free silver" party had actually run a presidential candidate in James Weaver who won 8.5 percent of the vote.[190]

The culprit was the Sherman Silver Purchase Act, though by 1893 its impact had expanded far beyond just silver and spread throughout the economy. Cleveland resisted calling a special session of Congress to repeal the act, but by June he could wait no longer. He issued a call for an extra session to begin on August 7.

In the midst of this, Cleveland was diagnosed with a tumor in his upper mouth and needed immediate surgery. He wanted this kept secret, leading to a surgical procedure on a yacht, the *Oneida*. Once the operation started, the doctor found more cancer. He took out two teeth, cut into the top of the mouth and removed the upper left jaw. Despite the extent of the surgery, Cleveland recovered well and with the aid of a prosthetic device could fool people at a distance that nothing had happened.

Meeting in special session, Congress repealed the Sherman Silver Purchase Act in October. The bleeding was stopped, but the patient continued to fail. Losing gold reserves, the banks continued their collapse. The repeal of Sherman had been followed with the Wilson Tariff, which Cleveland opposed. He had won on silver, but lost on the tariff.

As conditions worsened, in March 1894 an Ohioan named Jacob Coxey, a Populist who favored "free silver" had petitioned Congress to issue $500 million in unbacked paper money for highway construction. Coxey, of course, portended the New Deal of Franklin Roosevelt some thirty years later. At the time, however, the plan appeared goofy. Congress dismissed the petition. Coxey proceeded to organize a march to Washington, DC, to lobby in person—the first such national "march for…" event. He called his followers the "Army of the Commonwealth of Christ," but most referred to the thousands of marchers as "Coxey's Army" (which would be symbolized by Dorothy and her motley band in *The Wonderful Wizard of Oz* as they marched up the golden road to the Emerald City, or Washington, DC). Coxey lost many of the faithful along the way, arriving in Washington in May with only about 500 and tailed by Secret Service agents. Finally arriving at the Capitol, they were surrounded by police and arrested (sometimes clubbed for treading on the green lawns around the buildings), foreshadowing the harsh treatment of the January 6 (Patriot's Day) protestors in 2021. Coxey himself was arrested, found guilty of trespassing, and sentenced to twenty days in jail and a five-dollar fine.

By 1895 the decline in American gold reserves had become nearly fatal. The United States was on a gold standard, not a silver standard or a bimetallic standard. All banks kept *gold* as their reserve. Many failed. As the federal treasury started to see its gold reserves dwindle, there was a possibility that the United States itself might be forced into bankruptcy. Cleveland had to keep the federal government solvent. He met with banker J. P. Morgan to negotiate a massive loan of 3.5 million ounces of gold to the US government in return for a thirty-year bond issue (from which Morgan and the Rothschilds' financial firm in Europe netted a significant profit: Morgan's bank alone got $7 million for the deal).[191]

On top of these dislocations, the American Railway Union went on strike against the Pullman Company in May through July of 1894, throwing further economic dislocation into the mix. The federal government got an injunction against the Union and when the leaders refused, Cleveland ordered the US Army to stop workers from obstructing trains. Union organizer Eugene V. Debs was arrested in federal charges (which were later dropped). However, he received a national soapbox, which he then used to run for president. Thus, even with the Sherman Act's repeal and the gold loan by Morgan, Cleveland's second term was consumed by an ongoing depression that was not fully lifted until 1897.

Overall, as two pre-Donald Trump writers applying "public choice" theory note, "Currently it is difficult to imagine a politician following through on his campaign promises of limited government once he is in office."[192]

With his last first-term message to Congress, Cleveland alluded to another Swamp on the horizon, the Trust Swamp, noting:

> The gulf between employers and the employed is constantly widening, and classes are rapidly forming, one comprising the very rich and powerful, while in another are the toiling poor.... We discover the existence of trusts, combinations, and monopolies, while the citizen is struggling far in the rear or is trampled to death beneath an iron heel.[193]

Cleveland had attained a modicum of victory over the Swamp. He had enforced the Pendleton Act; he had increased the number of federal jobs put under Civil Service fourfold; and he had instituted important Navy reforms that limited the impact of spoils there. His efforts to ensure both efficient and honest government were mitigated by the Swamp, however. Over time, other presidents would suffer from the incompetence or outright criminality of their appointees. Warren Harding dealt with repeated scandals, the most notorious of which was Teapot Dome. Harding became so exasperated he once snapped to William Allen White, "I have no trouble with my enemies. I can take care of my enemies…. But my friends, my goddamned friends, they're the ones who keep me walking the floor at night."[194] Richard Nixon's vice president, Spiro Agnew, was investigated for kickback schemes that occurred under his governorship of Maryland. With an indictment likely, Agnew entered into negotiations before an indictment was delivered, claiming a sitting vice president could not be indicted. He resigned and pleaded *nolo contendere* (no contest) in 1973 in a deal that kept him out of jail. Of course, many others in Nixon's administration were indicted in the Watergate case, the motives of which are still murky to this day.[195] Reagan's secretary of defense, Caspar Weinberger, was indicted after his resignation from office for a role related to the Iran-Contra Affair, but a judge threw out the indictment.[196] These were but a few of the officials in the Swamp who violated the public trust. How much of the ongoing "scandal" culture in Washington was the result of genuine criminality and how much was due to perpetual sniping by the opposite party combined with a bloodthirsty press cannot be determined.

Abolition was a relatively straightforward process once the issue was decided on the battlefield. There has been no going back. But Spoils was Jell-O, amorphous, nearly impossible to define let alone pin down. As a result, Arthur and Cleveland, through no lack of effort, did not defeat the Spoils Swamp.

The Pendleton Act rechanneled patronage into a much larger arena of special interests and group lobbyists. What Martin Van Buren had created as a means to enforce party discipline to prevent a war in the 1820s had now metastasized into a much larger and more dangerous creature. Whatever Lincoln, Arthur, and Cleveland's difficulties were in dealing with job seekers on a personal level, it paled next to containing— let alone shrinking—the Spoils Swamp in the arena of special interests. Already veterans, farmers, the navy, unions and those industries seeking tariff protections for their businesses were emerging as powerful lobbying organizations. By the 1930s, the individual petitions for jobs would be dwarfed by the special interest calls for assistance here and aid there. Franklin Roosevelt's New Deal would institutionalize the Spoils Swamp in its new iteration; Lyndon Johnson's Great Society would color it in racial tones; and by the late 1990s, the environmental lobby with its so-called "green" agenda would seek to control every aspect of American life through its stated concerns over "saving the planet." What hath Martin Van Buren wrought?

Scorecard: Cleveland and the Spoils Swamp

- Moderately successful in reforming the Spoils Swamp
- Meticulously followed the wording of the Constitution in emancipation.
- Had mixed support from Congress
- Had good support from a significant portion of the press

CHAPTER 3

Teddy Roosevelt and the Trust Swamp

Abraham Lincoln's struggle with the Slave Swamp unfolded as the Spoils Swamp continued to grow—and indeed was accelerated by the Civil War—just as Grover Cleveland's tactical victory over the Spoils Swamp nevertheless concealed a long-term defeat. Just as the Spoils System had now transformed into jobs for special interest groups (as seen with the rise of agrarians and silverites), a new Swamp Creature had steadily risen to become a threat: the Trust Swamp.

Understanding the growth of trusts requires a brief foray into the history of American business in the 1800s. Beginning in the early part of the century, most businesses in the United States were relatively small, and most of those, single-owner shops or farms. The largest companies in the United States by the 1830s were likely to be a textile company with several mills, a steamship business that was still confined to American inland waters, or small manufacturing. Most businesses of the day were what were known as "mechanics." Today we would call them "artisans," and they consisted of candle makers, iron workers, coppersmiths, leather workers, and dozens of other small manufacturing businesses. Usually these were run by a single family, or a couple of partners, up to and including some of the bigger textile mills. There were also banks, again mostly run by partners. To form a corporation—at the time, mostly hospitals, schools, or banks—one had to present a petition to the state legislature for a charter. The charter was then viewed not only as a right to do business, but a *monopoly* right to do business in that area.

Major changes began to occur in the 1830s and 1840s when, first, petitions for new banks grew so numerous and burdensome to the legislators that they created "free banking" laws, known today as "general incorporation laws." These allowed any bank (then, later, any business) to open after posting a security of bonds with the state government. By the late 1840s, companies from all sorts of businesses were opening "corporations" under these laws. Another critical change, however, occurred with the US Supreme Court case of *Charles River Bridge v. Warren Bridge* (1837) that held that a charter did *not* necessarily imply a monopoly over an area, unless the charter specifically granted such a monopoly.[197] After the Charles River Bridge case, companies could freely enter the market with a minimum of paperwork, arm-twisting, and without fear of running afoul of someone else's charter. In other words, a free market was at work.

But already another massive transformation as under way with railroads. Capital demands of the "iron horses" were orders of magnitude different from even canals. No individual, or even partnership, could raise sufficient money to build and maintain a functioning railroad—it required stockholders. Thus, the new corporations acquired yet another feature largely unseen anywhere in the world, namely a large group of owners who could not attend to the daily management of the company. Instead, they selected a "manager," who soon became a professionally trained manager. This became the "managerial revolution" that Harvard historian Alfred Chandler wrote about in 1977 in his prize-winning book, *Visible Hand: The Managerial Revolution in American Business*.[198] In addition to the capital needs, railroads had a scope vastly larger than any other business, stretching ultimately from coast to coast. And finally, as Chandler points out, railroads operated at a speed that nothing else could match. An owner in New York, trying alone to control trains coming in different directions in Illinois at speeds of forty miles per hour or more could not possibly do so. Accordingly, the managers set up "managerial hierarchies" to control these giant organizations. Before long, each of the managers was professionally trained.

More important, the managers became permanent. After the Civil War, fewer and fewer companies were privately owned. If they were large by any measure, they were likely no longer run by the owner, but by a professionally trained manager.

And more important still, this new cadre of managers were (in their eyes) responsible to the owners—the stockholders—and as such, over time, they would increasingly be more sensitive to changes in stock prices than they were in ensuring a steadily improving product. This embedded a business conservatism in the managerial class that had not existed in most of the early run-and-gun entrepreneurs. Business after business found itself taken over by cautious, bottom-line-oriented managers who bore no thought of radical new systems, products, or applications. Indeed, revolutionary things scared them, for a company could sink its entire capital into a dramatic but risky new product or process and go broke. Instead, attuned to stock prices, the companies and their managers increasingly sought to avoid risk and seek slow, steady growth.

As Chandler explained, the key to this revolution was abandoning traditional forms of monopoly, known as "horizontal combinations." This is what most Americans think of when they hear the word "monopoly": a single company owning all the railroads, telephones, coal, whiskey, or internet services. Led by banker J. P. Morgan and oil tycoon John D. Rockefeller, a much different business model began to appear, known as the "vertical combination." This was largely derived from Rockefeller's obsession with lowering the price of kerosene ("We must remember we are refining oil for the poor man and he must have it cheap and good.").[199] He saw his kerosene as "the best illuminator in the world at the *lowest* price."[200] In that, Rockefeller's goals predated those of Sam Walton and his Wal-Mart by a century.

To achieve this objective of lower price combined with high quality, Rockefeller had examined the fate of other forms of combination or monopoly in other sectors, most notably the railroads. There, one of the early forms of stabilizing prices was the "pool," in which profitable lines that ran between frequently traveled routes associated with smaller lines that ran in less-profitable routes and agreed to profit share in return for some ownership. This generally failed because an unprofitable line was an unprofitable line, and ownership in a losing business seldom panned out unless new cities or industries needing rail were established along the way. Then there were cartels, an association of competitors divided by territory. Like the old mobs of the big cities, the railroads would agree not to compete in each other's "turf." Banker J. P. Morgan, who helped organize and finance many of these reorganizations (and who found them unproductive) called such arrangements "ropes of sand." They only worked when they didn't have to, similar to many United Nations treaties. Once a region became lucrative, other railroads would break their promise and move in anyway. Prices for travelers and shippers would fall, and railroad revenues would plummet. All of these developments are outlined in Alfred Chandler's book and in Vincent Carosso's biography of the Morgans.[201]

While early nineteenth-century magnates such as Cornelius Vanderbilt and his successors, Andrew Carnegie, John D. Rockefeller, and J. P. Morgan were all hardened and even ruthless at times, it is key to understand their motivation, which was never about money. It was always about control of their product or business in such a way that they could fully determine price. Yet under each, prices came down. Rockefeller lowered kerosene prices for the common man so much that he put the more expensive whale oil, and thus the entire whaling industry, out of business. Quite literally, Rockefeller saved the whales. Vanderbilt in his day had reduced steam travel and shipping prices even against competitors who were strongly subsidized by the US government so much that he drove them out of business. Carnegie's steel was the best in the world.[202]

Carnegie, though, was something of an exception. He maintained majority ownership until he sold his company in 1901, and ran it himself until he retired and turned management over to Henry Clay Frick in 1889. As a single-owner company, Carnegie Steel did not have stockholders to report to, and as a result was constantly on the cutting edge of new innovations in the industry. In that respect he was different from John D. Rockefeller, who never owned more than one-third of Standard Oil Company. Rockefeller still ran the company as the top manager, wielding an entrepreneurial spirit that kept the company in the forefront of innovation. Elsewhere, though, in most of the managerial-dominated companies, conservatism set in. Managers were wary of spending too much on new equipment or taking large risks. Companies became more interested in protecting market share and turf rather than continually refining their products and driving prices down.

By the late 1800s, major companies had started a transition from "horizontal" combinations—where they sought to buy up competitors or drive them out of business in price wars—to "vertical" combinations that focused the companies internally on achieving efficiency. The quest for efficiency drove the entire strategy from acquisition of raw materials (such as when Rockefeller acquired the Henry Clay Frick coal and coke works or when Carnegie acquired his own iron ranges) to sales and distribution (as when Cyrus McCormick created a new way of financing his reapers and developed a trained sales and maintenance network to sell and service them). The famous "managerial hierarchies" that resembled pyramids with their boxes of vice presidents appeared. And if companies gained market share, as did Rockefeller's Standard Oil, it was for one reason only: they were producing the highest quality goods at the lowest prices.

That's not to say that even before the trust the titans of prosperity did not push the envelope of the law. Rockefeller had popularized the "rebate," wherein with Standard Oil's massive railroad business, he could demand better rates through refunds (or rebates) than smaller competitors. Yet this is common in all businesses today, whether through "frequent-flyer" points or other sorts of price breaks for higher volume. No one bats an eyelash when they offer to buy a product in huge quantities and expect a price reduction over a single unit. Nevertheless, Judge K. M. Landis rendered a 1907 verdict against Standard Oil's rebates of $29 million. The *New York Times*—a shockingly different paper today than then—opined that the decision was a bad law and "a manifestation of that spirit of vindictive savagery toward corporations...."[203] (When told of the judgment, Rockefeller was playing golf. A member of his foursome asked what the judgment was. "Twenty-nine million two hundred forty thousand dollars...the maximum penalty, I believe." Then the non-plussed tycoon added, "Will you gentlemen drive?")[204]

Rockefeller, unable to make any of the other "horizontal" combinations work, initially came up with the first trust in 1879 when Standard Oil of Ohio was prevented from owning companies in other states. Standard Oil got around this by appointing three managers, Myron R. Keith, George Chester, and George Vilas, to serve as "trustees" who held stock in many subsidiaries outside of Ohio. When they received dividends, they paid them to Standard Oil's thirty-seven investors as individuals.[205] As biographer Ron Chernow noted, "This jerry-built structure enabled Rockefeller to swear under oath that Standard Oil of Ohio didn't own property outside of Ohio, even though it controlled most of the pipelines and refineries in Pennsylvania, New York, New Jersey, and Maryland."[206] Still, the structure was ramshackle and needed an overhaul.

A lawyer, Samuel C. T. Dodd, a "wizard at contriving forms that obeyed the letter but circumvented the spirit of the law," formulated a way for Rockefeller to put his family members in charge of new corporations—Standard Oil of New York, Standard Oil of New Jersey, for example—without each having to pay taxes outside the state they were incorporated in.[207] The new trust agreement went into effect in 1882. Essentially, Standard Oil was a holding company, though it could not make deals or sign contracts. But it did receive the stock of Standard Oil and some forty other companies in return for trust certificates. As the institution evolved, the exchange would work like this: Company A, a pipeline company competing with Standard, would be offered Standard trust certificates equal to Company A's full value. For a company about to be driven out of business, it was an offer they couldn't refuse.

Quite the opposite to how the trust was eventually perceived—and as it was pursued by Theodore Roosevelt—the trust as Rockefeller envisioned it was a form of "populist capitalism" with employee share ownership. Rockefeller wanted every employee to save some of his earnings in the form of Standard stock. Since Rockefeller abstained from reading critics in the papers and avoided reporters, he likely believed that was exactly what Standard Oil was doing. Yet the trend was both inevitable and ominous: a company, founded by pure individual enterprise had grown to the point it was stifling all other individual enterprise in its orbit.

Standard Oil became, as one newspaper put it, "parent of the great monopolies which at present masquerade under the newfound name of 'Trusts.'"[208] An anti-Standard paper, the *World*, delivered a scathing attack, calling the company "the most cruel, impudent, pitiless and grasping monopoly that ever fastened itself upon a country."[209]

Technically, what Rockefeller created was not a true "monopoly," as the focus (as in all vertical combinations) was in controlling the product from top to bottom to drive down the price, not (necessarily) in driving out competitors. Yet that was exactly what successful vertical combinations did. In the twentieth century, Wal-Mart and Amazon would pursue an identical strategy. The result was always to force out smaller competitors who had less ability to achieve the same economies of scale. In the 1800s, Rockefeller's trust structure was immediately copied by other companies in the sugar, tobacco, whiskey, and food industries. Rockefeller then established his "managerial hierarchy," which he called the committee system, that put each part of the production process under a different leadership that competed with each other for efficiency. Its success was such that Rockefeller was largely left out of the details of running the company. He set strategic direction, including the long oil war with Russia in which he girded his loins to cut oil prices to just 5.2 cents a gallon, leaving almost no profit margin. In doing so, Standard Oil captured two-thirds of the world's oil market by 1891.

Such low-cost petroleum "carried more cheap comfort into more poor homes than almost any discovery of modern times," according to William Libby, Standard's foreign agent.[210] A shocking, previously unseen rise in average American wealth and well-being began to take place. "An efficient kerosene lamp of 1875-85," wrote one economic historian, "provided a lumen of light at about a tenth the cost of a tallow candle from 1800."[211] Rockefeller agreed. "This is the poor man's light," he said of kerosene years earlier when he began his business.[212] While breakthroughs in electricity over the next thirty years would later dwarf these gains, the kerosene lamp was the equivalent of 73,000 candle hours per year at a cost of twenty dollars. The revolution in heating alone started a stunning increase in life span from birth beginning in the late 1880s—even before electricity.[213] And Rockefeller's quest for efficiency paid significant other dividends: he hired chemists to discover uses for all of kerosene's by-products, including turpentine. Standard Oil had a test laboratory at every refinery. One of Standard's chemists, Herman Frasch, had developed a process to remove the sulfur from Lima crude oil, enabling the company to span the gap between the depletion of the Pennsylvania fields and the Texas oil boom of the early 1900s. One key element of the new manager-dominated companies (which would later retard their innovation) was that they were constantly seeking to find a use for 100 percent of their product. Thus their research and development departments ignored radical new potential breakthroughs in favor of marginal gains from existing waste.

After insisting that Rockefeller almost certainly knew about his subordinates' shaky deals and relentlessly pushed his agents to more growth, Ron Chernow—hardly an uncritical biographer—concluded, "Rockefeller never had a single motive for any action and was surely motivated by more than altruism in championing cheap kerosene. He was obsessed with high-volume, low-cost production...even if he temporarily sacrificed profit margins."[214] Encouraging legislators was certainly on the table. One critic, Henry Demarest Lloyd, writing in the *Atlantic Monthly*, quipped that Standard Oil "has done everything with the Pennsylvania Legislature, except refine it."[215] Still, he knew he could go too far. Public sentiment, he was warned, would be against him if Standard actually refined all the oil.[216] Rockefeller vastly preferred controlled opposition to pure monopoly, and he also understood that once he raised prices, the threat of alternative fuels and future competition would present genuine competition. Consequently, he never got greedy, even if his moralistic personality would have allowed it. His observations on public concerns over getting too big would reflect the growing reality of giant businesses in all walks of American life. As with Amazon a century later, which had ruthlessly yielded profit and stock price to market share, Standard Oil gave people the lowest prices on kerosene they could hope for. But it came at a price.

The most obvious concern was, "What happens when someone less altruistic than a Rockefeller comes into control of so much of one product? The public would be at his mercy." At such a point the traditionalist free-market ideology of "just build your own" is rendered meaningless. In twenty-first century America, for example, it is virtually impossible to build a competitor to Twitter, YouTube, Facebook, Amazon, or even Wal-Mart from scratch. In these cases, after behaving responsibly for a decade, their social justice conscience suddenly made them more oppressive with their policies than Rockefeller or Carnegie could ever have been. Politically the same was true for the major news networks. After Fox News made a hard left turn during the Donald Trump presidency, there were virtually *no* nationally platformed alternative broadcast news media.

These concerns were already on the minds of Americans in the late 1800s, feeding the rising fires of the Populist movement that demanded regulation of big industry, especially railroads and the hated trusts. Already in 1876, in *Munn v. Illinois*, the US Supreme Court had ruled that a Chicago grain elevator was guilty of overcharging and that the state legislature could indeed regulate prices when it affected "the public good."[217] Then, in 1887 the Interstate Commerce Act created an Interstate Commerce Commission to combat unfair practices nationally.[218] The Commission could investigate and prosecute railroads, but only if they crossed state lines. Its edicts, however, lacked teeth. The US Supreme Court ruled in favor of the railroads in fifteen of the sixteen cases that came before it involving the Act.

Just as with Rockefeller's definition of "competition," problems arose with what constituted "public good" or "fair" prices. It could be noted that had Rockefeller joined with other producers to set prices, that would be considered collusion. Yet if he charged too much, he could be accused of "gouging." Charge too little? A new concept of "predatory pricing" could be invoked. The fact was, no matter how necessary it may be at times for the government to prevent abuses, almost any company at any time could be deemed in violation of pricing laws depending on who was doing the prosecuting. There was no doubt, however, that the public in the late 1800s saw itself as pawns in the grip of extremely large companies, no matter what the benefits to their everyday life.

And while Rockefeller knew public perception was important, nevertheless he sealed the company off from the press. "We have gone upon the principle it were better to attend to our business and pay no attention to newspapers...." he told a minister.[219] A May 24, 1887, letter from William Warden, one of Standard's insiders, warned Rockefeller that things were changing and that "men look askance at us, we are pointed at with contempt, and while some good men flatter us, it's only for our money...."[220] Warden concluded by telling Rockefeller that public approval would follow if he just made an effort to connect with working people.

The titan had no intention of such groveling. When summoned to give testimony to a New York Senate committee in 1888, Rockefeller appeared in person and skillfully negotiated the interrogation. He revealed more than he ever had before, cleverly withholding more damning key facts. Addressing concerns Standard Oil was a monopoly, Rockefeller cited over one hundred competitors as well as the Russians. Rockefeller, as prosecutor Samuel Untermyer later recalled, "could always read my mind and guess what the next six or seven questions were going to be."[221] New York's senators were not diverted, producing a report calling Standard the "most active and possibly the most formidable moneyed power on the continent" and labeling it, "the original trust." Its success proved "the incentive to all other trusts and combinations."[222]

Standard Oil's lawyers consistently underestimated their critics and the regulatory forces that were building. States had already passed their own antitrust legislation. But the most threatening of all was a new bill introduced by Ohio's Senator John Sherman, signed into law in July 1890. The Sherman Antitrust Act prohibited trusts and combinations "in restraint of trade." So amorphous was the language, and shot full of holes was the reasoning that it soon was known as the Swiss Cheese Act. Business historian Stuart Bruchey pointed out that the Act was so broadly worded as to be unenforceable. Businesses, he noted, "regarded the Act as impractical, unenforceable, and hence innocuous."²²³ Likewise the fact that with the trust form of combination as a matter of public record, it was difficult to hide anything. Two of the major tenets of antitrust doctrine were the "barriers to entry" argument (a monopoly prevented new competitors from springing up) and the notion that high concentration leads to high profits. By the 1980s, both came under sharp attacks, although the "barriers to entry" position began to have more validity after the rise of Facebook, Twitter, Google, and Amazon began to shut off all dissent from accepted "social justice warrior" and/or political speech.

Sherman's intentions in thwarting large combinations were thoroughly flanked: instead of creating trusts, big business more than ever established vertical combinations. Thus ironically, the Sherman Antitrust Act may have *accelerated and increased the power of big business*, sending companies into a more profitable and efficient form than horizontal monopolies. While the government's antitrust laws would eventually break Standard Oil, the more immediate target would be Rockefeller's contemporary, banker J. P. Morgan, who had made a living off reorganizing failing railroads into the newer managerial hierarchies.

The banker made no bones about the fact that he couldn't care less what the public thought. Morgan saw himself as essential to the prosperity of America and brooked no questions about his actions or decisions to ensure that prosperity continued. And no question he was essential. Whereas Carnegie had provided the skeleton to industrial America, and Rockefeller, the fuel for its muscles, Morgan gave it its bloodstream through a continued flow of capital. He wasn't the richest of the three, but his position on the boards of so many disparate companies—and the railroads the others relied on—likely made him the most powerful. Grover Cleveland had found out just how powerful when the nation teetered on the brink of financial collapse and he had to go, hat in hand, to Morgan.

They all knew that the America of the 1880s was rapidly changing and for all their wealth and power, they could only ride the beast, hoping once in a while to steer it gently. Already millions of new immigrants had poured into America—half a million in 1901 alone—and many of these from southern and eastern Europe had little experience with either free markets or democracy. Socialism was not a repellent term to them. They were accustomed to monarchs. At the same time, the standard of living for almost all Americans had started a 50-year upward climb unmatched in human history. The appearance of municipal water supplies played a key role in reducing disease and extending life spans, but so did Rockefeller's cheap kerosene until it was replaced by the far more efficient and powerful electric lights by Thomas Edison. Over the next half-century, electrification would make possible twenty-four-hour days manufacturing and entertainment, while cheap fuel would enable long-distance personal transportation with Henry Ford's new cars in ways no one even dreamed in 1870.[224] Breakthroughs in packaging and processing of cheese (James Kraft), vegetables (Henry Heinz), meats (the Cudahy brothers and Gustavus Swift), milk products (Gail Borden), soups (Joseph Campbell), cereals (William Kellogg and C. W. Post), and even cigarettes (James Duke) delivered low-cost semi-perishable foods and other goods to Americans in bulk.[225] These products lasted longer, were healthier because of their freshness, and cost less. They revolutionized shopping: housewives no longer had to rely on the grocery store merchant to select products, cut or pour them, then package them in the store. Through this, women became incrementally more independent, autonomous, and self-sufficient.

Whereas economic historians have for over a century measured mostly static changes in prices or output, newer estimates of economic growth in the era have included time savings and overall quality of life. For example, while the arrival of chain stores in 1911—a natural progression of the vertical combinations—may have "been quantitatively as significant as the arrival of Wal-Mart," the consumer price index has missed a massive "substitution bias" in which real prices may have dropped nearly 23 percent for food items.[226] Another largely un-captured development came from the advent of consumer loans. These were made possible only by the kind of mass capital J. P. Morgan and others made available to both industry and smaller banks, and resulted in higher productivity via hours saved. By the 1920s, with a washing machine hooked up to electricity and running water, a housewife no longer had to make trips to fetch and heat water, or with an electric stove, cook without soot or coal in one location. Without the creation of mass heavy industry and capital, such breakthroughs would never have reached ordinary people.

Cities changed as Carnegie's high-quality, yet less expensive, steel reshaped the new America into forests of metal and glass. It made possible bridges, railroads, and skyscrapers (which also needed other new industrialists such as Elisha Otis with his elevator and Erastus Corning with his high-quality glass). And all of them were still living off the contributions of earlier giants such as Cornelius Vanderbilt, who embodied the "Transportation Revolution" as historian George Rogers Taylor called it.[227] It was steam power that allowed the millions of immigrants to arrive; steam-powered railroads that allowed them access to the interior of America. Their capital demands, in turn, had spawned the rise of the New York Stock Exchange and of an entire investment banking industry, of which by the 1880s Morgan had emerged as the leader.[228]

As these changes occurred, a New Yorker, Theodore Roosevelt, entered an ascent to political stardom that would ultimately put him in conflict with many of the companies that wrought these changes. He clashed with Governor Grover Cleveland over his veto of a law that would arbitrarily reduce the fare on the elevated railroad in the city by half. Cleveland, who would later stand on principle in the Seed Corn Veto, gave a preview of his character when he said the law would violate the railroad company's contract with New York and that "the state must not only be strictly just, but scrupulously fair."[229] An outraged Roosevelt called the owners (or "swindlers") in charge of the railroad "that most dangerous of all classes, the wealthy criminal class."[230] For all his achievements and those yet to come, Roosevelt had a glaring gap in his résumé: he had never truly started or operated a business for profit.

Some historians might point to his ranches, the Maltese Cross Ranch and the Elkhorn Ranch in Dakota Territory (1883 and 1884). Those grew out of Roosevelt's keen interest at a young age in bird watching, then, as he got older, in hunting. It is true Roosevelt put up the money to the tune of $35,000 but it was more to purchase the equivalent of a personal spa, a vacation spot where Roosevelt could hunt and immerse himself in a romantic version of the Western lifestyle he adored. Elkhorn especially was a hunting lodge, a staging ground for hiking, hunting, and bird watching. He used it as a setting to document cowboy life for magazines such as *Collier's* and *Scribner's*.[231] What it was not was a business investment. He hired managers and cattlemen to handle both ranches and returned to New York as much as possible for regular escapes. His managers made regular detailed reports, but they handled the business side. When he did get involved in the ranches, it was as an outsider seeking to feel useful. He would do chores or mend a fence. Roosevelt saw a spring roundup as a fun event—a type of rodeo. He never negotiated their price with livestock buyers. While he did teach himself to ride well enough to accompany the cowboys never was thought of as a good rider. In his *Hunting Trips of a Ranchman*, the emphasis should be on "hunting trips" with little emphasis on "ranchman." He wrote six articles for *Outing*, "each time using Elkhorn Ranch as his lead."[232] One article called "The Ranch" was almost entirely dedicated to elk.

When it came to anything related to the business side of the ranches, it was with the Little Missouri Stockmen's Association. Just as he toyed with the idea of permanently moving to Dakota and making a living at it, a devastating winter hit in 1886–87. At the time, Roosevelt was abroad and again, had nothing to do with actually managing a business during a disaster. He knew nothing about the "Winter of the Blue Snow" until he returned. When he returned, he announced he was getting out of the cattle business for good (although he retained his brand and visited again as late as October 1918). He had never personally experienced the hardships of meeting payrolls in tough times; in having to beg and borrow money from others to fulfill a dream; or to grow his own enterprise. The "Winter of Blue Snow" had been his opportunity to leap in with both feet and do what countless other ranchers had done before: survive. Instead, he cut his losses and ran. Roosevelt's flirtation with ranching left him still well-versed in many things and a master of several, but having failed to experience the ebb and flow, agony and ecstasy of building a business and watching it grow. His financial losses, while not trifling, did not cripple him. Similarly, he never felt a direct negative impact of government regulations, taxes or laws. Nor did he experience any government constraints on what one was allowed to do with his own property, including selling his interest without any harmful effects on ordinary people. Had he seriously engaged in the ranching *business*, it is possible he may have looked differently at the "swindlers" and "criminal class" that he so cavalierly demonized and enthusiastically regulated. He might have held just a smidgen of respect and sympathy for the phenomenal sacrifices most entrepreneurs made to reach that "criminal class" status. Instead, he played at being a rancher, and the minute it got tough, quit, losing half of his inheritance.

It was an odd omission in his life, especially considering years later he gave a speech in Paris called the "The Man in the Arena" where he glorified "the man who is actually in the arena, whose face is marred by dust and sweat and blood, who strives valiantly, who errs and comes up short again and again, for there is no effort without error or shortcoming.... [and] if he fails, at least he fails while daring greatly...."[233] When it came to actually running a business, TR never got in the arena.

No matter: Roosevelt received a contract to write a four-volume *Winning of the West*, then decided to head to Washington, DC, in 1889. Named by Benjamin Harrison to the Civil Service Commission—where he worked well with Grover Cleveland—he nevertheless realized it was an "inefficient bureaucracy run in undemocratic ways."[234] That, of course, described almost every unelected body ever created. But bureaucracies weren't the only institutions suffering from inefficiency. Railroads were still in the early stages of figuring out how to take advantage of their massive fixed costs. The *price* of any particular shipment or ticket was less important than the necessity of filling every train every time. It seemed, however, that only a handful of the railroad men realized that—but Morgan did. John Moody, the financial analyst, wrote, "Morgan began to be looked upon as a rescuer of investors.... And he stood alone in this regard."[235]

Meanwhile, the year before the Sherman Act, Ohio's attorney general David Watson, almost by accident, discovered the original Standard Oil trust deed and realized that the Ohio company had transferred most of the control of the company to trustees in New York. He filed a petition against Standard Oil of Ohio in May 1890 seeking a dissolution of the company. Rockefeller and his lawyer, Samuel Dodd, had already considered the possibility of a court-ordered breakup, and had planned to make use of an 1889 New Jersey law that allowed corporations in that state to hold stock in companies outside of New Jersey. Watson's suit merely started Standard looking more closely at a complete reorganization with the movement of the headquarters to the Garden State. Complying with the court order in 1892 for dissolution, Standard reshuffled shares, calling in trust certificates and replacing them with the same value in some twenty companies. Then, Standard Oil relocated to New Jersey. As if nothing had happened, the new Standard Oil simply repurchased stock in other companies. Nothing really changed except a few titles. During the Panic of 1893 and the subsequent years, the gigantic Standard Oil was better able to ride out the depression than its competitors, and indeed (as Carnegie often did) bought more properties and wells.

Then something remarkable happened. While the Sherman Act was proving toothless so far, a group of 1,000 well-owners known as the Producers' and Refiners' Oil Company with its new United States Pipeline staged a competitive surge against Standard. As Chernow noted, "Several years before federal trustbusters mobilized to smash the Rockefeller monopoly, serious competition had already taken root...."[236] Nevertheless, Standard was showing yet one more aspect of vertical combination: it was becoming its own bank. The company could command massive loans from New York financial houses and thereby wielded great power over them in the "too big to fail" scenario.

Meanwhile, Theodore Roosevelt, after six years on the Civil Service Commission, resigned and took the position of New York City police commissioner, with an attending role as health commissioner. He accompanied street patrols where he saw the underside of the city, including living conditions for a large class of factory and shop workers. During this time Roosevelt also read *How the Other Half Lives* by muckraker Jacob Riis. The two became friends.

Had TR immersed himself in the business of ranching the way he did the supervision of the New York Police, it is safe to say his antitrust policies would have turned out much differently.

In 1896, William McKinley was elected president. He chose Roosevelt as assistant secretary of the navy, but within two years the country was at war with Spain. The main location of the conflict would be Cuba. Given the allure of war, and yet another opportunity to prove his own manliness to himself, Roosevelt resigned his secretaryship and raised a volunteer cavalry unit known as the Rough Riders. After becoming a legend for the "charge up San Juan Hill" (which really was Kettle Hill), Roosevelt returned home to a hero's welcome and the offer from New York power broker Tom Platt to nominate him for governor. Roosevelt won a close race, then proceeded to push his Progressive reform agenda with the state assembly.

To his credit, in 1899 Roosevelt sought to educate himself about trusts (keeping in mind that he had whiffed on his best source of business education with the ranches). Roosevelt concluded that the playing field was uneven, and that government needed to address the growing issue of monopolies. According to historian Leroy Dorsey, rather than engage in hostile attacks on trusts, Roosevelt sought to promote "the proper attitude in corporate leaders" regarding the role of business in society.[237] To Roosevelt, corporate America could only be regulated by instilling a sense of responsibility and ethics in its leadership. Dorsey notes, however, that the offensive against trusts was a two-sided coin that also involved reining in the muckrakers and the irresponsible journalists of the day. Roosevelt saw himself as the voice of the people against the trusts, not as one who wanted to dissolve the giant corporations or hinder their operations. He even viewed himself as protecting corporations from the sensationalistic yellow press. To Roosevelt, muckraker journalism posed as hideous a threat to American prosperity and the system of honor that undergirded it as did big corporations. He particularly feared that the muckrakers would inflame vicious attacks on big business by "ignorant agitation."[238]

When Roosevelt spoke in such a manner, he did so from the perspective of social Darwinism, an idea that were currently in vogue. In

1902 he had warned listeners to avoid trying to overthrow those "more prosperous" than themselves, as that would only bring disaster. A "spirit of rancor" toward the trusts that led to an overthrow of America's corporate foundations would endanger the natural order. Journalists, especially, who out of "ignorant zeal" stood ready to paralyze all industries. "Hysterical sensationalism," "gross and reckless assaults," and the "man with the muck-rake" promised only one of two ends: a violent crusade against business or a national malaise.[239] To be clear, most of the press supported Roosevelt. He manipulated the muckrakers as a convenient boogeyman to leverage for corporate control.

Contrary to notions that Roosevelt sought to establish a high moral plain from which to lead, his real intention was much craftier. It involved a strategy perfected some ninety years later by President Bill Clinton known as "triangulation," in which Clinton as president attempted to portray himself as above party and partisan politics and offer a third alternative to both parties. TR, of course, didn't need to worry too much about either party. Democrats already champed at the bit for regulation, and much of his own Republican Party had joined the so-called "Progressive Movement" that favored more government intrusion. Roosevelt's genius lay in his ability to triangulate between the giant interests of the corporations and the newspapers with their bent for "mobbing." By touting the violence and danger—even extermination—of large businesses from the "mob" as provoked by muckrakers, Roosevelt became their white knight. At the same time, he positioned himself as outside the muckraking, rendering journalists less powerful. In short, TR used the fear of what newspapers might unleash as a stick with which to smack trusts into line.

Historian Dorsey similarly explained Roosevelt's achievement as follows: "He took growing public resentment of big business, moderated its radicalism, and refocused it to create the pressure needed to persuade Congress to pass reform legislation...."[240] Another biographer claimed that there was "significance" in what TR said "rather than what he did."[241]

Those are rather loose yardsticks. All presidents influence and there is "significance' in what most presidents say. To argue that Roosevelt instigated change in national policy merely through rhetoric is a hard sell, though he may have been the most effective since Lincoln at doing so.[242] Roosevelt addressed the problems of corporations extensively, often within a metaphor of human biology, where the nation was a body and railroads were its arteries.[243]

While Roosevelt had gradually become more of a centralist, more of a "big government" guy, he had always had such inclinations bubbling under the surface. He endeared himself to the Progressive wing of the Republican Party, while his heroics in Cuba had stamped him as patriotic and fearless. In 1900, the Republican convention put Roosevelt on McKinley's ticket. To some, Roosevelt, described as a "brilliant madman born a century too soon," was too volatile to be left on a trajectory where he could become president himself.[244] When writer H. G. Wells met Roosevelt in 1906, he described his look as "a complex mingling of will and critical perplexity."[245] Novelist Bram Stoker, author of *Dracula*, wrote in his diary years earlier after meeting Roosevelt, "Must be President some day. A man you can't cajole, can't frighten, can't buy."[246] Thus, making him vice president could effectively move him out of the limelight and competition for the White House. Whether this strategy would have worked is unknowable, for McKinley was assassinated in 1901 and Roosevelt stepped into the presidency.

Many reformers viewed "ethics" and "uplifting the masses" as charms on a bracelet, distracting from their real motivations of social engineering. Not Roosevelt. Far from being a cynic, he devoutly believed that "no people were ever benefited by riches if their prosperity corrupted their virtue."[247] This was another factor in Roosevelt's disgust with corporations, the leaders of which he thought came from "new money," not from empires they built with their own hands. In this he was right: many of the new corporate leaders, as we have seen, were managers. Powerful managers they might have been, but still they had not created the companies they now ran.

As governor of New York, he supported a measure that taxed corporations. It marked a Jekyll/Hyde personality trait of TR's, namely that while he saw himself as the ally of the farmer, the mechanic, the small businessman, the oppressed, at the same time he (Lenin-like) thought a real revolution could only be led by a brilliant and visionary leader. Even at that, some historians saw his aggressive stance toward trusts coming less from a devout belief in antitrust law, and more from his self-identification as the head of a vanguard elite. To these scholars, Roosevelt wanted an issue to prove his administration's strength of will at the outset.[248] Marc Winerman notes that in 1899, Roosevelt saw fear of trusts as "largely irrational" and in 1900 labeled attempts to stifle concentration as not "one whit more intelligent than medieval bull against the comet."[249] Likewise, leftist historian Richard Hofstadter complained that there was "a hundred times more noise than accomplishment" in Roosevelt's record.[250]

Indeed, in his first inaugural, these views may have appeared sound. More than likely, TR knew that the nation was not quite ready for a Woodrow Wilson...at least not just yet. Therefore, President Roosevelt spoke in favorable terms of the great corporations and he endorsed the idea of expanding American markets. He cautioned, however, that the trusts were rapidly moving beyond the capacity of governments to control them and becoming laws unto themselves. Roosevelt signed the 1903 Elkins Act that prohibited railroad rebates such as those that had benefited Rockefeller, and implemented a new relationship between government and business by establishing a Department of Commerce and Labor. Within that was a Bureau of Corporations, which collected information on pricing and rates (in line with Charles Francis Adams's position that merely exposing corporations' practices through "Sunshine Laws" would prove sufficient regulation). But it would be the Northern Securities case that would provide the first clear trust-busting victory for Roosevelt. It offered the media event to consolidate his triangulation approach.

Northern Securities was a trust company established by Morgan to provide cover for railroad builder James J. Hill to control the Chicago, Burlington, and Quincy Railroad. Hill already had controlling interest in the Great Northern (his own), and the Northern Pacific (his long-time competitor that he had defeated). Edward Harriman of the Union Pacific, which he had rescued from decades of fraud. Both wanted the CB&Q, which provided access to the lucrative Chicago market. Each man drove the price up, and even though Hill stood to gain a majority of the Great Northern's common shares after 1901, Harriman might still fight the battle in the courts. Such tumult was unacceptable to Morgan, who had just finished saving the country once from bankruptcy and did not relish a second go.

Morgan and Rockefeller stepped in to bring Hill and Harriman together (under their company) with the Northern Securities Company, which would acquire controlling interest in the CB&Q, the Northern Pacific, and the Great Northern. The combination would result in a "rail megasystem covering seventeen states and thirty-two thousand miles of track."[251] Next to US Steel—which Morgan formed in March 1901 to combine all of Andrew Carnegie's steel works with Gary's Federal Steel, William Moore's National Steel, and "Bet a Million" Gates's wire company—the new Northern Securities would be the largest corporation in the world. And, it would combine two competitors that would act "in restraint of trade."

Morgan, Hill, Harriman, and Rockefeller were all confident their trust would hold up due to a recent favorable ruling in the E. C. Knight case, which seemed to support the principle that a trust could include formerly competing companies. When Roosevelt got wind of the new railroad monopoly, he called in his attorney general, Philander Knox. Roosevelt asked Knox to draft some paragraphs on trusts for his address to Congress. Alerted, Morgan sent over an attorney to urge the president to tone down the message. He refused. Indeed, Roosevelt and his attorney general thought that unlike the US Steel combination, Northern Securities provided the perfect villain for the public mind, easily explained and effortlessly symbolized. Vast railroads affected everyone with their steel sinews crossing the country, shaping travel, land prices, and daily life in ways that it was harder to see with steel.

The president began his blustery assault with terms about "evils," "despotism," "manipulation," and so on. He realized that by the twentieth century America was much more susceptible to the "news" and that newspapers of the day gleefully embraced conflict and bombast. Again, though, he carefully balanced his rhetoric with a Darwinian argument for the necessity of big business. In his address to Congress,

Roosevelt began by praising railroads: "The captains of industry who have driven the railways systems across this continent, who have built up our commerce, who have developed our manufactures, have on the whole done great good to our people."[252] He then delivered a backhand to the newspapers, saying, "Many of those who have made it their vocation to denounce the great industrial combinations...known as 'trusts,' appeal especially to hatred and fear...." Roosevelt could have added "class envy." Dealing with the malevolent aspects of trusts required a "calm enquiry and...sober self-restraint." Combinations, he argued, should not be prohibited but "supervised and within reasonable limits controlled...." The blessing of a corporate form included with it a commitment to "truthful representations" and a commitment to work in harmony with American institutions. Government, therefore, had the authority and the duty to inspect and examine a corporation's inner workings, and to regulate them at the interstate level. Specifically, he claimed the "railway is a public servant. Its rates should be just to, and open to, all shippers alike."[253] Concluding, Roosevelt made clear he was making policy for generations: "We are dealing with a new and momentous question, in the pregnant years while institutions are forming, and what we do will affect not only the present but the future generations."

Knox soon issued a statement that announced a bill would be filed by his office to test the Northern Securities agreement. Having reviewed the E. C. Knight case, Knox thought it failed because it was badly argued, and that a tighter antitrust brief would do the trick. Northern Securities, he stated, flatly violated the Sherman Antitrust Act. Wall Street immediately flew into a panic. Morgan paid a visit to the White House, urging Roosevelt to give him a bill of particulars and let him fix the trust, but Roosevelt was focused on setting a standard, not allowing further flexibility in the laws. Nevertheless, the banker was perfectly willing to settle immediately while James J. Hill was incensed, seeking to take the case to the US Supreme Court.

Hill wasn't the only one trying to press legal actions to a conclusion. In 1902, Roosevelt had asked Knox if he could go after the coal companies as a trust during a coal strike. Knox, citing the ongoing *Northern*

Securities case, replied that the Sherman Antitrust Act was still too narrow to employ and that at present the president had "no power or duty in the matter."[254] At a speech in Providence, Rhode Island, the following day, Roosevelt again laid out what he thought was a balanced approach toward combinations:

> Where men are gathered together in great masses it inevitably results that they must work far more largely through combinations.... Under present-day conditions it is as necessary to have corporation in the business world as it is to have organizations, unions, among wage workers.... The great corporations which we have grown to speak of rather loosely as trusts are the creatures of the State, and the State not only has the right to control them but it is in duty bound to control them whenever need of such control is shown...."[255]

Newspapers blared the message, PRESIDENT WOULD REGULATE TRUSTS.[256] The Washington *Evening Sun* labeled the president "trust-buster" and the sobriquet stuck.[257]

In "stalking" Standard Oil, though (as Chernow put it), Roosevelt found a valuable ally in the press. Ironically, just as hatred for Donald Trump fueled cable television ratings in the early twenty-first century, Rockefeller's trust had given modern journalism much of its power by expanding the ranks of advertisers and providing the cash papers needed to churn out muck. Such was the *McClure's* series by Ida Tarbell, daughter of a disgruntled oilman, which started in 1902. Of course, Roosevelt read the articles. They continued over a three-year period.

From 1905 to 1908, Roosevelt shifted his position again, championing a "Square Deal." Government would not deal anyone the "best hand," but instead would assure a square deal in which "if the cards do not come to any man or if they do come and he has not got the power to play them, that is his affair."[258] At the time, he still maintained (at least in public) that enacting more legislation would not "make any community happy and prosperous" or even be among the "chief factors in security such happiness and prosperity."[259] Nevertheless his stance was purely elitist, reasoning that he alone could bring a sort of moral awareness to both business leaders and the masses. Tycoons of "swollen fortune" were a "bad example" whose success created a "false standard" for people to follow. Their wealth and status aroused envy and "sour and discontented feelings."[260] That "venomous envy of wealth," a "cringing servility toward wealth," derived from a "fantastically twisted" prioritization of wealth itself. But this, again, was largely the fault of corporate leaders who "awaken[ed] in our breasts...the mean vice of worshipping [*sic*] mere wealth... or the equally mean vice of viewing with rancorous envy and hatred the men of wealth merely because they are men of wealth."[261] Either way, the fault lay with those who were successful. (One cannot be but shocked by the hypocrisy of someone who had inherited *all* of his wealth condemning those who had actually worked for theirs!)

Roosevelt wasn't finished lambasting business: corporations had produced the evil of excess wealth out of the "carelessness toward the rights of others." This made them "malefactors of great wealth," whose sin had nothing to excuse it. Profits alone could not take the place of "a high standard of conduct—honor, integrity, civic courage."[262] (For a glimpse at what happens when business puts profits aside to act on its perceptions of "honor, integrity, civic courage," look no further than the decade beginning after 2010, with "woke" corporations jamming their marketing departments' views of social justice down the throats of consumers, profits be damned.)

After Roosevelt was reelected in 1904 his tone changed dramatically in its view that some large combinations were acceptable (US Steel and International Harvester, to whom he had promised he would not file antitrust actions). At the same time, however, TR concluded that his Department of Justice had spent too much time prosecuting individual antitrust cases and that a new national law was needed. His tone grew more hostile to big business, and more statist. In 1908, he likened corporate leaders to blackmailers and "bribe-givers" who made "an enormous fortune by corrupting legislatures and municipalities" and "fleecing"

stockholders and the public, making them no different than "the creature who fattens on the blood money of the gambling-house and the
saloon." [263] Note that Roosevelt was already laying the groundwork for
Prohibition by labeling saloons as evil.

It is also of interest that when discussing bribes, Roosevelt focused on
the "bribe-givers" and not the recipients, his fellow elites in Washington.
As they say, it takes two to tango, and TR had little interest in identifying
political Swamp creatures.

Roosevelt's post-election rhetoric was a universe away from the
man who just nine years earlier had said fear of trusts was "irrational."
Now in a special message to Congress he demanded that corporations
"show they have a right to exist" [!].[264] Roosevelt had grown substantially
fonder of big government in his first term, now envisioning the Bureau of
Corporations as an agency that would manage big companies and avoid
corporate dissolutions. His brush with death from an assassin's bullet in
October 1912 and his "New Nationalism" platform led him to deem the
Sherman Act obsolete ("rural toryism") and as antiquated as the "flint-
locks of Washington's Continental."[265] He concocted a doctrine of "good
trusts" and "bad trusts" with no one other than himself able to determine
what constituted one or the other. His criteria largely rested upon how
supplicant the corporations were to him personally. After he had been
reelected (with a large campaign donation from banker J. P. Morgan),
Roosevelt met with Elbert Gary of US Steel, which Morgan had helped
create four years earlier. Gary told Roosevelt that if the government ever
suspected his company of doing anything wrong, US Steel would "convince you that we are right or we will correct what is wrong." TR replied,
"Well, that seems to me to be about the fair thing."[266]

The Progressive reformer in him emerged with full fury: the country
needed yet another new commission to set rates. Standard Oil, again,
was the target. Knox, now, was a US Senator; William Moody had taken
his spot at Justice, and public sentiment had been stirred up by a series
of articles in *Collier's* against the beef trust—already the focus of investigation by journalist Upton Sinclair. One of the more volcanic articles,
however, came from the opening article in a series in the *Cosmopolitan* on

January 15, 1906, called "The Treason of the Senate." In it, David Phillips had alleged that Senators Nelson Aldrich, Henry Cabot Lodge, Arthur Gorman, Thomas Platt, Chauncey Depew and half a dozen others were in the pocket of Standard Oil.[267]

With words that could have come from Cleveland's era, or our own, Phillips wrote, "The combination of bribery and party prejudice is potent everywhere; but there come crises when these fail 'the interests' for the moment." In Rhode Island, he wrote, "The Aldrich machine controls the legislature, the election boards, the courts—the entire machinery of the 'republican form of government.'"[268]

Still, for his Progressive inclinations, Roosevelt also knew where the radicals were headed: toward full-blown government ownership of railroads, utilities, and virtually everything else. When pushed on this, he reminded people of how "inefficient and undependable" federal employees were and that it would be a "disaster" to put them in charge of any enterprise.[269] Once again, it seemed the only one capable of making wise decisions about whether corporations were charging unfair rates or oppressing the masses was Roosevelt himself.

The regulation impetus received a sharp stimulus from an unexpected source. Sinclair's novel, *The Jungle*, came out in 1906 seeking to spark a socialist uprising in America. Instead, it ginned up support for the new pure food and drug bill. Roosevelt, of course, supported this as well: "I recommend that a law be enacted to regulate interstate commerce in misbranded and adulterated foods, drinks and drugs."[270] Too often, however, Roosevelt just wanted legislation, whether effective or not. This was his Progressive character poking through, the confusion of activity for achievement. However, Roosevelt constantly saw himself as speaking on behalf of the people, and even novelist H. G. Wells in 1906 commented that in TR, "America for the first time [is] vocal to itself."[271] This was a trait characteristic of all six of the Swamp fighters: Lincoln, Cleveland, John Kennedy, Ronald Reagan, and Donald Trump all spoke for largely unheard (within government at their respective times) majorities or near-majorities of the public.

Congress had provided the Pure Food and Drug Act in 1906 with its Food and Drug Administration. (Its first target was that dangerous product, Coca-Cola: the FDA insisted there was cocaine in the mixture, then when proven there was not, abruptly switched its claims in court to harangue Coke for false advertising!)[272] Then there was the coal strike, another opportunity for TR to make general point about combinations in restraint of trade on both sides of the ledger. But he didn't. Roosevelt had already more or less decided that a union could not be "in restraint of trade," even though non-union men were beaten, harassed, and otherwise tormented for not wishing to associate. His increasingly strident tone suggested that the president felt he had not accomplished much in the area of actual "trust-busting." His appeal to the "common man" had been usurped by Populist William Jennings Bryan of Nebraska, who found himself the nominee of the Democrat Party in 1896, 1900, and 1908. Bryan, after all, flat-out said he would put Rockefeller in jail. Fittingly, Grover Cleveland, the last sensible Democrat in the party's history, died just days before the actual nomination.

Another panic had swept the nation in 1907 when speculators Augustus Heinze and Charles Morse failed in their attempt to take over the United Copper Company. Their failure sent ripples through the banking community, particularly the Knickerbocker Trust, which had financed their speculations. Before Roosevelt could act, Morgan flew into action, organizing relief from syndicates of banks. He was joined by the very people Roosevelt had made war upon—Harriman, Rockefeller, and Henry Clay Frick. These titans mobilized previously undreamed-of capital, averting the "Roosevelt Panic." It was an unfair appellation, as the president had nothing to do with it either way. There were still mines left to explode, however, and in October 1907 another big bank, Moore & Schley appeared to be sinking. Morgan conceived a plan to have US Steel buy its collateral shares, then reinvest them in the Tennessee Coal and Iron Company. Many of Morgan's colleagues feared Roosevelt would merely use the incident to launch new antitrust actions, but the president, meeting with Elbert Gary and Frick, instead leaped at the opportunity to avoid a new "general industrial smashup" as he called it. Within hours, confidence returned.[273]

That panic, however, proved the last straw for the titan J. P. Morgan to stand as the final bulwark against national financial collapse. He informed anyone who would listen that the next crash would extend far beyond even the resources of his and his colleagues' ability to plug the dike. Substantive reform of the financial system was needed.

Here was Morgan doing exactly as Roosevelt supposedly advocated, leading out of courage and conviction. Indeed, Morgan knew that whatever institution or institutions arose from the national banking reform, his own banking business would find itself more regulated and less powerful than ever. Still, he knew it was needed. The irony of what emerged—the Federal Reserve Act of 1913—was that far from being a creation of a handful of conspirators on Jekyll Island, it emerged almost entirely from small-town American bankers who sought help from international economic storms over which they had no control. While Morgan may have laid the first brick, it was thousands of small-town bankers who, through the American Bankers Association, built the structure of the Fed. Passage of the Federal Reserve Act, though, while entirely mirroring what Roosevelt would have wanted, came long after he was out of office.

Just as Cleveland had exited without gaining full control over the Spoils Swamp, now Roosevelt—with only months left—faced departing before the Trust Swamp had been corralled to his satisfaction. One wonders if he had taken a more forceful stand against *labor* as well as business, insisting that *all* large combinations were suspect and dangerous, he would not have had more success. Certainly the Republicans seemingly moved to endorse TR's antitrust positions by nominating William Howard Taft, the former governor of the Philippines, as the presidential choice.

Taft would later be chief justice of the US Supreme Court (the only person ever to have been both president and chief justice). When Roosevelt tabbed him as his successor, he was serving as TR's secretary of war. Tipping the scales at 300 pounds, Taft, while governor of the Philippines, received a cable from Secretary of War Elihu Root, who had heard Taft had taken ill. No, Taft replied in a cable, he was fine. He had just taken a twenty-five-mile ride on his horse. Root cabled back, "How is [the] horse?"[274]

Taft supposedly had the right "street cred," and certainly he had the president's support. Roosevelt said the two shared the same views. Taft referred to Standard Oil as "an octopus that holds back the trade in its tentacles...."[275] Taft's speech to the convention likewise seemed to indicate the GOP was on a course to continue the assault on the Trust Swamp. He certainly seemed more energetic than Roosevelt in pursuing antitrust violations: his attorney general's office brought seventy cases against businesses in four years, whereas TR had brought forty in seven years. The biggest victories came after Roosevelt was gone. In 1911 the US Supreme Court ruled in the case of *Standard Oil Co. of New Jersey v. United States* in which the oil giant sued to prevent the Sherman Antitrust Act from being applied to it.[276] The court ruled on May 15, 1911, that the decision to dismantle Standard Oil was upheld. Standard was broken up into thirty-four separate companies, including (subsequently named) Standard Oil of New Jersey (Exxon), Standard Oil of New York (Mobil), Standard Oil of Indiana (Amoco), Standard Oil of California (Chevron), and Standard Oil of Ohio (purchased by British Petroleum and called Sohio). And, as one might predict, it wasn't long before they began to recombine, as in the case of ExxonMobil.

The legal reasoning, according to the Sixth Circuit's Chief Judge in an 1899 case violated the "rule of reason," in which only unreasonable combinations in restraint of trade could be considered monopolies. That Chief Judge? William Howard Taft. In the *United States v. American Tobacco Co.*, also decided in 1911, the Court ruled that the company was also in restraint of trade, but that having a monopoly by itself did not constitute restraint of trade.[277] In 1918, the Supreme Court would reaffirm the "rule of reason" in the *Chicago Board of Trade v. the United States.*[278]

U. S. Steel had, in fact, expanded under Roosevelt by acquiring the Tennessee Coal, Iron, and Railroad Company as TR sought to end the Panic of 1907. That was Roosevelt's sop to Morgan. Taft also defended the deal.[279] With the Standard Oil case, breaking up Rockefeller's company into several smaller businesses, As with most government regulation, it came after there was no longer any real need for it. As Ron Chernow noted in his biography of Rockefeller, "Standard Oil attained its peak influence in the 1890s," and yet after "years of harrowing prophecies that the industry might vanish, the business outlook had never looked brighter."[280] Foreign competition from Russia cut into Standard's market; Shell Oil from Holland constituted a growing threat; and Spindletop in Texas led to the formation of the new Gulf Oil Company. Chernow, no friend of Rockefeller's, concluded, "It might not be much of an exaggeration to say that the antitrust cases brought against the trust in the early 1900s were not just belated but were fast becoming superfluous."[281] By the time Roosevelt came into office, "cooperation" via discussion among the industrialists had replaced monopolies and trusts. Rockefeller laughed at the government's efforts, calling the legislation "not one whit more intelligent than the medieval bull against the comet...."[282] Indeed, the same could be said for the lack of action against the tech monopolies in the early twenty-first century, when they were begging for regulation.

Not only had the trustbusters pushed Standard and every other trust into the more effective "vertical combinations," but by breaking up Standard into many smaller profitable companies owned by Rockefeller, they helped make him the richest man in the world. As for the Sherman Act, it fell into a morass in which, eventually, judges had to decide whether the combination in question was a "good trust" or a "bad trust." In other words, the Sherman Antitrust Act had made it impossible to apply a clear and unambiguous standard.

But Roosevelt had succeeded in the mind of the public. His nickname "Trust Buster" would follow him into history. He rode the crest of the Progressive assault on the Trust Swamp, emerging as more victorious in perception than in reality. America's antitrust legacy, however, proved completely inadequate to control or even mediate the trust threat of the twenty-first century, that of media and tech conglomerates. Those merged, combined, and gained almost unchallenged control over America's entertainment and speech: some six corporate giants dominated *all* of the entertainment and news. Websites such as Facebook, Google, and Twitter actively censored political speech to advance their own causes, safe from regulation by claiming they were simply platforms for speech with their own codes, not public utilities subject to oversight. As such, they engaged in behavior that would dwarf the evil excesses of the worst of TR's trusts. Their censorship of ideas, speech, and advertising in the public square made a mockery of the virtues Roosevelt championed—honor, integrity, civic courage. Whether Big Tech and Big Media could be controlled or even tempered remains perhaps the most important question of the age as of this writing.

Roosevelt's war against the Trust Swamp had another completely unintended consequence, and one that over time unraveled almost all the gains made in his predecessor's battle against the Spoils Swamp. With antitrust came a growing federal government, with more agencies, more bureaus. Roosevelt was oblivious to that. After all, as Louis the XIV would say, "*L'etat? C'est moi.*" TR would not live to see the Bureaucracy Swamp that one of his successors, Ronald Reagan would have to struggle with, but to no small degree it was TR who loosed the levies to fill the swamp. The dangers of the Bureaucracy Swamp, though, would only become apparent after Roosevelt's cousin, Franklin, dropped truckloads of alligators in it.

Unlike Lincoln, whose clear triumph over the Slave Swamp was unique, Cleveland and Roosevelt found their enemies more slippery, less easy to attack legally, and well-supported and financed. Each, however, still benefited from largely supportive parties, somewhat or entirely positive press (or in TR's case, a slice of journalism he was able to parlay against the corporations) and the presumption that for better or worse the elected president was the voice of the people. When at all possible, his will should be accommodated. By 1960, the Bureaucratic Swamp that TR helped unleash revealed its malignant side in the form of the Central Intelligence Agency that seemingly answered to no one.

Scorecard: Roosevelt and the Trust Swamp

- Temporarily successful in regulating the Trust Swamp
- Along with the courts, frequently applied antitrust laws based on questionable constitutional bases.
- Had solid support from Congress and the courts
- Had generally positive support from the press and used the "muckrakers" as foils
- Narrowly focused antitrust actions in such a way that they seldom applied to new problems created by the digital media

Part 2

Failures

Abraham Lincoln, Grover Cleveland, and Theodore Roosevelt all to one degree or another succeeded in defeating or severely attenuating their Swamp creatures. Lincoln, the most successful, was able to end slavery in America permanently. While he certainly desired racial harmony and equality of opportunity in the nation's economy, Lincoln knew that those goals lay way beyond the reach of any president.

Grover Cleveland had benefited from ground-breaking work by James Garfield and Chester Arthur. Cleveland, though, could not entirely eliminate the Spoils Swamp—it was far too deeply embedded and, more important, constituted a key mechanism for the operation of the American party system. But he dealt it powerful blows, reducing much of the direct control any president had when it came to handing out jobs as political plums. His actions and the Pendleton Act may have unwittingly shifted the Spoils Swamp onto a different playing field, but for the time being Cleveland could claim a split decision.

Likewise, Theodore Roosevelt was able to use the powers he had at the time to restrict the growing dominance of trusts in America. The

Trust Swamp did not disappear: like the Spoils Swamp it underwent a metamorphosis into vertical combinations that were legal, but also more capable of acquiring unrelated businesses to create massive conglomerates highly resistant to any kinds of regulation or public control. Like Cleveland, however, Roosevelt could leave office with his crusade considered a success.

Each of the three benefited from a largely positive press. Lincoln and TR especially faced Swamp creatures that were more narrowly defined, hence more easily attacked. All three presidents were popular—Cleveland won three straight popular votes; Lincoln and Roosevelt were reelected overwhelmingly. Finally, for the most part, the Slave Swamp and the Trust Swamp existed outside of government, thus were more vulnerable to government action. But while the Spoils Swamp in essence "was" government, it nevertheless had a strong and unified core of one of the major parties aligned against it. In short, the battlefield in each case was at worst neutral for these presidents and at best slightly in their favor. Such would not be the case with the next three, whose Swamp monsters either defeated them outright or successfully deflected attempts at reform. John Kennedy, Ronald Reagan, and Donald Trump all failed to beat the Swamp, which emerged more powerful than ever at the end of the tenure of each president.

CHAPTER 4

John F. Kennedy and the CIA Swamp

ohn F. Kennedy's struggle with the Central Intelligence Agency in the early 1960s saw one sharp distinction between his battle and those waged by Abraham Lincoln and Teddy Roosevelt in that Kennedy needed his CIA Swamp to further his foreign policy objectives. Far too often, he used it to do the dirty jobs he did not want to be seen as doing. Often, he was controlling it. But just as often it was controlling him. In the decades since his assassination, those who insist that the CIA played a role in his death have been required to develop a counterfactual about JFK, namely that immediately after the Bay of Pigs disaster, he set himself to draining the CIA Swamp. That hinges on a central premise, namely that JFK was not knee-deep in the CIA Swamp himself until he began to resist its overtures. Far too often—much like Grover Cleveland's relationship with the Spoils Swamp—Kennedy could not eliminate the Agency altogether. He needed it too much.

As the various stories about "who killed JFK" unfold, we are left with two versions of John F. Kennedy. One is the "Saint Jack" interpretation, whereby he was a world-class peacemaker who was on the verge of "secret talks" with Fidel Castro, a number of peace deals with Nikita Khrushchev, and at the cusp of "pulling out" of Vietnam. The other is the "Sinner Jack" interpretation, whereby Kennedy was a Cold Warrior, a hard-line anti-Communist who supported the Bay of Pigs until it turned ugly then abandoned his allies, who raised the number of American "advisors" in Vietnam from 500 to 16,000 in three years, and who nearly brought the world into a nuclear war with the Cuban Missile Crisis. One's view of the Kennedy assassination itself largely rests on whether one subscribes to the "Saint Jack" or the "Sinner Jack" interpretation.

Determining the degree to which Kennedy was committed to eliminating or greatly constraining the CIA constitutes a fundamental building block in any narrative as to who killed Kennedy and why. But to what degree was he half-submerged in the CIA Swamp itself? When JFK's facility with using the CIA to his own purposes is fully realized, the story of JFK and the Agency is far murkier than some of the other episodes we have examined. Neither the "Saint Jack" nor the "Sinner Jack" view may be entirely correct.

President Harry Truman, who signed the National Security Act of 1947 establishing the Central Intelligence Agency, was asked by a biographer many years later what he thought of what he'd done. Truman replied, "I think it was a mistake. And if I'd known what was going to happen, I never would have done it."[283] In 1963, just a month after John F. Kennedy was assassinated, Truman wrote an op-ed for the *Washington Post* in which he said

> There is something about the way the CIA has been functioning that is casting a shadow over our historic position and I feel that we need to correct it....[The CIA has been] diverted from its original assignment [and has] become an operational and at times policy-making arm of the Government (emphasis mine).[284]

The CIA as we know it was created by Harry Truman as the Central Intelligence Group (CIG) in January 1946 to "accomplish the correlation and evaluation of intelligence relating to the national security," but according to the CIA's chief historian, the straightforward statement left room for a power struggle within the government over just who would control this agency.[285] By September 1947, now established as the Central Intelligence Agency, the CIA reported to an interdepartmental body known as the National Intelligence Authority (NIA) with the main task being to prepare a Daily Summary (DS, or now known as a presidential daily brief [PDB]) for the Chief Executive. This DS was to remain between four to six pages so as to not overwhelm a president. Truman approved of the process, and thought the Daily Summary made him the "best-informed Chief Executive in history on foreign affairs."[286] However, it also meant that the CIA was setting the agenda for the president and shaping what intelligence he received. After all, what if the Daily Summary ignored a key development the CIA did not want the president aware of?

Other senior officials in the Truman administration were not nearly as thrilled with the Daily Summaries: Secretary of the Navy James Forrestal thought it valuable but not "indispensable" and Secretary of State George Marshall quit reading it after two weeks because he already saw almost everything in the DS in his State Department traffic. Truman's military representative, Adm. William Leahy, said the president "was pleased" with the reports and had a "coordinated method...and a practical way" to keep informed.[287]

Others, however, recognized the dangers right away. A survey group established to examine the new CIA warned of the Daily Summary that "there is an inherent danger that it will be misleading to its consumers... because it is based largely [90 percent] on abstracts of State Department materials, not in historical perspective, lacking a full knowledge of the background or policy involved and with little previous consultation between the [CIA] and the State Department."[288] (This may well have been an attempt by the State Department to wedge its way back into policy.) But the survey also observed that at times the CIA's comments "appear gratuitous and lend little weight to the material itself" and often was "beyond the Agency's area of responsibility."[289]

Truman intended the Agency (or "the Company" as some called it) to be a center for informing the president as to what was happening in the world at the time, not as a "Cloak & Dagger outfit" (as Truman called it).[290] When he left office, he praised the agency and boasted that the "Agency puts the information of vital importance to the President in his hands."[291]

In 2017, when Democrats were panicked about President Donald Trump's election and sought to undermine it by claiming there was "Russian collusion" (a hoax that was thoroughly disproven even by the Special Counsel investigation of Robert Mueller), the leftist *Huffington Post* issued an outraged editorial claiming the CIA was the last organization in the world with the credibility to make such a claim. "Seriously?" the HuffPo asked.[292]

It probably shouldn't come as a surprise that Senator Joseph McCarthy was the first to actually attempt to investigate the CIA. In July 1951, after Republican Dwight Eisenhower won the presidency, McCarthy's permanent subcommittee on investigations issued a subpoena to William Bundy, the CIA liaison to the National Security Council. McCarthy had found Bundy had given $400 to his arch enemy Alger Hiss's defense fund.[293] Vice President Richard Nixon, Eisenhower's point man on Congress, met with the senator and forced him to withdraw the subpoena. Typically, McCarthy was staring at a mountain of dung and instead focusing on a single mouse dropping in the corner. With Allen Dulles's help, the flap blew over. Both parties agreed to a general mushy formula where the subcommittee would be within its rights to call CIA employees without endangering national security. For McCarthy, it was a typical missed opportunity to expose a malignant cell within the federal government. For Eisenhower, Nixon, and the CIA, it was a successful attempt to keep the Agency out of Congress's oversight so it could be useful.

President Dwight D. Eisenhower saw the CIA as a means to pursue Cold War ends without the public scrutiny of wars. He "relied frequently on covert action to avoid having to take public responsibility for controversial interventions. He believed that the CIA, created in 1947, was an effective instrument to counter Communist expansion and to assist friendly governments."[294] Still, he saw weaknesses in the Agency, which had expanded too fast with too many incompetent employees. He remarked upon a "complete lack of security consciousness throughout" the CIA and suggested there was "too much information" being "leaked at cocktail parties."[295] Nevertheless, Ike first employed the spy agency in the realm of gathering information on the Soviets' space activities. This alliance soon led to the construction and use of the U-2 and SR-71 spy planes, whose success actually undermined the CIA's on-the-ground human intelligence capabilities.[296]

But quickly, as Chester Pach, writing for the Miller Center on the presidency at the University of Virginia, noted, Eisenhower authorized those actions against leaders and nations under the logic of Cold War realities. He did so with "plausible deniability" which was sanctioned in 1948 with the National Security Council directive NSC 10/2." Under Ike, in 1951 the CIA overthrew Prime Minister Mohammad Mossadegh in Iran because of his pro-Communist tendencies (although the Shah of Iran, Mohammad Reza Pahlavi, remained in power). The following year, the CIA assisted in the overthrow of the Guatemalan government, which was falling under the influence of Communists. Of course, it was the last of these ventures—against the man Ike called a "madman," Cuba's Fidel Castro—that drew in John Kennedy.

During the campaign of 1960, John Kennedy had hammered the Eisenhower administration for weakness against the Soviets. He lied about a "missile gap" (which he knew didn't exist). More important, he called Ike's Cuba policy "a glaring failure of American foreign policy" and mocked Richard Nixon for not "standing firm on Cuba.... If you can't stand up to Castro, how can you be expected to stand up to [Soviet Premier] Nikita Khrushchev?" JFK attacked Eisenhower for "two years of inaction" on Cuba and called for "fighters for freedom" to overthrow Castro."[297]

By the time John F. Kennedy assumed the presidency in January 1961, the CIA was well entrenched first under director Allan Dulles from 1951–1961, then John McCone. Did the CIA control Kennedy? Did it seek to undermine or evade his intentions—even his orders? These are complex questions that demand a great deal of interpretation of events. The first thing to understand is that John Kennedy was a "cold warrior."

His central campaign issue was largely a lie, namely that there was a "missile gap" that existed between the US and the Soviet Union, and that the USSR was well in the lead. JFK knew this was untrue. He was receiving briefings from the Eisenhower administration. If anything, the US had a substantial lead in missiles of all types.

Kennedy's inaugural address further debunked any notion that he would be weak on the Soviets. He promised that "we will pay any price, bear any burden, meet any hardship, support any friend, oppose any foe, to assure the survival and the success of liberty."[298] Stories about JFK's "turning" to a man of peace and his intentions to withdraw from Vietnam—which shall be discussed presently—are based almost entirely on assertions by Kennedy aides Dave Powers and Ken O'Donnell about supposedly private conversations they had. Those stories appeared in 1971, when the US was embroiled in the Vietnam War and when Democrats who had originally supported the war now opposed it and were attempting to saddle Richard Nixon (who got the US *out* of the war) with its origins. Bizarre indeed.

Upon assuming office, Kennedy inherited some of Ike's troubles. The situation in Laos was still dismal: Eisenhower had refused to send troops in, but in all likelihood it would soon fall to the North Vietnamese-backed Pathet Lao. Kennedy knew that even for the US military, Laos was a long reach. Then there was the new problem of Cuba, which in December 1958 installed the Communist Fidel Castro in power over the deposed Fulgencio Bautista.

More pressing was a plan already in motion by the CIA, which had been training 1,500 Cuban exile troops in Guatemala, to invade Cuba. Long glossed over by the "Jacobite"/St. Jack interpreters of Kennedy's administration (i.e., that he was a peacemaker who wanted to get along with Castro), he was meeting in secrecy with the "eventual leaders of the Cuban Exile brigade that landed on the beaches at the Bay of Pigs" in March 1960.[299] Recent evidence has shown that Juan Almeida Bosque, the commander of Cuba's Army, whose identity was concealed during the early major JFK assassination investigations, was being prepared to take over for Castro by the Kennedy administration.[300] (Some assassination theorists maintain that both Lyndon Johnson and then-Attorney General Robert Kennedy, John's brother, kept Almeida's identity away from the investigators because he remained secretly placed and had played a role in preventing the Cuban Missile Crisis from escalating.) Kennedy rejected a more ambitious "Trinidad Plan" in March 1961, in which the CIA wanted an amphibious/airborne assault on Cuba in favor of a night landing with "no basis for American military intervention."[301]

This element is key: while Eisenhower had authorized Operation Mongoose in March 1960, establishing a program of "Covert Action Against the Castro Regime," he never ordered nor authorized any amphibious invasion.[302] In fact, on January 18, 1960, the White House (CIA) division organized a task force stationed in Washington, Havana, and Santiago Base, to run the Cuban operation. At that time, no assassination attempts were authorized, but increasingly (especially after the Bay of Pigs) it became clear that central to any plan to liberate Cuba required the CIA to assassinate Castro first and install Almeida. By August 1960, the company openly negotiated with representatives of the Mafia, specifically asking Robert Maheu, a businessman and lawyer who worked for the agency, to contact mob boss Johnny Roselli to "dispose" of Castro.[303] A suspicious Roselli demanded to meet directly with someone from the CIA. Maheu then introduced him in September 1960 to the "Support Chief."

This unidentified "Support Chief" had been compartmentalized and did not realize he was working not only with Roselli, but Roselli's associates Momo ("Sam") Giancana and Santos Trafficante, the bosses of Chicago and formerly Havana, respectively. By that time, the Support Chief noted, he realized "we were up to our ears in it."[304]

Some results were comedic and loopy. The CIA wanted to discredit Castro by changing his appearance and influencing his behavior. Among the methods the CIA considered, spraying his broadcast studio with an LSD-like substance was rejected as too unreliable. But a plan to line Castro's shoes with thallium salts that would cause his beard to fall out gained support, only to have Castro cancel the trip where the CIA would have access to his shoes.[305] The CIA via the mob also tried to employ poison cigars, to no effective result. Whether Roselli actually tried to kill Castro or merely sucked up government resources remains unclear. He purportedly dispatched two three-man teams, to no effect. By September 1962 the Agency prepared to pull the plug on the mob aspects of the JM/WAVE operation.

Years later Richard Helms, who replaced Dulles as the head of the CIA, testified that "it was the policy at the time to get rid of Castro, and if killing him was one of the things that was to be done...we felt we were acting well within the guidelines.... Nobody wants to embarrass a President...by discussing the assassination of foreign leaders in his presence."[306] Where hagiographers of JFK saw deception and manipulation by the CIA, others saw the fingerprints of the Kennedy brothers cleverly wiped away by "plausible deniability."

However, new evidence from CIA agents at the time suggests that in fact the CIA was not nearly as anti-Castro as the Oliver Stone school thought. Former CIA officer Brian Dean Wright told Fox News that the agency had a history of pushing a leftist agenda.[307] Robert Weicha, a CIA operative in Cuba, said, "Everyone in the CIA and everyone at State was pro-Castro, except [Republican] ambassador Earl Smith."[308] Robert Reynolds, the CIA Caribbean Desk chief from 1957–1960 said, "Me and my staff were all Fidelistas."[309] The ambassador to Cuba from 1957 to 1959 said, "Without US help Fidel Castro would never have gotten into power. The press, the Chief of the CIA section are also responsible...."[310]

In fact, one wing within the CIA actively worked to ally with Castro. Alfred Cox, Chief of the Para-military Division, Political and Psychological Staff, wrote

> A practical way to protect United States interests [in Cuba] would be to make secret contact with Castro, assure him of the United States sympathy with some of his objectives, and to offer him support. (emphasis mine)....
> Obviously, the support must be given covertly so as not to endanger United States relations with Bautista.[311]

Cox went on to argue for shipping arms to Castro. The unclassified history of the Bay of Pigs notes: "Not all Agency reporting out of the Cuban area was biased against Castro." It cited an unnamed CIA source—a Catholic priest—in Cuba who said, "The United States should not be taken in by President Fulgencio Batista's attempt to label the revolutionary movement as Communist inspired, dominated, or influential."[312] Another Catholic source, the representative of the archbishop of Havana, urged private meetings with Castro, and "Havana Station" (of the CIA) agreed that the "proposal merits serious State/ CIA consideration."[313] In 1959, after the KGB had dumped a number of undercover agents in Cuba, the CIA was still arguing that "Cuban Communists do not consider [Castro] a Communist Party member or even a pro-Communist…Our conclusion, therefore, is that Fidel Castro is not a Communist."[314]

Even the Dark Prince of the "St. Jack" version of events, the CIA Director Allen Dulles in late 1959–60, could not say that Castro was a Communist. In a December 1958 meeting involving high level foreign policy and defense advisors, Dulles for the first time changed his opinion of Castro, saying, "Communists and other extreme radicals appear to have penetrated the Castro movement…. [and if] Castro takes over, they will probably participate in the government."[315] Astonishingly, as late as 1959 the CIA did not have a "qualified Communist expert" in Havana to brief embassy officers on Communist doctrines or operations.[316] Significantly, however, in the critical memorandum from J. C. King, Chief of the CIA's White House division, presented for the first time in December 1959 a plan for removing Castro. Dulles had written corrections to the King memo that called for the "elimination of Fidel Castro" to the "removal from Cuba" of Castro; then again later in the same memo Dulles changed King's wording regarding the "disappearance of Fidel would greatly accelerate the fall of the present government" to "the *removal*" of Fidel.[317]

In short, 1) the CIA was still quite ambiguous as to whether to support or oppose Castro as late as 1959; 2) Dulles did not support assassination of Castro then; and 3) large elements within the CIA were convinced Castro was not a Communist.

Meanwhile, after winning the election, Kennedy restructured the National Security Council in such a way that it "diminished the voice of the Joint Chiefs of Staff (JCS) in national security matters."[318] Consequently the JCS lost direct access to the president and its role in decision-making was limited. He abolished the two NSC committees that took that organization out of the loop in favor of a more personal, ad hoc process. Kennedy placed a premium on intellect, and especially on academic qualifications.

Kennedy thought he had effectively squelched any direct US involvement in the Bay of Pigs operation—the air support came from unmarked CIA B-26 bombers on Cuban airfields two days before the 1,400-man force landed on the night of April 17 at the Bay of Pigs. But as H. R. McMaster pointed out, his informal style never permitted a systematic review of the invasion, consulting the JCS only after he had decided to launch the attack.[319] After early success by the Cuban exiles, Castro took over military counteroperations and crushed the invasion. Did the CIA intend to draw in American military forces through the failure of the initial invasion? Was the CIA attempting a covert operation on the *president* as well as the Cubans by forcing his hand? Stories from some of the anti-Castro leaders surfaced later in which they supposedly were told that the CIA would "make some kind of show, as if you were putting us, the CIA advisors, in prison to override Kennedy's orders"—a development Attorney General Robert Kennedy called "virtually treason."[320]

It is here that John Kennedy commented that he wanted "to splinter the C.I.A. in a thousand pieces and scatter it to the winds."[321] Arthur Schlesinger related that JFK had told him during the Bay of Pigs invasion that "we will have to deal with the CIA...no one has dealt with the CIA."[322]

These are odd comments for a commander in chief who, just seven months later would huddle with CIA director John McCone, Bobby Kennedy, Brigadier General Lansdale, and others to discuss Operation Mongoose. By the end of that month, Kennedy himself approved details of Mongoose. *Robert Kennedy was in effective control of the operation.* Far from "scattering the CIA to the winds," JFK was indeed "dealing with it." But not in the way some interpreted his words.

The notion that St. Jack was the object of a secret operation by the CIA to make end runs around him falls apart when it is seen that Operation Mongoose was in fact directed by Lansdale out of the Department of Defense along with William Harvey at CIA. But according to the CIA co-organizer Samuel Halpern, the "CIA and the US Army and military forces and Department of Commerce, and Immigration, Treasury, God knows who else—everybody was in Mongoose. It was a government-wide operation run out of Bobby Kennedy's office with Ed Lansdale as the mastermind."[323] This would have been utterly impossible without John Kennedy's full knowledge and unequivocal approval.

Part of the problem was that the CIA was not alone in trying to manipulate Kennedy. According to a March 1962 memo, the Joint Chiefs were hip-deep in the plan to draw America in through a "logical build-up of incidents to be combined with other seemingly unrelated events to camouflage the ultimate objective and create the necessary impression of Cuban rashness and irresponsibility."[324] In other words, JFK was aligned against much more than the CIA Swamp.

Nevertheless, Kennedy did reorganize the government to minimize the power of the CIA Swamp. In National Security Action Memoranda (NSAM) 35 and 36, Kennedy removed military-style operations from the CIA. NSAM 55 made the Joint Chiefs of Staff the principal military advisors of the president, not the CIA. In fact, this was always expected to have been the proper arrangement. JFK just put it into words. He reduced the CIA budget in 1962 and 1963, and forced the masterminds behind the Bay of Pigs (Dulles, Deputy Director Richard Bissell, Jr., and Deputy Director General Charles Cabell) to resign.

That hardly meant that JFK was at war with the CIA Swamp. As the Church Committee documents showed, from June 1963 onward Kennedy's administration actually intensified its war against Cuba with the assassination plots in full swing. (The Church Committee would identify eight separate plots to kill Castro.) Ironically, one of the attempts to eliminate the Cuban dictator occurred on November 22, 1963, at *exactly* the same moment as JFK himself was being assassinated.[325] Other sabotage actions that included attacks by CIA-funded teams on petroleum storage facilities, a power plant, a sawmill, and a railway bridge continued through October 1962—the Cuban Missile Crisis—although historians differ on whether Kennedy temporarily halted those actions as the Crisis escalated.[326] Historian Jorge Dominguez noted that the most striking aspect of the entire Cuban Missile Crisis was that the central player, Cuba, wasn't even included in any of the talks!

In large part due to the Bay of Pigs invasion and the ongoing attempts to assassinate Castro, both the USSR and the Cubans examined options to counter American moves. Of more concern was the genuine "missile gap" in which the US held a commanding lead. Soviet First Secretary Nikita Khrushchev saw an inexpensive way to address the Soviet disadvantage by putting intermediate-range missiles in Cuba. In May 1962 Khrushchev began moving teams into Cuba to prepare the facilities.

Soviet concerns, as historians have later shown, were based on terrifying numbers. They only had twenty missiles capable of hitting the US from the Soviet Union.[327] In truth, though it is never mentioned in the literature, it was worse than that. Soviet missile failure rates were kept secret for decades. American failure rates were 15 percent, and most analysts think theirs were far worse. That would mean that of the twenty missiles—if all were launched at once, perhaps only fifteen would actually exit the atmosphere, and more still would fail en route or upon impact. Any atomic explosion is horrific, but looking at the total retaliation the Soviets would expect, firing your entire arsenal for a dozen explosions knowing you would be wiped out in return was beyond lunacy.[328] Then there was the whole issue of Cuba as a net drain on the Soviet economy, for which the Russians were receiving nothing in return. At least Castro could offer them a missile base. Anastas Mikoyan, the second-highest ranking Soviet official, confirmed this, saying the move was designed to achieve "a definite shift in the power relationship" between the US and the USSR.[329]

What became the "Cuban Missile Crisis" originated not just in Cuba, but in Berlin, where tensions were high. In 1948, Joseph Stalin had attempted to force the United States, Britain, and France out of West Berlin by a blockade that cut off all ground traffic, including railroads, into and out of West Berlin (though that name did not take hold until a year later). The city was buried 100 miles deep within the eastern part of Germany (known as "East Germany"), which then was controlled by the Soviets. It constituted a major thorn in the side of the Communist Germans, who watched West Berlin recover faster than the East. Because most people, especially those in the West, thought the Soviets would honor their commitments to withdraw from the portion of Germany they controlled (Winston Churchill excepted), Berlin was left as an administrative city that would be reunited. With Stalin's blockade in 1948, all illusions of a peaceful reunification of Germany vanished.

President Harry Truman backed the Soviet dictator down through an airlift that supplied food, medicine, and other goods to Berlin. Soon thereafter, however, the Communists separated the electrical grids, sealed the borders around the city, and blocked roads heading in and out of the east zone. Anyone who thought Stalin's successor, Nikita Khrushchev, would be more reasonable was disappointed when, beginning in August 1961, he had a concrete barrier known as the "Berlin Wall" erected that separated the two Berlins and made utterly clear the difference in living standards. Between 1946 and 1961 when the Wall went up, some 3.5 million Germans had fled the Communist zone for West Germany, many of them through West Berlin. As Marc Leif and I noted in our 2010 film *Rockin' the Wall*, East Germany was "rapidly becoming depopulated."[330]

A third trouble spot existed that prompted Khrushchev to use the Cuban missiles for leverage. The United States had placed Jupiter missiles in Italy and Turkey. These medium range ballistic missiles had a range capable of reaching the inner parts of the USSR. To Khrushchev, the Jupiters and the Cuban missiles were linked; to JFK, they were separate. Khrushchev viewed the Jupiter missiles as a "first strike" threat, especially dangerous given the unreliability of Soviet missiles.

Kennedy's refusal to support the Bay of Pigs invasion convinced Khrushchev that the young president would not challenge the new deployment of Cuban missiles. Publicly, the Soviets denied they were deploying any missiles in Cuba. However, already US intelligence services had observed Russian light bombers in Cuba and the U-2 spy planes found surface-to-air missile sites at eight locations—a clear sign they were about to deploy something worth protecting from attack. As members of the Senate began to warn of the emplacement of ballistic missiles, Air Force General Curtis LeMay developed a bombing plan to eliminate the sites.

Concerns that the Soviets might shoot down a U-2 had resulted in a "photo gap" period in which there was no coverage over Cuba five weeks. Finally, on October 9, Kennedy authorized new U-2 flights. Kennedy began to consider responses on October 16, and immediately he felt the weight of the Berlin issue and its connection to Cuba: taking out the Cuban missiles might provoke the Soviets to respond in Berlin, if not Cuba itself.[331] To say Kennedy was pressed hard by the Joint Chiefs to use military force is an understatement. General LeMay, in particular, was insubordinate and his comments bordered on treason at times. In the White House meeting, LeMay compared Kennedy's inaction to the appeasement at Munich.[332] The unflappable Kennedy refused to be bullied. When LeMay said, "You're in a pretty bad fix," Kennedy just laughed and replied, "You're in it with me...."[333]

Offered the options of a military strike to take out the missiles, pursuing the (so-far-useless) diplomatic route and employing the United Nations, or establishing a naval blockade to keep the missile sites from being completed, JFK opted for the final choice. American ships would set up a patrol zone and board any suspicious ships bound for Cuba. In one instance, a Soviet ship was on a direct course to challenge the "line" when literally at the last second a message from Moscow halted all forward movement. That order may have prevented a war. Only later was it revealed that there were 162 nuclear warheads in Cuba, and the missiles were in fact ready to be fired. Meanwhile, the United States was on DEFCON 2 for the only confirmed time in history. American bombers were dispersed and some B-52s laden with atomic bombs were aloft 24/7. This impressed the Russians, who were "thoroughly stood down."[334] After the US intercepted and boarded the Lebanese freighter *Marcula*, it was clear to the Kremlin that Kennedy was not going to relent. A Soviet cargo ship, the *Kislovodsk*, turned back toward the Baltic. Still, publicly the Soviets gave no indication of backing down.

Even before the secret negotiations started, Kennedy had told the Executive Committee that he thought only an invasion would remove the missiles. Still, he agreed to wait and increased low-level flights over Cuba from two per day to twelve. Sergo Mikoyan, who served as the personal secretary to his father, the second-highest-ranking Soviet leader, Anastas Mikoyan, found in the transcripts and memoirs that in fact the implicit threat of military strikes weighed heavily on Khrushchev.[335] As Khrushchev got more desperate, he sought a way out. Dean Rusk, the secretary of state, would later say the Soviet boss "blinked."

The story of the back-channel negotiations that used ABC's John Scali as a messenger to Aleksandr Feklisov, the KGB station chief in Washington, to broker a deal are well known. Through the Brazilian government, JFK sent a message to Castro saying that the United States would be "unlikely to invade" if the missiles were removed, and late on the 26th, Khrushchev's first long message (twenty-six pages) arrived. According to Robert Kennedy, it was long and emotional. Yet at the same time—literally the messages crossed in transmission—Castro was urging Khrushchev to launch a pre-emptive nuclear strike on the United States. (Khrushchev reportedly saw the "Armageddon Letter" from Castro on the 27th.)[336] Even worse, the CIA reported three of the four missile sites were operational. By that time, Khrushchev had to know that Castro was an unstable maniac seeking war. But he also had the Politburo breathing down his neck wanting him to get more from the negotiations than an American promise. An evening broadcast of his newest message indicated Khrushchev now wanted the Jupiter missiles removed.

JFK recoiled at this. There were already plans to retire and withdraw the Jupiters, but he could not let them become part of the Cuban discussions. McGeorge Bundy, Kennedy's National Security Advisor, put it plainly: "The current threat to peace is not in Turkey, it is in Cuba."[337] As Khrushchev was receiving Castro's Armageddon Letter, a Soviet submarine B-59 was being tracked by the US Navy, which was dropping "signal" depth charges on it. B-59 in fact had nuclear torpedoes on it and had been ordered to fire if damaged by depth charges. Unable to acquire radio traffic, the captain, Valentin Grigorievich Savitsky prepared to launch but protocol required he have agreement of all three officers on board. One, Vasili Arkhipov, refused to order to launch and war was averted.

Khrushchev insisted the Jupiter missiles had to be part of the deal, and Kennedy relented. But the removal of the Jupiters was to remain secret: the only public aspect that Kennedy agreed to was the promise not to invade Cuba. Any suggestion that Castro was mellowing or seeking a rapprochement with Kennedy seems absurd, given that the Cuban strongman reportedly threw a fit, kicking a wall and smashing things. Years later, Castro told US Senator George McGovern, "I would have taken a harder line than Khrushchev.... [But if] my position had prevailed there might have been a terrible war."[338] And, undoubtedly, there would have been no Cuba.

So who won?

First, in averting war, Kennedy and Khrushchev saved countless millions of lives. Tactical nuclear weapons which were unknown stayed in Cuba for a time, but Castro had shown his unhinged nature to the general secretary, and Khrushchev ordered the tactical missiles out as soon as possible. One year to the day before Kennedy was assassinated, Anastas Mikoyan firmly told the Cuban dictator that all rockets with nuclear warheads would be removed. The clear unstated message to Castro: "You can't be trusted."[339] Because of the secret nature of the Jupiter removals and the (unknown to the US) tactical nuclear weapons that were withdrawn, JFK came out looking like the victor. When Khrushchev was sacked in 1964, the Soviet Presidium cited his scheming and rash decisions—clearly alluding to the installment of Cuban missiles. Some, including British historian Paul Johnson, however, claims "both Castro and Russia did very well out of Khrushchev's brinksmanship." Even French president Charles de Gaulle observed that going in, the Soviets had no advantage. Khrushchev later admitted that Cuba was 10,000 miles from the USSR and air communications were sporadic. Johnson claims that JFK "could have gone further: he could have insisted on punishment—on Soviet acceptance of a neutral, disarmed Cuba...."[340] While rationally, later, this may seem possible, at the time, in the heat of the crisis, with all forces on a hair trigger, *any* delay could have been catastrophic. (Just consider the dropping of "signal" depth charges on the Soviet submarine.) It is true, as Johnson points out, that Castro was a pain in the neck to the United States for the rest of his life. His support of Marxist guerrillas in Central America would plague President Ronald Reagan two decades after the Missile Crisis. Unloading of Cuba's criminals and scum class in the Mariel Boatlift of 1980 greatly affected Reagan's immigration reform policy and his decision to pursue an amnesty plan for illegal aliens that resulted in the 1986 Simpson-Mazzoli Act.[341]

In 1962, however, Kennedy's main concerns were simply removing the missiles and not leaving the world a radioactive heap. He succeeded in both instances. Contrary to some claims, JFK had not given up his strong anti-Communist stand in the slightest. For example, in June 1963, he made a dramatic speech in Berlin where he promised the continued existence of a free West Berlin and said, "There are some who say in Europe and elsewhere we can work with the Communists. Let them come to Berlin."[342] The wall, he noted, "is the most obvious and vivid demonstration of the failures of the Communist system...." These were not the words of someone capitulating to communism simply for peace.[343]

However, as Cuba faded into the rearview mirror, another battle-ground lay straight ahead. Already, Kennedy found himself engulfed in a new morass, Vietnam.

After the division of French Indochina into four countries in 1954 (Cambodia, Laos, North Vietnam, and South Vietnam), the United States had aligned itself firmly with the South. As the *Pentagon Papers* noted, Vietnam was "essentially the creation of the United States."[344] That also meant that its premier at the time John Kennedy assumed power, Ngo Dinh Diem, was the special instrument of American policy. Kennedy, handed Laotian turmoil by Eisenhower, quickly agreed to the neutralization of the country—which historically (perhaps with the exception of Austria and Finland) meant that that the Communists would infiltrate, force sham elections and overthrow the government, or, more likely, merely institute a revolutionary coup.

Despite warnings from the JCS and State Department, Kennedy acquiesced to the Communist plan for the Laotian accord that would in essence be a partitioned country in which the coalition government would be dominated by the Pathet Lao Communists. Worse, the corridor on the eastern side of the country that ran alongside part of South Vietnam, soon to be known as the "Ho Chi Minh Trail," would prove an open sore after American troops arrived. The North Vietnamese—literally within eyesight of American troops who were barred from killing them or even interfering with their movement of war materials and troops—would funnel in massive reinforcements to the Viet Cong. Failing to eliminate the Ho Chi Minh Trail (or even *attempt* to close it) constituted criminal negligence and dereliction of duty at the highest levels, namely that of JFK and Lyndon Johnson.

During the Laotian discussions, the JCS, to the degree the Chiefs were allowed to submit a recommendation, made it clear that *if* ground troops were sent in, unambiguously they not suffer from the lack of will or firepower that had doomed the Bay of Pigs. Contrary to conspiracy critics, the JCS did not push for ground troops in Laos but rather sought to make sure that insufficient forces then required still more forces—exactly what transpired in Vietnam.

Diem saw the future of South Vietnam in Laos. Attempting to reassure Diem, Kennedy sent Vice President Lyndon Johnson to the region in May 1961. The president did not like Johnson's report: "Laos has created doubt and concern about intentions of the United States through Southeast Asia. No amount of success at Geneva [the pending meeting with Soviet dictator Nikita Khrushchev] can, of itself, erase this…. Our mission arrested the decline of confidence in the United States. It did not—in my judgment—restore any confidence already lost."[345]

It is worth keeping the post-World War II history of the Cold War in mind before one rushes to criticize Kennedy, Johnson, or anyone else for the Vietnam morass: when the Soviets began expanding, taking East Germany, Poland, Czechoslovakia, Romania, Hungary, Estonia, Latvia, Lithuania, then supporting the Communist takeover in Cuba and indirectly supporting the North Koreans in the Korean War, there existed a very long history of the USSR taking territory and *never* giving it up. Mao Zedong's Communist victory in China continued that onslaught. Only Yugoslavia, a somewhat independent Communist state, bucked the trend. All of this was reinforced by the genuine concerns of the "Red Scare," where dozens of Soviet spies were found in the Roosevelt and Truman administrations, one at the highest level of assistant secretary of the treasury (Harry Dexter White). Joe McCarthy, it turns out, was right about virtually every Communist he publicly named. With such a track record, the "domino theory," which held that if a third-world country fell, its neighbors were next, seemed quite valid. (And, after South Vietnam fell, indeed Cambodia also fell to a murderous Communist regime before receding.)

Ho Chi Minh, the Communist leader in the North was the embodiment of Communist terror wherever it landed. A reign of state-sponsored murder had ensued under Ho with a ratio of one execution for every 160 villagers, or roughly 100,000 executions.[346] The Communists in the North were not about to let a free South Vietnam escape their clutches and began funding and arming a "revolutionary" guerrilla movement, the Viet Cong. Kennedy hoped this could be handled by a vigorous counterinsurgency effort, and in December 1961 announced the United States would increase aid to South Vietnam, including an increase in American troop commitments. South Vietnamese Premier Diem actually balked at any American troops, fearing it would be a propaganda feather in the cap of the North. Kennedy assented based on advice from his chief military advisor, Maxwell Taylor, and his special assistant for national security affairs, Walt Rostow.

Taylor was another of Kennedy's ad hoc moves. Rather than listen to the JCS, Kennedy brought in the former Army Chief of Staff as a personal advisor: he "became enamored of Maxwell Taylor's ideas."[347] Taylor, in turn, recommended that a "new type" of JCS member, General

Earle Wheeler, be sent to Vietnam in 1963 to investigate. The South Vietnamese had just suffered a costly defeat at Ap Bac, but Wheeler glossed over the South Vietnamese Army's deficiencies and presented a rosy picture of the counterinsurgency. Kennedy was listening to Taylor and McNamara only, not the Joint Chiefs.

Contrary to the view of those who thought the military sought a gigantic war with hundreds of thousands of American troops, Maxwell Taylor and others hoped that a quick and decisive, but overwhelming, effort by the US early might preclude the necessity of many more American forces later. They wanted 8,000 troops immediately under the guise of "flood relief," and argued strongly for an overwhelming air campaign against the North. In short, the JCS consistently sought a proactive deployment that would stop the war before it got rolling. But Kennedy was "convinced that military advice based on the objective of achieving victory was outmoded."[348] Far from seeking to put troops in, Marine Commandant David Shoup insisted that the United States should not, "under any circumstances, get involved in land warfare in Southeast Asia."[349]

Indeed, Kennedy and McNamara had engaged in a massive shift away from nuclear weapons and toward "flexible response." McNamara added almost 300,000 men to the army. But flexible responses often turn into quagmires if goals and objectives of military actions are not clearly spelled out.

Kennedy undermined the Joint Chiefs on various occasions, including when he leaked a story to the *New York Times*—hardly a responsible or reliable source in the first place—that the JCS was reluctant to send troops into Vietnam. JFK deliberately misled the public, with the assistance of what would eventually become known as the "fake news media" in the twenty-first century, while at the same time increased the number of "advisors," including US noncombat military and CIA agents there. In Laos, Kennedy had tried to win on the cheap by adding 500 CIA and military advisors to buttress the 11,000 anti-Communist Hmong tribesmen.

Kennedy said that "to introduce US forces in large numbers there today, while it might have an initially favorable military impact, would almost certainly lead to adverse political and, in the long run, adverse military consequences."[350] Then he proceeded to do just that. Almost immediately, it became clear that the Army of the Republic of Vietnam (ARVN) was incapable of defeating the Viet Cong. Hanoi's support of the Viet Cong was important, but the corruption and leadership in the South under Diem and his brother Ngo Dinh Nhu was atrocious. Slowly the number of military and CIA "advisors" grew, until by 1963 there were at least 16,752 in Vietnam.[351] However, in a speech Kennedy alluded to over 25,000 military personnel in "Southeast Asia," likely referring to naval forces and air force personnel in Thailand or other neighboring countries.

The CIA at that time was already engaged in a vigorous training program in Thailand to stop the Pathet Lao Communist forces coming in from the north. Under Project Ekarad, which trained Royal Lao troops in northern Thailand, the Kennedy administration was embedding Thais and American military advisors with Laotian forces. In May 1962, more than 6,500 Marines landed in Thailand, making this—and not Vietnam—the first overt deployment of American combat soldiers in Southeast Asia since World War II.[352]

Kennedy also authorized a "limited crop destruction operation" in which South Korean helicopters sprayed herbicides in a Communist held region, recommended by McNamara.[353] He did order a review of withdrawal as an option in 1962, but JFK did not push McNamara on it, nor did the secretary of defense push his generals.

As Michael Allen and I wrote in *A Patriot's History of the United States*, "No president did more to ensure the quagmire of Vietnam than John Kennedy."[354] Informed by the Joint Chiefs that at least 40,000 American troops would be needed to defeat the 17,000 Viet Cong—but the JCS warned that if the North Vietnamese got involved, it would take at least three times that many—Kennedy still straddled the fence. He put in 500 Green Berets (a newly created counterinsurgency unit touted by

Kennedy) but still resisted full ground combat units: the 16,500 men in there at the time were "advisors."

Kennedy kept sending "fact-finding" missions to Vietnam. None gave him the answer he wanted (i.e., that Diem was doing a great job and that the remaining Americans there would be home soon). In December 1962, JFK sent Senator Mike Mansfield, who had helped create the Diem regime in Vietnam, to Southeast Asia. Mansfield told the president that the Viet Cong controlled the countryside, and that Diem now headed an unpopular government. He urged withdrawal. Within a few months, though (March 1963) Kennedy told a press conference he didn't see how "we are going to pull out of Southeast Asia and turn it over to the Communists...."[355]

This constituted a problem for the St. Jack view. Kennedy didn't pull out when he had the chance. A new explanation had to be concocted: according to the apologists' new view—Kennedy first had to be reelected before he could withdraw. Mansfield (as told by JFK hagiographers Kenneth O'Donnell and David Powers, who published their book in 1970—long after Kennedy was dead) reportedly said Kennedy told him, "If I tried to pull out completely now from Vietnam, we would have another Joe McCarthy on our hands, but I can do it after I am reelected."[356] What makes this little more than political talk is that *at best* JFK was describing something that might happen nearly two years in the future.

In fact, however, Kennedy and his advisors were already planning a coup that would, as John Roche once said, nail the US flag to the flagpole in Saigon and ensure the full commitment of American troops. South Vietnamese Premier Ngo Dinh Diem, once hailed as the "Jefferson of Asia," instead proved nearly as thuggish and intractable as the Communists. His open oppression of Buddhist leaders (Diem was a Catholic) may not have been as brutal as some claimed but chafed at JFK. At the same time, as of early 1963 Diem told the US Ambassador Frederick Nolting that America had begun to run his country like a "US protectorate." He planned a number of measures to restore South

Vietnam's control over its own actions. He and his brother Nhu both wanted fewer Americans in South Vietnam.[357]

When the Buddhist crisis exploded in May 1963, the Ngo brothers feared more than ever that the US was trying to take over the country. Premier Diem told the *Washington Post* that South Vietnam could get by with almost all of the American forces removed.[358] They well understood that the majority of the advisors at the local level were CIA agents. Some claimed JFK was seeking a way out of Vietnam—but if so, when asked by his aides Dave Powers and Kenny O'Donnell, how he could withdraw, he answered, "Easy.... Put a government in there that will ask us to leave."[359] There was only one problem with that answer: Kennedy already *had* a government asking the US to leave and instead of complying, Kennedy arranged to have that government removed.

For the advisors at Camelot, Diem's actions worried them less than the public relations damage they caused. Kennedy's team wanted the president to replace Diem. A search began for generals who could perform a coup.[360] Kennedy's CIA had already planned to fund the overthrow by three generals, including the eventual temporary successor, Duong Van Minh (or "Big Minh"—no relation to Ho). Lt. Col. Lucien Conein arrived in Vietnam in October and met with the generals, informing them that the US would secretly support their effort. Big Minh was to take the lead.

Typically the pro-Kennedy St. Jack press described Big Minh as a "deceptively gentle man...[who] when he spoke of the coup d'état that lifted him into office...[had] a discernable tone of apology in his voice."[361] On November 1, 1963 Conein handed a bag filled with three million Vietnamese piastres into a bag for Big Minh. Minh was indeed "deceptively gentle" as he, having given Diem and his brother assurances that they would be safely seen into exile if they stepped down, saw to it that the two were shot and stabbed several times while in the armored car en route to their exile. Now, having supported the coup, JFK supposedly expressed shock that Diem was killed, having fooled himself into thinking that his administration could topple a third-world regime and expect participants to behave as if they were at Harvard Yard.

In fact, Kennedy knew Diem's assassination was incoming and, according to James Douglass, tried to derail it. Kennedy sent Torby Macdonald, an old friend and special emissary, to meet with Diem personally. Macdonald bypassed the CIA, the State Department, and the ambassador. In his meeting with Diem, he pleaded with the premier to take refuge in the American Embassy in Saigon and to ditch his brother and his sister-in-law, Madame Nhu. Diem flatly refused.[362] It is therefore pure fantasy to claim that Kennedy was surprised or shocked by the assassination of a foreign head of state he had essentially ordered.

The North Vietnamese knew who their most effective enemy was, and called Diem's removal a "gift from heaven for us."[363] Diem's murder ironically came less than one month before Kennedy's own assassination, on November 22, 1963. With Diem gone, American withdrawal was impossible—as JFK well knew.

Based on his conflict with the Joint Chiefs during the Cuban Missile Crisis, JFK and his secretary of defense, Robert McNamara weakened the authority of the JCS: the Chiefs did not receive briefings critical of the war or even objective assessments because McNamara—a Kennedy's urging—kept them from the group. By the time of JFK's assassination, the military had to some degree been cut out of the planning for a war they were expected to fight and win.

By his last inaugural, Kennedy still had not "turned," as some suggest. He said in that speech, "For us to withdraw...would mean a collapse not only of South Vietnam but Southeast Asia [the infamous domino theory]. So we are going to stay there."[364] Much controversy has arisen over the National Security Action Memorandum 263, in which 1,000 troops were to be withdrawn on the basis of recommendations from the Chairman of the Joint Chiefs, General Maxwell Taylor, and McNamara. The Memorandum accepted their recommendations based on an improvement in the performance of the South Vietnamese military, having a training program "so that essential functions can be carried out by Vietnamese by the end of 1965," by which time "it should be possible to withdraw the bulk of US personnel by that time."[365]

Yet Kennedy dithered. First, he ignored Diem's public statements to reduce American strength in Vietnam. Then he removed Diem. Then he used the necessity for reelection as the excuse for why he could not reduce the number of troops in Vietnam. He had sent Johnson and Mike Mansfield to Vietnam, and appeared to be unhappy with each report. To conspiracy theorists who cling to the "1,000-man withdrawal" as evidence that Kennedy, following a 16,000-man *buildup*, had changed his mind, Kennedy was a hapless whaler, clinging to the harpoon of a leviathan bureaucracy that he could not control. Douglass, for example, claimed "the President's increasing isolation from his bureaucracy was evident in the resistance and outright manipulation he was beginning to experience even in his inner circle."[366] Such theorists return to Kennedy's reelection as the motivation for staying: "I can't give up a piece of territory like that to the Communists and then get the American people to reelect me," he told reporter Charles Bartlett.[367] Yet Bartlett's comments conveniently came over twenty years later, when in liberal circles it was becoming critical to make Vietnam "Nixon's War" or, at the very least, "LBJ's war." Thomas P. "Tip" O'Neill, the speaker of the house under President Ronald Reagan, likewise told a story about how Kennedy was "pulling the American troops out of Vietnam *once the 1964 elections were over.*"[368] O'Neill's purported comments were even further removed from the time JFK supposedly said them by yet another twenty years. In other words, in the immediate aftermath of Kennedy's death—when Vietnam was a divisive issue and when hundreds of thousands of anti-war protesters marched regularly against the war, not one of these "memories" of Kennedy pulling out managed to surface.

Virtually all of these "pull-out" memories came decades after the fact. Not one of those who conspiracy theorists such as Douglass cite came public with their comments in the immediate aftermath of JFK's assassination or, more important, Johnson's 1965 escalation. One of the Joint Chiefs, Marine General David Shoup, reportedly told his wife that Kennedy told him during a walk to the Tomb of the Unknown Soldier that he was withdrawing American forces from Vietnam. Likewise, Kennedy supposedly told Senator Wayne Morse, another critic of the

Vietnam policy, "I've decided to get out. Definitely."[369] (Morse's memory only came a decade later.)

And, to return to a key point, after the 1964 election in late October when supposedly some of these comments were made was a full year away. Even assuming that the removal of Diem would have had a beneficial impact, assuming that a combat zone would remain static for eighteen months is a leap of faith indeed.

Supposedly Kennedy was hearing from aides that it would take a million men to win in Vietnam, and that, according to Michael Forrestal, the odds were 100:1 that America could win. But Kennedy's own secretary of defense, Robert McNamara, was running war games showing that it would be impossible to lose. Always a "bean counter," McNamara rhapsodized about the differences in US and North Vietnamese military production, GNP, industrial capacity, and so on. He never formulated a plan for victory—a disastrous development that plagued the Johnson administration. On paper, the US looked unbeatable. But what was the end game? Kennedy never came close to developing a plan for victory, and therefore had no real idea about what it would take nor about the odds.

The president continued to issue contradictory orders, telling the new ambassador Henry Cabot Lodge, who had been instructed to proceed with the coup against Diem, to delay removing him. "We see no good opportunity for action to remove the present government in [the] immediate future," Kennedy wired Lodge. Then he turned around and told Lodge, "This is a matter for your judgment."[370] Lodge proceeded to request CIA operative Edward Lansdale, to "take charge" under his supervision.

Meanwhile, McNamara, far from being boxed in by the military brass, was manipulating them and everyone else at the Pentagon. Even as he and Maxwell Taylor were on their fact-finding mission in Vietnam and cabling back their information, General Victor "Brute" Krulak met constantly with both JFK and Bobby, who "dictated to Krulak the recommendations of the 'McNamara-Taylor Report.'"[371] To be clear: the Kennedys were dictating the recommendations that the people making the recommendations were sending to them! After issuing the resulting NSAM 263 ordering 1,000 troops withdrawn "by the end of the year" (i.e., 1963), the order also directed that "no formal announcement be made." Publicly, Kennedy had insisted the US would stay, telling Walter Cronkite, "I don't agree with those who say we should withdraw. That would be a mistake."[372] And as if that wasn't clear enough, he told Chet Huntley and David Brinkley one week later, "I think we should stay [in Vietnam]. We should use our influence in as effective a way as we can, but we should not withdraw."[373]

By the time of his assassination, the picture that emerges of Kennedy is not positive whichever view is taken: either he was completely incompetent in his appointees (with his new ambassador to Vietnam, Lodge, being just the most recent), or in fact he really did agree believe his own public statements to "not withdraw" and was feeding the "dove" crowd just enough (to coin the phrase of a later president) hope and change to keep them pacified at home. The former view can be supported by the fact that in two years Kennedy had failed to substantially restack the Joint Chiefs; to appoint a secretary of defense who had control of the Pentagon; to appoint ambassadors and other representatives to Vietnam who would enforce his withdrawal policy; to demand *any structural change* at the CIA whatsoever; or to make public even the slightest intent of withdrawing combat troops from Vietnam—again, having escalated them *himself* from 600 to over 16,000 in just two years.

Support for the Sinner Jack approach rests on much of the same evidence. Kennedy seemed to be doing nothing to control the bureaucracy with which he supposedly disagreed; to fire any of the individuals at any agency (save the three fired immediately after the Bay of Pigs); to call any kind of top-level public meeting in which his intentions to leave would be made clear in a way the generals and others could not ignore; or to continue to support Diem—who wanted America out. Indeed, in an October 5, 1963, meeting that drafted a cable to Lodge, Kennedy instructed the ambassador to "maintain sufficient flexibility to permit [the] US to resume full support of the Diem regime," and then *praised Lodge's policy* of, as JFK put it, "cool correctness in order to make Diem come to you [as] correct. *You should continue it*" (emphasis mine).[374] Lodge, likely covering his own exposed rear, replied to the cable by telling Kennedy flat-out "we cannot remove the Nhus by nonviolent means against their will."[375]

The conspiracists' case, therefore, relies on JFK being either a weakling or a liar, and the exchanges with Lodge suggest the latter. Clearly not only did Kennedy realize that removing Diem would happen, but that it would be bloody. Lodge even warned that there was a growing possibility that Diem would himself demand a withdrawal—something Kennedy would not permit.

In September 1963, as part of the coup momentum, David Bell, head of the Agency for International Development (AID), noted that the US had already cut off the Commodity Import Program that supported Diem. Kennedy asked who told him to do that, apparently unaware of his own government's policies to stop aid to governments which had "differences" with the US. It was a reasonable and predictable result. Why would anyone give money and commodity support to a country that was ignoring American recommendations? As conspiracist Douglass noted, "The message was meant for the man staring...in disbelief. He was being told who was in control. It was not the president."[376] And the generals planning the coup in Vietnam took this as a clear "go" signal.[377] And, as after the Bay of Pigs, when Diem was murdered, Kennedy blamed the CIA: "I've got to do something about those bastards," he told his friend Senator George Smathers. They "should be stripped of their exorbitant power."[378] Once again, in the ensuing weeks before his own death, Kennedy did nothing about the CIA.

As the inevitable momentum built to remove Diem, the FBI discovered a plot to assassinate Kennedy in Chicago—hardly "nut country" as the president described Texas. Indeed, Chicago was the hotbed of the very corruption that possibly gave JFK the presidency in the first place. The attempt, according to the FBI, involved "rightwing para-military fanatics."[379] (It is interesting that few plots the FBI has ever uncovered seem to involve "left-wing fanatics.") In both the Chicago and Dallas assassination plans, the killers (according to the theorists) were placed in particularly good shooting spots via employment. Yet presidential travel routes not only regularly change but in Dallas, at least, Kennedy was supposed to have had a bulletproof glass bubble on the convertible—which he rejected. In either scenario, a changed route or a bulletproof bubble, the assassination attempts would have been futile. As it was, in Chicago, the police and the FBI broke the case and arrested the gunman.

Conspiracy theorists proceed along whatever conspiracy pathway they have created—whether the mob, the CIA, "right-wingers," or whomever—in a vacuum, as if all of the others didn't exist. It is useful, however, to review the list of those who presumably wanted Kennedy dead in 1963, and for what reasons:

- The Mob. After Giancana, Trafficante, and Roselli failed to eliminate Castro, one might conclude that the "deal" with the feds was over. But not in the mind of the mob bosses. They tried. Now it was up to Kennedy to instruct his brother the attorney general to cease all anti-mob Justice Department offensives. When RFK did not (so the theory goes), the mafia decided to take out the "head," (i.e., John Kennedy).[380]

- The anti-Castro Cuban community. Feeling betrayed by JFK's unwillingness to support the Bay of Pigs invasion or to kill Castro, the American Cubans could rightly feel stabbed in the back.

- Castro. Certainly with the continued assassination attempts on his life, Castro could not know that JFK and the CIA finally abandoned "Project Mongoose." Castro would have powerful reasons for wanting to have Kennedy dead. Thus, one of the very few new documents to come from President Donald Trump's order in October 2017 to release another 2,800 documents on the assassination that has been viewed in any way as significant is a record of the Cubans seeking to assist Lee Harvey Oswald. A transcript from the recently released documents showed that a man named Angel Salazar was interrogated at the Cuban Embassy in Mexico City in 1967 and Salazar mentioned that Oswald was a good shot: "He was quite good.... I knew him."[381] Whether Oswald or an impostor showed up in Mexico City to meet with Cuban and Russian consular officials, the CIA was convinced someone using the name Oswald was seeking rapid travel or a "quick escape."[382]

- The CIA. This is the favorite villain of most theories in that the CIA had it in for Kennedy after the Bay of Pigs and Vietnam. Certainly the Agency had means, motive, and opportunity, although it is hard to see Kennedy not doing pretty much what the CIA wanted in Vietnam. Moreover, it was the Joint Chiefs of Staff, not the CIA, who was upset with JFK's response to the Cuban Missile Crisis.[383]

- The Secret Service. Bonar Menninger's 1992 book *Moral Error* claimed that, based on the work of ballistics expert Howard Donahue, although Oswald fired two shots including the "magic bullet," Oswald did not fire the head shot. Donahue argued that the "kill shot" that hit JFK in the head was in fact an accidental discharge by Secret Service Agent George Hickey riding in the car behind Kennedy. Hickey, Menninger claims, was in the process of standing up and grabbing his AR-15 which was leaning against his seat. As he turned toward the sound of Oswald's gun, the AR-15 went off.[384]

- Lee Harvey Oswald, either as a "lone nut" or as a "cutout" or "patsy" from either the CIA or the mob or someone else.[385]

Whichever theory one accepts, it is important to realize that the *physical forensic evidence* remains daunting. Other than the three Oswald Mannlicher-Carcano rifle shells found, no other bullet or lead of any sort has ever been produced, despite thousands of treasure-hunters, conspiracy theorists, and official investigators. Second, the only surviving sound footage of the day comes from a police motorcycle recording that clearly picks up three of Oswald's shots and a much different pop, which the patrolman said was his motorcycle. Gerald Posner has conclusively shown there was nothing "magical" about the "magic bullet," but rather the majority of researchers have failed to properly place the jump seat where John Connally rode on that day. (It was down and to the right of Kennedy, not directly in front of him, meaning the "magic bullet" traveled on a perfectly straight line from JFK's throat to the governor.)

And Oswald? Claims that he could not have fired three shots in the allotted time do not hold up to real-world tests. In the late 1960s, a Baltimore television station recreated the route JFK's limousine would have taken. Using a platform of the same size and height, with silhouette cutouts for JFK and the others in the car, the station conducted a test in which it invited ten marksmen to see if they could a) fire three shots in 6.6 seconds (all did) and b) score two hits (all of them did).[386] The last shooter, firing in a rainstorm, got three hits on "JFK" in 6.6 seconds. But even then, the time allotted (as Postner discovered) was in error, pegged to the movie camera of Abraham Zapruder. A correct calibration of his camera put the "shooting window" at closer to *ten seconds*, at which point all ten of the test shooters would have scored three hits. And as noted before, Oswald not only was a Marine marksman, but a Cuban contact of his claimed he was a very good shooter.

All JFK assassination documents were to have been released by law fifty years after the assassination, or 2013. But they were not. President Donald Trump promised to release them and after his election, in October 2017, he ordered another 2,800 documents related to the Kennedy assassination declassified, leaving about 300 files whose release was objected to by the CIA and other intelligence agencies. For all practical purposes, the Trump release effectively made public all of the remaining documents— with no big bombshell other than the fact that Oswald was well known to Cuban officials. The most important other recent revelations have come from Lamar Waldron, who made public the name of the CIA contact inside the Castro government, Juan Almeida. While there is sufficient room to view Oswald as having assistance, more of the recent theorists point to him as the shooter. But at the behest of whom? The absence of any physical or sound evidence showing any other shooters means that the "grassy knoll" theories have been debunked. But was Oswald either directly working for the CIA or was he a dupe? No one can prove either claim at this point, and given that almost all of the documents have been released, hoping for a "smoking gun" remaining in the handful of as-yet unreleased documents makes a new bombshell unlikely. Indeed, given the cross-referencing of names and other information in the released materials, a shocking fact yet to be unearthed seems further away than ever.

In J. R. R. Tolkien's *Lord of the Rings* trilogy, the nine rings of power were governed by a single, more powerful, ring. "One ring to rule them all." It was inevitable that over time, even the bureaucracy itself would be stratified to the point that one agency would "rule them all" by virtue of its control of information over the others.

Kennedy's attempt to bring the CIA under control failed. Whether it cost him his life is unproven, but his inability to subjugate the Agency would have long-term ramifications, not the least of which sent the US to war with Iraq in 2003. And when Donald Trump became president in 2017, he would find that the CIA, acting in concert with other agencies, effectively obstructed some of the most important agenda items he had been elected to implement. Trump should have taken note: if a media darling insider like John Kennedy, some half a century before Trump entered the Oval Office—when the CIA was far less entrenched and less funded—with his own brother as the attorney general of the United States, could not bring the rogue agency under control, then it was unlikely that an outsider hated by the hierarchies of both political parties and detested by the media and Hollywood ever stood a chance.

Scorecard: Kennedy and the CIA Swamp

- Unsuccessful in controlling, let alone defeating the CIA Swamp
- Used an extremely loose interpretation of the Constitution largely manipulated by Allen Dulles
- Had no support from Congress to rein in the Agency
- Had good support from most newspapers for his policies, but never made the public case to control the CIA
- Relied far too heavily on the Agency he needed to control

CHAPTER 5

Ronald Reagan and the Bureaucracy Swamp

The connections between Ronald Reagan's battles with his swamp and JFK's struggle with the CIA Swamp are strong, but Reagan and Donald Trump really were fighting the same war extended across a 40-year span. In many ways, Reagan was also dealing with the unfinished Swamp battle of Grover Cleveland (the Spoils Swamp) but with one significant difference: the parties had ceased to be the major regulating mechanism on the bureaucracy as they had been in Cleveland's time. Instead, insiders in each party had formed what would often be called the "Uniparty" that cooperated in graft rather than competing to oust their opponents. By 1981, when the Gipper entered office, he faced a vastly transformed administrative state that had attained a life of its own. It grew so bad that Reagan once quipped that the closest thing he had ever seen to eternal life on earth was a government agency.

A new dynamic had accompanied this profound shift. Not only were the bureaus, agencies, and offices immune to political pressure from their own parties, but they were also beyond the control of either Congress or the president. This new unconstitutional counterstate had gotten a toehold in the Great Depression and Franklin Roosevelt's New Deal, then entrenched itself in Lyndon Johnson's Great Society. Briefly, as John

Marini notes in *Unmasking the Administrative State*, Congress sought a regulatory role by using the budget in the late 1960s and early 1970s, before it capitulated.[387] Courts became the last resort for reining in the runaway bureaucracy, but more often than not, rather than striking at the *constitutionality* of the agency itself (or its mission), the courts have by and large merely confirmed their right to exist and then attempted to define the parameters in which they operate.

Short of a court telling a particular agency it has gone too far, the bureaucracy "has established the purpose, unity, and the rational authority of the political branches.... [and has] sought to progressively replace politics by substituting administrative rulemaking for general lawmaking."[388] It has become its own political faction whose "platform" is administrative rule. In that process, it deliberately eroded or destroyed any institutions in civil society that provided a foundation for self-government, including private organizations, churches, and the family. The actual practice of the political branches of American government found themselves bound to accommodating various interest groups and lobbies that have carved out niches in the administrative state. Of course, throughout this evolution, partisans were pushed to the side in favor of trained "experts." Nothing showed that more clearly than the response to the Covid-19 "China virus" in 2020 when the Center for Disease Control, and its power mad director of the National Institute of Allergy and Infectious Diseases, Anthony Fauci, became a health dictator for national Covid policy.

As Reagan would find out, it was in the area of budgets that Progressives first achieved a major victory. Congress historically had controlled the budget, but Progressives argued for a president to formulate a budget and submit it to Congress—which removed a major separation of powers obstacle to the administrative state. Reagan soon found that he was to a large degree in thrall to his own budget director, David Stockman, whose mastery of the numbers could, within limits, move Reagan's policy any direction he wanted it to.

Reagan had to look no further back than a pre-Watergate Richard Nixon, who warned in 1972, "If this kind of growth [of the administrative state] were projected indefinitely into the future, the result would be catastrophic. We would have an America top heavy with bureaucratic meddling, weighed down by big government, suffocated by taxes, robbed of its soul."[389] It is not a trivial fact that the Watergate Affair began as an illegal effort on the part of Nixon's subordinates reacting to the leak of the *Pentagon Papers* (or, if you believe the more conspiratorial theory, a reaction by John Dean to information that his fiancée's name appeared in a madam's address book that was in the position of the Democratic National Committee). The Watergate break-in was a criminal act responding to another criminal act of the leak by the bureaucracy.

Nixon, it should be noted, attempted a reorganization of the federal government, including abolishing a number of departments, only to replace them with others. Resistance came, as he saw it, "because the plans and programs…threatened the entrenched powers and prerogatives that they had built up over many decades."[390]

Strangely enough, the Bureaucratic Swamp began with our earlier Dragonslayers who were somewhat successful, Chester Arthur and Grover Cleveland. And, like most problems, the bureaucracy's origins in Cleveland's time ironically sprang from another instance of contagion, animal diseases.[391] As historians Alan Olmstead and Paul Rhode showed in their book *Arresting Contagion*, concerns about livestock disease prompted new public policy in the late 1800s: "The constitutional necessity to gain state support [for such measures] led to novel cooperative agreements…. [that] occurred earlier in animal health than in many other policy areas."[392] Previously historians had laid the groundwork for the regulatory and bureaucratic state at the feet of the Interstate Commerce Act (1887) and the Sherman Antitrust Act (1890) as a response to "big business." This, of course, brought Theodore Roosevelt to battle the Trust Swamp. But in fact it started earlier, with the creation of the Bureau of Animal Industry (BAI) in 1884 under Arthur following an eruption of CBPP (contagious bovine pleuropneumonia) in the Midwest.

America's cattle business was no small thing in the late nineteenth century, when the value of capital stock in livestock exceeded that in railroads. Of course, the public health aspects of the livestock industry were national in scope, as individual states often had incentives to merely ship diseased livestock outside their borders. States also enacted quarantines to prevent animals from other states from coming in. Within two years of CBPP's appearance, the nation's major distribution channels were endangered. Yet Chicago, the state of Illinois, stockyards, and livestock owners all became enmeshed in turf battles that led to paralysis. With national control, CBPP was stopped, but a new livestock disease, foot-and-mouth Disease (FMD) arose in 1914–1916. Olmstead and Rhode argue that the presence of the BAI and expanded powers granted after FMD prevented the US from suffering the way other countries did.

Foreign nations barred American beef and pork due to diseases in the 1870s, leading many to consider applying the Commerce Clause (Article 1, Section 8) of the Constitution to address measures that regulated diseased animals. Already, in 1879, Congress empowered the National Board of Health as an independent agency to impose national quarantines where state rules failed (as in the New Orleans "Great Fever" epidemic in the late 1870s when states and other cities quarantined New Orleans).[393] After a major failure of the Bureau to snuff out an outbreak of CBPP in Chicago in 1886–87, President Grover Cleveland—no big government zealot—requested that Congress grant even more authority to remedy the contagion problem within "the limits of a constitutional delegation of power [that] the General Government will permit."[394] Those powers included the ability for commissioners to issue quarantines.

The BAI was successful. As the historian of the agency noted, "The United States was the first of the large nations of the world...which, having been extensively infected with contagious pleuropneumonia, was able to extirpate it completely.... It accomplished the first great thing it undertook, the paramount purpose for which it was created."[395] BAI constituted an appropriate constitutionally created and empowered agency. Its goals were simple, attainable, and quite necessary. It addressed a problem that the states could not handle on their own and which brought them into conflict, exactly in keeping with the ideals of the Constitution. But it was one of the very few such agencies that appeared after 1887 that could make that claim.

Instead, during World War I, the numbers of such bureaus exploded, and the oversight declined. In wartime, few Americans cared if there was waste or duplication—the goal was to end the war as soon as possible. After the war, Presidents Warren Harding and Calvin Coolidge shrank the wartime federal government by selling off federally owned railroads and shipping, then cutting taxes, but even they could not return it to its pre-WW I size. But the bureaucracy bounced back once the Great Depression hit, when President Franklin Roosevelt with full support from Congress, instituted an explosion of federal agencies, bureaus, and commissions. The press dubbed it the "Alphabet Soup" of bureaucracy, most of it oriented to finding ways to get money into the pockets of Americans who, in Roosevelt's "demand side" economic theory, would lead consumers to spend their way out of the depression. It didn't work. As Jesus said, the poor were with us always, but now so were the agencies. Once entrenched, they were nearly impossible to remove.

Reagan's political hero as a young man, Franklin Roosevelt, did not initiate the shift to unaccountable bureaucracies, but he institutionalized it and greatly expanded their power. Roosevelt claimed that while at the beginning of the republic American government existed to protect the inalienable rights of free speech, free press, free worship, and so on. But then Roosevelt added, "As our Nation has grown in size and stature...these political rights proved inadequate to assure us equality in the pursuit of happiness."[396] FDR had slyly worked in the word "equality" in the pursuit of happiness, which is not listed as an inalienable right. He later, in that address, inverted the relationship between people and the government, suggesting there was a "contract" where rulers "were accorded power, and the people consented to that power on consideration that *they be accorded certain rights.*" This was a fundamental and inexcusable interpretation of the Declaration and the Constitution, where the people accorded the government certain powers, but they ultimately retain *all* rights.

Despite leaving the Democrat Party (or, as he was famous for saying, "I didn't leave the Democratic Party, it left me"), and despite firing blistering salvos at the welfare and regulatory state created by Roosevelt, Reagan never once attacked Roosevelt personally. It was as if FDR had nothing to do with his own policies. Dutch refused to ever name him personally in his attacks on the New Deal. Reagan observed that Americans have "been tempted to believe that society has become too complex to be managed by self-rule, that government by an elite group is superior to government for, by, and of the people."[397] Somewhere, Reagan insisted, "A perversion has taken place." Any businessman could point to "his own tale of harassment," and our "natural, inalienable rights are now considered to be a dispensation of government...." A large centralized government was "the very thing the Founding Fathers sought to minimize.... A government can't control the economy without controlling people," which, he pointed out, inevitably required force.

What Reagan had missed was that since the New Deal, the Bureaucracy Swamp had slithered out of the control of Congress—*not under the control of presidents*—but rather the courts. Further, Congress found that by "delegating authority to the bureaucracy [it] could avoid responsibility for the obtrusive regulations foisted upon society."[398] Congress could, from time to time, make agencies responsive to its will through language in its committee reports, but mostly through authorizations and appropriations. This tactic, unfortunately, was undercut in part by Congress's desire to avoid blame for agencies' regulations but also by its laziness. A process called "baseline budgeting" ensued. Instead of a bureau or agency appearing before Congress to justify why it needed, say, $1 million (its request), Congress just assumed that said agency would start with *last year's budget* and justify the increase for the new year. Thus no budget ever, ever fell.

When Ronald Reagan announced his candidacy for president for the third time on January 13, 1980, he stated that "the people have not created this disaster in our economy; the federal government has. It has overspent, overestimated, and over regulated."[399] Then he bored in on the real problem: "We must put an end to the *arrogance of a federal establishment* which accepts no blame for our condition, cannot be relied upon to give us a fair estimate of our situation and utterly refuses to live within its means. I will not accept the supposed wisdom which has it that the *federal bureaucracy has become so powerful that it can no longer be changed or controlled* by any administration" (emphasis mine).[400] The Gipper specifically referred to the 10th article in the Bill of Rights that reserved power for the people, and noted that the savings to the government in administrative costs would be considerable and there would be "increased efficiency and less bureaucracy."[401]

Under Jimmy Carter, Reagan noted, "There were more than 130 indictments, and GSA [Government Services Administration] auditors estimated they were looking for $100 million lost to fraud and another $130 million lost to mismanagement every year." According to Reagan, Carter's answer to all of this was "politics-as-usual. The GSA mess is still not cleaned up and the men who tried to clean it up are no longer in the GSA."[402]

Reagan usually spoke of bureaucracy, though, in terms of waste: Americans, he said on election eve in 1980, "have always known that excessive bureaucracy is the enemy of excellence and compassion...."[403] Because of who he was and how he grew up, it was nearly incomprehensible to Ronald Reagan that there would be Americans—not Communist plants—who were so fundamentally opposed to true republican government that they would sabotage efforts to hand power over to the people. Reagan didn't even really think most Democrats were capable of that. But employees of the federal government? Preposterous. In that, he shared with Donald Trump a fundamental failure to grasp the nature of the enemy he was up against.

Intuitively, though, he knew the entrenched Bureaucracy Swamp was a threat. In his first inaugural, Reagan said, "In this present crisis, government is not the solution to our problem; government is the problem."[404] From time to time, he continued, "we have been tempted to believe that society has become too complex to be managed by self-rule, that government by an elite group is superior to government for, by, and of the people." He wanted the nation to "take inventory":

> We are a nation that has a government—not the other way around. And this makes us special among the nations of the Earth. Our Government has no power

except that granted it by the people. It is time to check
and reverse the growth of government which shows signs
of having grown beyond the consent of the governed.

Reagan stated his intention to reduce the size and influence of the
"federal establishment and to demand recognition of the distinction between the powers granted to the Federal Government and those reserved
to the States or to the people."[405] And he wasn't finished. The Gipper
insisted that "our present troubles parallel and are proportionate to the
intervention and intrusion in our lives that result form unnecessary and
excessive growth of government." He promised to restore the balance
between the states and the federal government.

Upon taking office, Reagan instituted his economic recovery plan
which consisted of three major parts: tax reform (lowering taxes); regulatory reform (reducing the size of government); and monetary reform (controlling inflation). Having been prepared through the most
thorough transition plan in American history—cited by the Harvard
Business School for its efficiency—the administration saw tax cuts as key
to achieving every other goal. Reagan personally not only believed tax
cuts were key, but as I noted in *Reagan: The American President*, his teams
had been actively preparing a budget that would incorporate them as a
major component of restoring the economy.[406] Even David Stockman, the
backstabbing budget director, "believed them utterly critical to growing
the economy," although he disavowed them later.[407] They were not gim-
micks or band-aids. Reagan thought that, naturally, with less tax money
available, Congress would be forced to rein in the bureaucracy's budgets.

But it was on the reduction side—what the Gipper frequently called
"fraud and abuse"—that the administration hoped to actually reduce
government. Speechwriter Tony Dolan, warned that waste had gotten so
bad that the bureaucracy no longer even saw it as a problem.[408] During
the transition, Ed Meese had already proposed a federal government
hiring freeze and urged that Reagan move as many federal employees
as possible out of DC to save money.[409] Dolan insisted that people who

stayed in the Capital ended up with a "severe case of Washingtonitis"—
another way of saying they became part of the Swamp.

Immediately after the inauguration, David Stockman organized a
meeting in which all attendees were handed one hundred new regulations Carter had instituted at the last minute. (They were known as the
"Midnight Regulations.") Lyn Nofziger told the group to go through
the regulations. Joe Wright, one of the budget advisors, asked, "Do you
want comments?" Nofziger pointed them to the last page where Dutch
had written his signature and under it a single line: "Eliminate all of
these." Wright observed that the "shortest meeting you could have with
the president was to come in and propose a new regulation."[410] Reagan's
first official act was to sign an executive order eliminating price controls
on oil and gasoline. But most important, on January 27, 1981, Reagan
sent a memo to all departments ordering that they reduce spending on
consulting contracts, office redecoration, and any other nonessential
items. It constituted an immediate reduction in the bureaucracy—but
they soon slipped back into their bloated ways.[411]

Reagan could count on Democrats in Congress to be sympathetic
to his tax cut policies, as even they knew the economy had to recover.
Getting them to sign on to actual budgetary cuts and reduction in the size
of government was a wholly different matter. However, he had one major
advantage that Donald Trump never had: despite the fact that the media
was still overwhelmingly liberal and biased, it retained a modicum of
fairness and objectivity at times. One of the biggest, earliest battles came
over the definition of a "cut," which, as we have seen when it involved
baseline budgeting never was an actual cut but a reduction in the rate of
growth. This issue arose early in a March 17, 1981, meeting with James
Baker, Senator Pete Domenici, and others over cost of living allowance
(COLA) *increases* in Social Security checks.

This particular incident was quite revealing about the Bureaucracy
Swamp and its allies in Congress. Reagan had always wanted to convert
Social Security into a voluntary program on the grounds it was inefficient,
and that people who would have put that same money into a mutual fund
would have had many times the return. (Franklin Roosevelt himself in

his 1935 Social Security message had stated that "voluntary contributory annuities by which individual initiatives can increase the annual amounts received in old age" were to be a part of Social Security and that "ultimately those voluntary self-supporting annuity plans would supplant the 'old-age pension plan.'")[412] Reagan's understanding of Social Security as a fund that people paid into also involved the entire notion that if indeed people "paid into" Social Security, and died before they had recovered all they paid in, then their families should be entitled to the remainder as an inheritance. Asked about his past views on Social Security, Regan said, "Since it is billed as an insurance program...a person who paid into it should have the right to choose his beneficiary."[413] Senator Pete Domenici of New Mexico, who headed the Senate Budget Committee, was another of those Washingtonians obsessed with budget deficits and with South Carolina senator Fritz Hollings proposed a freeze on the COLAs. Even Stockman knew this was a cut. (The proposal got no further than Domenici and Hollings: Reagan's chief of staff, Jim Baker, sensing political fallout, went into "red alert" to derail the proposal.)

When Reagan, Stockman, and Baker met with Domenici, however, the senator argued that freezing the *growth* of a program was not the same as cutting it (in which he was correct). Budget Director David Stockman wanted to reduce those increases, but Jim Baker insisted, "Compared to what [recipients] would expect to get there will be a cut from expectation."[414] Domenici warned that that was "Democrat" thinking and that the same argument could be made to every government program. Reagan dug in, seeing the issue as a campaign promise. Little did Reagan know he was not just making a judgment on COLAs, but on virtually every welfare program that had been grafted onto it over time. Stockman, still in his budget-cutter persona, drafted a nearly incomprehensible proposal he took to Reagan on May 11 that would have substantially cut retirement checks for early retirees, but downplayed the date. Reagan of course like the proposal until he found that it was an immediate cut, not something phased in over time. When word leaked out, the *Washington Post* screamed, "Reagan Proposes 10% Cut in Social Security Costs," without mentioning that it was on *some* Social Security costs, and only for those taking early retirement. But the damage was done. Democrats and their media allies pounced, and as Lou Cannon somewhat gleefully recorded in his book, *President Reagan: the Role of a Lifetime*, "Reagan recovered politically from this calamity, but he would never again mount a major assault against the basic premises of the federal government."[415]

Raising the boogeyman flag of "cutting Social Security" helped the Democrats win the mid-term elections. Reagan was urged to form a bipartisan commission (which was Washington-speak for a body that accomplished nothing significant) to address the Social Security crisis. Baker played a key role in the deliberations, as did Alan Greenspan. Ultimately the commission boosted payroll taxes, taxed the highest-income recipients, and raised the retirement age from sixty-five to sixty-seven in the year 2027. Overall, the entire episode reflected the Swamp's attitude, which was to tax instead of cut whenever possible. Meanwhile, Reagan in part had become a slave to the budget and deficits—which never constrained a single Democrat president.

Just as everything Donald Trump accomplished—or tried to accomplish—was affected by the Russia hoax probe, Reagan's first term was profoundly shaped by the assassination attempt on him in March 1981. His tough survival and overall cheery attitude was received enthusiastically by the public, and it made whatever he did (at least for his next three years) much easier.

Reagan's ability to attack the Bureaucracy Swamp, bolstered by public support, still depended in large part upon the economy. The press routinely accused the Gipper of pushing overly optimistic projections and estimates. Quite the contrary, the administration's estimates, while quite positive, *always understated real growth*. For example, in June 1981, a compilation of real GNP estimates by six private firms or universities put the expected growth rate at 6.5 percent, well above that the administration projected. In fact, however, the real rate was revised upward to 8.4 percent. Similarly, the Reagan team publicly stated the velocity of money would come in at 5.5 percent but in fact the internal estimates were a much lower 3.6 percent.[416]

Meanwhile, as the first round of proposed budget cuts hit Congress, Reagan grew concerned. He saw weakness among his coalition to stick with the cuts: "I think they have '82 election jitters," he remarked.[417] On September 23, he withdrew his reductions on Social Security and admitted, "We won't get all we ask for but we'll do fairly well."[418] Soon, however, he found himself resorting to a whole bag of tricks to reduce the size of government, including calling for the bipartisan commission and going public with an appeal for support to cut $57 billion more, including abolishing the Departments of Energy and Education. His poll numbers fell.

What ensued was a struggle by Reagan's advisors to control his bureaucracy-chopping instincts. Biographer Lou Cannon, who saw the Gipper as entirely the product of his staffers and who thought him "poor at doing his homework," advanced the notion that Reagan hardly made few decisions of his own.[419] Instead, as I have shown in *Reagan: The American President*, other advisors such as Secretary of State George Shultz, were impressed with Dutch's "extensive preparatory effort" and his "vision that was always well beyond that of his cabinet."[420] That said, David Stockman from the outset was devious: Reagan biographer Steven Hayward called him a "disastrous" appointment, the equivalent of the "Robert McNamara of the Reagan administration."[421] Stockman would describe himself as the "Trotsky of the supply-side movement."[422]

Indeed, Stockman was all over the map, beginning as a radical New Left-er at Michigan State University who burned his draft card and went to divinity school. Supposedly he had a political conversion at Harvard (probably the first time such a salvation moment ever moved someone from the left to the right at that institution). But his newfound conservatism only went so far: while in Congress he worked with liberal Congressman John Anderson who later ran against Reagan as an independent in 1980. Stockman voted with Anderson 80 percent of the time, voted against school prayer, and supported abortion. He described Dutch as a "cranky obscurantist."[423] Democrat Senator Patrick Moynihan leerily observed of Stockman, "I have never known a man capable of such sustained self-hypnotic ideological fervor."[424] And initially, even many of

Reagan's inner core were in awe of him. Martin Anderson likened him to a "new puppy, eager and urgent, bounding and leaping through the federal budget…. [a] superb leader for OMB [Office of Management and Budget]." Alan Greenspan, later the chairman of the Federal Reserve Board, called him "the brightest guy around."[425] Even at that, however, Stockman told William Greider, "A lot of people criticize [Reagan] for being short on the details, but he knows when something is wrong. He just jumped all over my tax proposals."[426]

At the time, however, Stockman was Budget Cutter Stockman, planning to abolish over 140 programs and lower spending in almost all those remaining. Significantly, in William Greider's book based on Stockman's extensive interviews, *The Education of David Stockman*, when it came to listing Reagan's goals, all he mentioned was tax cutting and "tight monetary control," *not* a revolution that eliminated the New Deal.[427] Quite the contrary, Stockman always spoke in terms of economic growth as the factor that reduced (proportionately) the size of government. Stockman's early cuts failed to include any of the major money-suckers, such as Head Start, the Supplemental Security Income program, or the largest, Medicare, later saying he intended to work on these at a future date. Stockman *never* spoke to Greider in terms of a vast, conceptual attack on the *premises* of the New Deal, or of the notion of the administrative state.

The problem, which Stockman well knew, was that a narrow window existed for *any* cuts, and by failing to include these programs initially, Stockman led Reagan and everyone else to believe they were off limits. But, as he described his job to Greider, the new administration would have to find $40 billion in budget cuts. "Do you have any idea what $40 billion means?" he asked Greider.[428] "It means I've got to cut the highway program. It means I've got to cut milk-price supports. And Social Security student benefits. And education and student loans."[429] Stockman's goal was less to actually achieve reduction in government and more—from his perspective—in tricking Reagan into feeling the pain of the cuts. His budget still came up short of balancing by 1984 without an additional $44 billion that Stockman put in with an asterisk as "future savings to be proposed." He had in mind Social Security and other programs

Reagan had specifically taken off the table. (Later this became known as the "magic asterisk.")

While the liberal media continually referred to Reagan and Stockman's "rosy" scenarios about growth, as shown earlier, in fact the projections for growth were *low* and the White House's own higher estimates were never shared with the public specifically because they would be labeled "unrealistic." Contrary to myth, no one in the Reagan administration ever argued that cutting taxes alone would be sufficient to cause the economy to recover. Rather, budget cutting, regulatory reform, and monetary tightening were always considered the other three pillars of recovery.

Even then, Reagan and Stockman both had fundamentally misjudged the nature of their enemy. "Budgets" and money alone were not the problem. The problems rested on *assumptions* that the bureaucracy was made up of patriotic Americans who had the common good at heart. In this view, bureaucrats knew that their jobs were counter-constitutional, occasionally superfluous, and at the very worst they were merely employees of the federal government who could find work elsewhere and who would gladly make the sacrifice of closing down shop if it meant the improvement of America. Stockman sensed some of this when he carped to Greider about packaging the tax cuts:

> All those guys [in various departments] are looking for ways out. If they can detect an alleged pattern of preferential treatment for somebody else or discriminatory treatment between rural and urban interests or between farm interests and industrial interests, they can concoct a case for theirs.[430]

By the 1980s, if not much earlier, the bureaucrats had ceased being ordinary citizens who worked *for* the government, and instead had become vested instruments who saw themselves now as part of a new "ruling class." Their expertise meant they knew better than others. Their control over fiefdoms meant they were superior to the country class who merely voted on issues. During the budget battles, really only the secretary of agriculture, John Block, who suffered from mass lobbying by peanut farmers to increase their subsidies, stood up to the special interests.

Reagan failed to see this because of his inherent goodness and optimism. It revealed itself in the way he refused to attack FDR personally (or, later, Mikhail Gorbachev). Dutch even avoided publicly blasting his main enemy on the Hill, Speaker of the House Thomas P. "Tip" O'Neill. Indeed, Reagan almost never publicly campaigned against members of his own party who undercut him.

The signs were all around him. Even his "friends" at *National Review* sniped at the "disarray" and "untidiness" of Dutch's foreign policy, which should have sounded a warning claxon about their real agenda. Of course, the liberal media—which was to say, the media—fell lock-step into place after the Reagan tax cuts hit, with CBS warning "Hunger in America is back" and Charles Osgood on CBS warning that the budget-cutting wind has been "blowing strong enough to uproot some government programs...."[431] George Will, a supposed "conservative" who despised Reagan in all aspects except his anti-communism, had warned that when it finally came down to cutting programs, the president would find that the number of "liberals" in Congress "approaches 535."[432] Will hardly dripped with any insight. Rather what should have at least started to become clear was that Congress had lost all practical authority over the bureaucracy by Reagan's first term. Realistically speaking, there was no means by which congressmen could vote to eliminate or remove programs wherein they would not lose their seats.

Biographer Steven Hayward, a strong supporter of the Gipper, nevertheless misread what had happened in his two-volume study *The Age of Reagan*. In the wake of the 1981 budget fight, Hayward wrote

> the media's formidable onslaught on the Reagan budget plan helped Democrats achieve the long-term victory for control of future budgets, even after losing the initial battle. Social spending over the next few years

would grow in real terms and as a proportion of the
federal budget.[433]

Yet Congress *never* was going to reduce the bureaucracy. It had lost
control of that in the late 1960s and early 1970s to courts, who were
focused only on determining whether agencies were operating by the
rules Congress established. As Philip Hamburger noted, though, the
bureaucracy expanded largely through evading real oversight via administrative adjudication, whereby they could ignore such basic protections
and liberties for businesses as due process, while denying discovery and
reverse the burden of proof.[434]

After Stockman's article with William Greider, "The Education of
David Stockman," came out in the *Atlantic Monthly* in which Stockman
criticized Dutch's program, Nancy was furious and demanded he be fired.
Ed Meese agreed with her. Although Stockman offered his resignation in
a face-to-face meeting with the Gipper, Reagan told him that wasn't want
he wanted. But just as Stockman thought he was off the hook, Reagan
used a frequent ploy of his referring to his other advisors: "Oh, the fellas
think this is getting out of hand. They want you to write up a statement
explaining all this and go before the press tomorrow afternoon."[435]

Stockman's significance was that overall the budget *deficits* remained
the top priority on the domestic side as opposed to cutting the size of
government. Reagan assumed that because he had put many like-minded
people in his cabinet and in much of the bureaucracy, they would behave
appropriately and seek cuts. Meanwhile, the Democrats and the traditional deficit-hawk Republicans were bent on balancing the budget. (The
Democrats only cared about budget-balancing as a means to hurt Reagan
and force him to raise taxes, which they did eventually.) Reagan justified
the 1982 negotiations to raise taxes as "the price we have to pay to get
the budget cuts."[436] Whatever Stockman's malignant intentions, though,
he correctly identified cutting the bureaucracy as an essential element of
regaining control of the government. For him, however, it was entirely a
budgetary issue. He did not appreciate how deeply entrenched culturally
the bureaucracy had become.

When Stockman had tried to cut, he encountered strong resistance. For example, in the Energy Department, which candidate Reagan had proposed to eliminate, the secretary resisted even cutting the department in half. At the Department of Transportation, where Secretary Drew Lewis claimed Stockman was "seeking power for himself," resistance was strong.[437] Lewis demanded to know, "What kind of bureaucracy are you building up over at OMB?"[438] Stockman, still in his revolutionary budget-cutting phase, fumed that the Gipper was not up to the task. Forty years, he said, of "promises, entitlements and safety nets issued by the federal government to every component and stratum of American society would have to be scrapped or drastically modified," and Reagan didn't have the stomach for it.[439] Yet it was Stockman who flat refused to even discuss cuts with Caspar Weinberger at the Pentagon. "As soon as we get past this first phase of the process," he told Greider, "I'm really going to go after the Pentagon.... We're going to get our case in line and just force it through the presses."[440]

In 1988, the Office of Management and Budget under director James Miller had this exchange with Commerce Department over forty-three congressional add-on programs to the Department totaling $73 million that could be cut. When Miller requested a response from Commerce on what wasteful or unnecessary spending could be chopped, the Commerce Department responded that 51 percent of the money had already been obligated, meaning the department couldn't touch it. "Of the remaining $36.1 million," it replied, "Commerce intends to comply with $23.9 million as earmarked and partially comply with another $1.1 million." In other words, the Commerce Department planned no cuts.[441]

Holding a harder line on cuts of any sort was difficult considering Reagan needed Democrat support to defeat the USSR in the Cold War. That was the second major campaign promise Reagan made, to rebuild the US military and stand up to the Soviets. Few people, however, knew that Reagan actually intended to *defeat* the USSR, despite the fact that he was asked early on about his intentions regarding the Soviets and he said, "It's easy. We win, they lose." This strategy involved a massive naval, air, and ground forces buildup; and soon also brought a full court press by the CIA in Afghanistan and in allowing the Soviets to "steal" critical—but deeply flawed—technology that later resulted in catastrophic losses. Reagan had resisted the Soviets on every battlefield, including spiritual, cultural, political, and military wherever he could. Then in 1983, in his Strategic Defense Initiative speech, he added the straw that broke the Soviets' back, "Star Wars," a missile defense system that rendered useless the Soviets' massive edge in (intercontinental ballistic missiles, or ICBMs).[442]

Even without the Iran-Contra Affair, which weakened Reagan, the time and energy consumed by defeating the Soviets and rebuilding the economy exceeded that of most normal men. Reagan repeatedly championed the line-item veto, knowing full well that Congress would never cede such authority. He observed, almost in resignation, that subsequent generations my have to do some of the heavy lifting, and that he couldn't do it all. Congress increasingly overrode his spending vetoes. Cutting government and attacking the Bureaucracy Swamp would require a full-time effort by a president.

Through no fault of the Gipper's, the bureaucracy experienced other triumphs in his terms. In 1984, the US Supreme Court ruled in *Chevron v. Natural Resources Defense Council* that judges needed to defer to administrative interpretations of ambiguities in the statutes. Put another way, the Bureaucracy Swamp got to determine what its own regulations meant and whether they were constitutional.[443] One expert on the threat from the bureaucracy, Philip Hamburger, identified another power-expanding tactic by the administrative state as "evasion," wherein new regulations or rules avoid acts of legislation through legal edicts stemming from their previous administrative decisions. Another method by which the Bureaucratic Swamp could avoid the natural consequences of its poor regulations—which Barack Obama took advantage of endlessly—was through waivers. Friends and cronies could escape damages from regulations by being friends of the administration. Finally, Hamburger noted, the bureaucracy used licensing rights to regulate words and speakers (as is evident today with "critical race theory" being forced on federal employees).

Reagan fell into the trap of fighting the Bureaucratic Swamp on the battlefield of the budgets. In fact, the enemy had prepared a "defense in depth" in which the budget process was the first, and in many ways least important, battlefield of all. For one thing, fighting budget battles usually required horse trading. To obtain the support of the conservative Southern Democrats known as the "Boll Weevils," the Gipper had to woo them. He invited them to a barbecue at Camp David; he telephoned them personally, promising to refrain from campaigning against them in the next election cycle. One of them, Texas congressman Charlie Wilson—who would work closely with Reagan in supporting the *mujahadeen* in Afghanistan—quipped that he was bought and would stay bought. "You're not worth a damn around this place if you don't keep a commitment like that," he noted.[444]

When the Air Traffic Controllers Union (PATCO) went out on strike, Reagan reluctantly fired the striking employees for violating their federal contract that prohibited them from striking. He successfully replaced them amidst dire predictions of a wave of airline crashes, and sent a message that he would stand strong against union thuggery. But while the PATCO strike carried implications even for dealing with the Soviets (who were taking by Reagan's strong will), it did nothing to change the scope or size of the bureaucracy. Indeed, once he rolled out the Strategic Defense Initiative (SDI), it created yet another powerful agency within the Pentagon.

By the 1980s, the Pentagon had emerged as a major spoils trough. It may have been necessary to counter the Soviet buildup, but the waste and fraud associated with the Reagan ramp-up were significant. For example, auditors found that defense contractors charged $7,000 for a coffeepot on C-5A cargo planes; $435 for a claw hammer one could purchase at a hardware store for $5; and $640 for a toilet seat. An inspector general report from the Pentagon of 15,000 spare parts found two-thirds of the parts had price increases of more than 50 percent since the early 1980s and some had price increases of up to 500 percent.

Beset on one side by Democrats wanting higher taxes as a bludgeon to smash supply-side economics with, and on the other by Reagan's own swampy staff, who still didn't understand the essence of dynamic tax cuts that changed incentives, Reagan accomplished the near impossible by getting tax rates down for most people, permanently.

Moreover, he did have significant success against the Swamp when it came to regulations. In 1981, the number of pages in the *Federal Register* (a good barometer of the number of regulations being issued) fell by one-third. New rules by agencies dropped even faster, by 50 percent. In the area of antitrust policy, Reagan reversed a dramatic intrusion of the federal government into the market. Federal antitrust actions fell by a third and for the first time since TR, the government began losing anti-trust actions. Reagan's administration also imposed cost-benefit requirements on new regulations. For example, in a case involving Adirondack mountain fish, the new requirements reversed a policy that would have cost more than $12,000 per fish saved![445] Dutch may not have been able to substantially change the numbers of offices in the bureaucracy, but at least he significantly limited their scope and power.

A similar goal of prohibiting the blatant use of race-based quotas and other regulations epitomized the administration's work in the civil rights arena. Even when his appointees arrived ready to implement a different approach, the entrenched civil rights interests in the bureaus and agencies viciously resisted. One major exception was Clarence Thomas at the Equal Employment Opportunity Commission (EEOC). Thomas announced that the EEOC would follow the dictates of the Justice Department and direct its remedies to individual victims with specific claims, not to classes or groups. But Thomas even went further, abolishing the EEOC's unit that brought discrimination claims based solely on disparate impact and restrained the EEOC in other ways. Because of Thomas's modifications, the number of EEOC enforcement actions actually increased, resulting in settlements that included a major suit with General Motors for $42 million.

In his second inaugural, Reagan returned to the theme of a government that had far too much influence in people's lives. "We asked things of government," he noted, "that government was not equipped to give. We yielded authority to the National Government that properly belonged to States or to local governments or to the people themselves."[446] He left it at that. There was no more mention of cutting government in his inaugural speech.

Based on his unsuccessful first-term experience with cutting government at all, by 1985, Reagan had given up on any ideas of battling the bureaucracy: he needed the new bureaucracy of the Pentagon to defeat the Soviets; he had already put Social Security and Medicare off limits. He had trimmed where he could, closing one small aviation-related agency and reining in PATCO. Then, other, darker issues came to the fore.

Reagan became embroiled in the Iran-Contra Affair, a convoluted mess that resulted from lack of oversight of his national security advisor, Bud McFarlane, and his subordinate, Marine Col. Oliver North. The imbroglio started with Islamic forces taking Americans hostage in Lebanon, acts that deeply troubled and affected Reagan. He thought relentlessly about the hostages, and constantly pondered ways to get them released. At the same time, two trouble spots in Central America, El Salvador and Nicaragua, erupted. Reagan sent military advisors and money to El Salvador. Nearby Nicaragua, however, was collapsing due to a Communist insurgency there, and in 1981 the National Security Council had proposed military assistance to the Nicaraguan exiles with echoes of the Bay of Pigs looming. The Nicaraguan resistance, or the "Contras," were too small a group to be effective, and regardless the money they received was largely wasted. Reagan found himself limited even further by the 1981 Boland Amendment, named for Democrat Edward Boland of Massachusetts, who chaired the House Intelligence Committee. His amendment banned any American support for the purpose of overthrowing the Government of Nicaragua.[447]

Just how the Middle East hostages and the Nicaraguan Contras intersected was one of those strange twists of history. Reagan asked McFarlane if there was any way to fund the Contras, and he, in turn, handed the project off to North. The colonel devised a byzantine arrangement whereby Saudi Arabia would send money to bank accounts held by the Contras. At the same time—right as Dutch was undergoing surgery for a polyp in his colon—he sent McFarlane to the Middle East to negotiate for the release of hostages. Iran, while not claiming to actually hold these captives, nevertheless implied it could get them released by those who did. What did the Iranians want in return? Arms.

The whole scheme was harebrained, convoluted and violated many of Reagan's most fundamental beliefs about negotiating with terrorists. Yet his omnipresent concern with the fate of the hostages led him to do just that, reasoning that the Iranians (in this case) weren't the hostage takers (terrorists). As Secretary of State George Shultz said, Dutch "worried about them personally.... It just drove him crazy."[448] Reagan's Secretary of Defense, Caspar Weinberger, and Schulz, who seldom agreed on anything both united to tell Dutch it was "almost too absurd to comment on" (as Weinberger put it).[449] As I pointed out in *Reagan: The American President*, it is important to keep in mind that the Israelis had already worked with Congressman Charlie Wilson (D-TX) to coordinate weapons sales through the Egyptians to the *mujahideen* in Afghanistan, blurring the lines of such third-party "negotiations." While some hostages were released, including Rev. Benjamin Weir, a secondary justification for the shipments—that Iranian "moderates" would be empowered—never even remotely came to pass.

What the Iran arms deals demonstrated contradicted Lou Cannon's (and others') depiction of Reagan as a puppet in the hands of his advisors. He went ahead with the exchanges despite the opposition of everyone in his cabinet. Matters grew worse, however, when the next step in the hostage initiative unfolded in January 1986, when not only the US would have to supply anti-tank missiles but would also have to convince the Israelis to release twenty Hezbollah captives in order to gain the release of five more hostages. By that time John Poindexter had replaced McFarlane who had, before his departure, moved oversight of the Iran dealings from the CIA to the National Security Council. Poindexter wanted to bypass all intermediaries and sell arms directly to Iran for the hostages. On January 17, 1986, Poindexter gave a new "finding" to Reagan that was the same as the old one, but with a new cover memo from North and Poindexter indicating that the United States would sell the arms directly to Iran. Reagan signed it without looking at the new cover letter. "I gave the go ahead," he wrote in his diary.[450] Reagan told one audience, "I don't care if I have to go to Leavenworth: I want the hostages out," suggesting he knew exactly what he was doing.[451] Reagan maintained a powerful faith that the public would support him if fully informed, and that the only way to release the hostages was through trading arms.

He did not know that North had transferred some of the money from the sales on his own to support the Contras. News broke publicly on Election Day, 1984, when an Arabic-language paper in Lebanon ran a story that before his departure McFarlane had shipped arms to the Iranians. After Poindexter took over, though, North exercised much more autonomy. When Reagan sent Peter Wallison, Don Regan's counsel at Treasury, to look into the matter, Wallison found that North and Poindexter had lied about the whole arms transfer affair.

Iran-Contra demonstrated yet again how the Bureaucracy Swamp had gotten out of control. However well-intentioned North and Poindexter had been, they had evaded the chain of command and engaged in personal diplomacy to the point of arming a military force outside of a US government office without telling the president or Congress. It seriously damaged Reagan, especially once the Reagan-hating media got hold of the story and smelled blood in the water. When Reagan's pollster, Richard Wirthlin met with Wallison, he knew the Iran-Contra Affair was of Watergate proportions when the term "high crimes and misdemeanors" came up. The White House called Ed Meese back, who was away giving a speech when it was discovered that North and Poindexter had concocted two different timelines—which were important because Reagan was legally vindicated in selling the arms if there was a "finding" that was sent to Congress prior to the sale. Now, Meese discovered that the missiles and other arms may have been sold without such a finding. Once the whole group involved in the episode met on November 24, 1986, Meese showed the president the evidence of the illegal transfer and the missing money that North sent to the Contras. Meese told Reagan that both North and Poindexter had concealed this from everyone. As Meese related these findings, the color drained from Reagan's face. Don Regan, who had since moved from treasury secretary to be Reagan's chief of staff, later wrote, "Nobody who saw the President's reaction that afternoon could believe for a moment that he knew about the diversion of funds before Meese told him about it."[452]

For the second time in twenty-five years, the National Security Council had failed catastrophically to oversee foreign intrigue. North had circumvented Congress, the State Department, and the Department of Defense. A single colonel had engaged in a one-man arms sale operation *and* funding a rogue army in defiance of Congress's strict warnings. While Reagan paid the political price and narrowly avoided impeachment, the larger threat of uncontrolled bureaus and agencies within the leviathan government wasn't even addressed.

Under Reagan, another disaster befell the country, again stemming from oversight failures within the bureaucracy. In January 1986, the Space Shuttle *Challenger* exploded shortly after liftoff, killing all seven crew aboard. The National Aeronautics and Space Administration (NASA), which up to that time had possessed a stellar reputation, quickly came under scrutiny. Reagan set up a special commission, the Rogers Commission, to investigate the accident. What the commission found was that NASA's organizational structure and decision-making processes had caused the agency to violate its own rules for safety. Since 1977, NASA managers had been alerted to a problem with the "O-rings" that sealed parts of the Morton-Thiokol solid rocket boosters, but did not address them. NASA managers also ignored warnings about cold weather causing the O-rings to fail.

Like other bureaucracies, NASA had become its own fiefdom, obsessed with the public relations victories from launches that ensured continued large budgets from Congress. NASA downplayed safety concerns and displayed "poor technical decision-making over a period of several years by top NASA and contractor personnel...."[453] What emerged from the investigations was that NASA behaved like any other big bureaucracy: it never did anything wrong, no one was ever to blame, and its existence became its mission.

When the Gipper left office in 1989, most people had forgotten one of his original "big three" goals—to reduce the size of government. The

Bureaucracy Swamp managed to turn the narrative to taxes and deficits, rather than the structural rot causing the deficits and requiring the taxes. Actual reductions in government gave way to perceptions that Reagan had changed the system, which in many ways he did. None other than President Barack Obama admitted as much, saying,

> I think Ronald Reagan changed the trajectory of America in a way that…Richard Nixon did not or Bill Clinton did not. He put us on a fundamentally different path because the country was ready for it…. I think it's fair to say that the Republicans were the party of ideas for a pretty long chunk of time over the last 10, 15 years, in the sense that they were challenging conventional wisdom.[454]

Conservatives, though, saw that little had changed in the Swamp. Thomas Silver pointed out that Reagan's goal was "nothing less than a realignment of the American political order, in which the primacy of the New Deal was to be challenged and overthrown. It cannot be said that Reagan in any fundamental way dismantled or even scaled back the administrative state…."[455] Stephen Hayward, generally favorable toward Reagan, argued that rolling back the bureaucracy was more difficult than defeating the Soviet Union. Both public opinion and constitutional obstacles impeded him—and Hayward cited the failed 1994 Republican "revolution" under Newt Gingrich as evidence that the public did not support shrinking government. Conservatives such as Hayward thought the Reagan Revolution did not go far enough because it did not begin as a full-fledged constitutional effort of its own.

Yet these criticisms miss the mark, and entirely fail to grasp the nature of the Bureaucratic Swamp Ronald Reagan inherited. Gone were Lincoln's and Cleveland's days when a president (often via a party) had significant control over the administrative state with his appointments. Since the Pendleton Act, party control over the Swamp all but disappeared; Congress ceded its budgetary control to the White House in the 1920s; and by the 1970s—while Reagan was still governor of

California—the courts abandoned all serious effort at restraining the Bureaucratic Swamp. If the Gipper is to be faulted, it is for not recognizing how deep and fast his enemy was, and how much ground had already been surrendered to it. Expecting Dutch to fundamentally transform that with a mostly oppositional House, a thoroughly hostile media, and at the same time defeat the greatest threat to life on planet earth (the USSR) and, oh, by the way, *also rebuild the US economy* is perhaps a fantasy.

Early on, Reagan had an opportunity to impose significant cuts in the administrative state's budget, but he got distracted by Stockman, who though all control flowed through the budget. In fact, all control flowed through the *perception* held by the Bureaucratic Swamp of its own entitlement, its own power, and most of all, its own permanence. Some early elimination of a dozen agencies, even if insignificant, may have sufficed to reorient the thinking in Washington DC, though it is unlikely. In the end, Reagan failed to do much damage to the Bureaucracy Swamp.

Scorecard: Reagan and the Bureaucracy Slave Swamp

- Completely unsuccessful in curbing the size or reach of the bureaucracy
- Followed the Constitution
- Had minimal support from Congress when it came to the reduction of the size of government
- Overall had a hostile media
- Had to place control of the Bureaucratic Swamp as third priority behind reviving the economy and winning the Cold War

CHAPTER 6

Donald Trump and the Deep State Swamp

Understanding Donald Trump's success requires an apprecia-
tion for Barack Obama's political achievement. Obama's team
was highly superstitious and "completely immersed in their
own mythology" (as if that was a surprise to anyone).[456] The connection
between the two became apparent only after Obama left office. One of
the Obama team's biggest mythological stories was that of Iowa, where
he had surprised everyone by winning the Iowa caucuses in 2008. In
2016, after Hillary Clinton lost, Obama's advisors wanted to do one
last focus group—in Iowa. They chose only people who had voted for
Obama twice and then for Donald Trump. To their shock and amaze-
ment, Obama's advisors found that the voters saw Trump and Obama
as similar: both wanted change, although many believed Obama failed
to deliver. One independent voter, a woman, said, "We'd sent this young
man to Washington hoping to make a change [and] I want somebody to
get in there now and drain the swamp."[457] When the team presented the
data and the responses to Obama, he only said, "I get it."

To traditional party loyalists, this development would remain a mystery. They only saw things in terms of Democrats and Republicans, not
"the ruling class" vs. the "country class," as Angelo Codevilla described it

in his insightful 2010 article, "America's Ruling Class—And the Perils of Revolution."[458] Yet the idea of a Swamp or a Deep State was not new at all.

In 1956, C. Wright Mills, a sociologist at Columbia University, wrote the first book on the Deep State, *The Power Elite*, which maintained that a group of men who held key positions in the military, finance, communications, and politics dominated the country. Mills claimed that "a few hundred giant corporations," a group of government elites, and the military establishment have combined to control the country.[459] While asserting that the power elite might not be aware of their status, or might be uncertain about their roles, they nevertheless had become a quasi-hereditary class almost exclusively emerging from Ivy League schools, especially insofar as the elites had access to inner clubs such as Porcellian and Fly Club (and, later, Skull and Bones).

Mills traced the decline of small-town America—within thirty years, "middle America"—and the rise of self-contained worlds of fashion, style, literature, thought, and above all power in East Coast (and later, West Coast) metro areas. He saw an interlocking directorate at the top of the American power structure, showing how the bureaucracies (the Swamp) had become interchangeable. Generals were appointed as directors of large corporations, businessmen moved into government posts. (What he did not see at the time was the incredible inbreeding of politicians and journalists, with many of Bill Clinton's "war room" or Barack Obama's cabal going on to be prime-time "journalists" or commentators or vice versa with journalists serving in various administrations, including George Stephanopoulos, Jay Carney, Linda Douglass, Jill Zuckerman, Douglas Franz, and Stephen Barr.) Regular contributors included Matthew Dowd, who worked for both Democrats and Republicans, and David Gergen.

To fully understand the depths and expanse of the Deep State that President Donald Trump found when he came into the presidency in January 2017, look no further than a pathbreaking book from Charles Murray, *Coming Apart*. He traced a noticeable, nay, shocking shift in the college admissions process whereby test scores increasingly decided who would go to the elite schools. And those test scores shot up like a rocket on nearly a 90-degree angle. In 1997, ten schools took 20 percent of all the students who scored in the top 5 percent on the SAT or ACT. In other words, a mere ten schools siphoned off one-fifth of the brainiest students in America. The immediate problem here was that "the segregation of the college system now means that the typical classroom in a third-tier public university is filled with students who are not much brighter than the average young person in the nation as a whole, whereas the typical classroom in an elite school has no one outside the top decile of cognitive talent, and many who are in the top hundredth or thousandth of the distribution."[460] This by itself would be a problem for the nation: a tier of geeky nerd geniuses who will occupy all the top jobs and have no clue how the other 99 percent live. But the problem was much deeper than that. These graduates would go on to take the top jobs in law firms, tech companies, journalism, hedge funds and banks, and, of course, politics. They infested the top staffing jobs in Washington, DC. Murray's term for this was "homogamy," or the inbreeding of individuals with like characteristics.

They settled in "superzips," or zip codes identified as being in the top 5 percent of both wealth and university status. Those areas were overwhelmingly on the East Coast, in the Boston to DC corridor. Some twenty states did not have a *single* superzip and a half dozen more only had one. But the area outside Washington, DC, is filled with superzips. One member of the elite noted with amusement that every person on his block graduated from an Ivy League school. Outside of picking up dry cleaning (if they did it themselves), or filling their gas tank (if they did it themselves), or ordering Starbucks, the inhabitants of the superzips would literally encounter *no one* outside their wealth/IQ class in normal daily interactions. (It is getting so bad that even the left is now assaulting the elite schools, calling them "obscene.")[461] This was the group that had staffed much of the Swamp that Donald Trump encountered.

To appreciate the breadth and depth of the Swamp Trump encountered, it was exponentially bigger than the Spoils Swamp Cleveland fought; it had lobbying elements vastly more influential than the Trust Swamp Roosevelt beat; and it had all the worst inhabitants of both the

CIA Swamp and the Bureaucracy Swamp JFK and Reagan fought. As Tom Engelhardt, author of many books on the Deep State, argued

> In recent times, that labyrinthine structure—of intelligence agencies morphing into war-fighting outfits, the US military (with its own secret military, the special operations forces, gestating inside it), and the Department of Homeland Security (DHS), a monster conglomeration of agencies that is an actual "defense department," as well as a vast contingent of weapons makers, contractors, and profiteers bolstered by an army of lobbyists—has never stopped growing.[462]

And as former campaign manager to President Donald Trump, Stephen Bannon, noted, many non-defense agencies including the Post Office, the Bureau of Land Management, and the Internal Revenue Service, have their own *armed* agents. The armed Deep State is deeper than ever.

Liberal critics of the Deep State pointed with glee to the system's targeting of al-Qaeda as the "great Satan" in the rationale for its existence, only to be horrified that it was Donald Trump who became the central victim of this apparatus. In that context, it is interesting that it was a member of the Deep State, Mark Felt, an FBI official, who was "Deep Throat" in the Watergate Affair, meaning that it was the bureaucracy that really brought down Nixon. As John Marini wrote, "Bureaucracies have developed the instinct for self-preservation at all costs. They cannot, however, defend themselves on the basis of self-interest. Rather, they see themselves as defenders of institutional rationality...."[463]

One might go further, particularly with the military arms of the Deep State. "Security" of the United States has become a religion permitting, and even demanding, that the American public be lied to for its own good. Not once or twice, but constantly. They do this, noted Engelhardt, "based on the belief that the deepest secrets of their world and its operations can only truly be understood by those already inducted into their orders."[464] (In this context, from the left's viewpoint, the Masons have nothing on the Deep Military State!) Some 92 *million* pages of Department of Defense documents are classified. When Barack Obama said that the National Security Agency was under the supervision of all three branches of government, the opposite was likely true, namely that because of the secrecy imposed, they were at best co-opted and muzzled and at worst complicit in shielding the secret intelligence from those seeking to protect President Trump from the very conspiracy against him that the intel agencies initiated.

In 2012, the Defense Intelligence Agency—which supposedly existed for analysis and coordination of information—launched a human intelligence arm (HUMINT) by filling US embassies with up to 1,500 new clandestine operators (spies). The outcome of such an expansion could be seen in the Russia hoax, where such operators were feeding information to those compiling the "Steele dossier." At the same time, the Obama administration—after promising openness and transparency—cracked down hard on whistleblowers, launching an "unprecedented program" to train millions of employees and contractors to profile coworkers for "indicators of insider threat behavior."[465] Obama more than doubled the total number of whistleblower prosecutions over all previous administrations combined. When the US Senate Armed Services Committee and Senate Select Committee on Intelligence sought to investigate the CIA's drone-killer program under Obama in a "joint classified hearing," the White House refused to provide security clearances for committee members to question the witnesses.[466] And Obama's head of national intelligence, James Clapper, brazenly lied to Congress on March 12, 2013, when Senator Ron Wyden asked if the NSA had gathered any data on millions of Americans. Clapper, with a straight face, replied, "No sir, not willingly."[467] These were just a few examples of the Deep State Trump was about to walk into over and above the ongoing Russia hoax.

Trump used the term "Drain the Swamp" for the first time in October 2016 when he pushed several ethics reforms in Colorado Springs that he said would "drain the swamp" of Washington, DC.[468] These included proposals to strictly limit lobbying, a ban on senior government officials lobbying for foreign governments, a ban on members of Congress from lobbying for five years, and a term limits amendment to the US Constitution. He used the term in this context over 75 times in the le-adup to the 2016 election.[469] Both Ronald Reagan, in 1983, and Reagan's speechwriter and presidential candidate, Patrick Buchanan in 2000, had used the term sparingly before Trump.[470] Of course, the Washington media got the concept entirely wrong, thinking it just referred to eliminating lobbyists or special projects. Throughout the 2016 campaign, it had been a hallmark of elites and especially those in what would be called the Hoax News or Fake News media to take Trump literally but never seriously. He was less concerned with (as Cleveland did) canceling one unconstitutional office or program and getting to the root of the corrupt enterprise.

How and when the term Deep State came to replace the Swamp is another matter. Slowly, after Trump took office, it became obvious that the traditional rules of Washington, DC, did not apply: he would not see quick action on his nominees requiring confirmation in the Senate, and countless appointees were stalled—not just the high-profile cabinet positions. Some cite the expression "deep state" as originating in Turkey in the 1990s; Bill Moyers, press secretary under Lyndon Johnson, claimed on a talk show in 2014 that there was a "deep state hiding in plain sight" that favored military conflicts regardless of the party in power.[471] This was a throwback to Dwight Eisenhower's warning of the military-industrial complex.

Whether the news media or journalism as it once was called is a part of the Deep State is a legitimate question. The most likely answer is, yes. One telltale sign of news organizations being interconnected with the Trump resistance in Washington was how quickly they rushed to deny the existence of a Deep State. "As Leaks Multiply, Fears of a 'Deep State' in America," blared the *New York Times*.[472] "Deep State: How a Conspiracy Theory Went From Political Fringe to Mainstream," explained *Newsweek*.[473] "Five Myths About the 'Deep State,'" intoned the *Washington Post*.[474] Thus, the top two newspapers in America in terms of influencing the political class, plus one of the two biggest remaining magazine weeklies, all managed to put out stories debunking the Deep

State from February to August 2017—without ever once questioning the legitimacy of a now-debunked (and embarrassingly so) Deep State "investigation" into so-called "collusion" between the Trump White House and Russia.

A few admitted that the Deep State was real, but it was either benign or simply misunderstood. Political scientist George Friedman, openly admitted that a Deep State existed, pointing out that the bureaucracy was a "very real thing" that was "created to limit the power of the president."[475] Of course, as we have seen, Friedman's explanation for the purpose of the Deep State is entirely wrong. It was never created to "limit the power of the president," but rather to *relieve the president of a massive burden.* Not one advocate of the Pendleton Act, discussed in the chapter on Grover Cleveland, justified it as a means to limit the powers of a president. Neither James Garfield, nor Chester Arthur, nor Grover Cleveland, the three presidents most responsible for the civil service bureaucracy, in any way sought limitations on their powers but rather an *increase* in their powers by eliminating a mind-numbing and time-consuming task. And contrary to Friedman's astonishing claim that the bureaucracy existed to "shield the government from politics" the Deep State bureaucracy, as many have shown, exists to shield itself from any reduction of its own power.

Another early indicator of the incestuous nature of the new journalism class and the Deep State was how quickly leaks that harmed Trump (but never any that helped him) found their way into the pages of the *New York Times, Politico,* or other media outlets. Later, the Office of the Inspector General would investigate these leaks, but conclude nothing illegal really happened—or at least nothing worth prosecuting.[476]

Just seven months after Trump's inauguration, Barack Obama's CIA director, John Brennan, said that executive branch officials (i.e., the Swamp) had an "obligation…to refuse to carry out" outrageous or anti-democratic orders from the president.[477] Just whose definitions of what constituted "outrageous" or "anti-democratic" of course would depend on who was carrying out such actions, in Brennan's case, the Deep State itself. As *Politico* writer Michael Crowley noted, "For a generation, the people who saw something like an American deep state—even if they rarely called it that—resided on the left, not the right."[478] Yet as we have seen, this went back on the left far longer than "a generation," all the way back to Mills' "power elite." And even as candidate Barack Obama campaigned against George W. Bush-era surveillance and security policies, he not only continued them but expanded and enhanced them, releasing the National Security Administration to delve into phone calls of Republicans (a crime for which no person has even been charged).

Since JFK's failure to tame the CIA Swamp, it became inevitable that one of the intelligence agencies would, as with Tolkien's ring, "rule them all." And it became likely that the CIA or FBI would emerge as that "ring." The government, as writer "Sundance" has argued in his "ConservativeTreehouse" blog, puts information into "containment silos." This has the effect of blocking the free flow of information between agencies and branches.[479] When the FBI started its fraudulent Russia investigation, it did not inform anyone in the Department of Justice because of the "sensitivity of the matter." To FBI Director James Comey, even informing the National Security Council (!) would have been the equivalent of notifying Trump himself. Indeed, throughout the Russia hoax investigation, the intelligence community deliberately notified *only* the director of national intelligence (James Clapper) as a means to *avoid* oversight, not enhance it—because Clapper was a Trump hater and part of the intelligence operation itself.

Sundance's argument here is critical, for the intelligence community now operates without any authority from Congress, the president, or the court system. It is not, as he notes, "a subsidiary set of agencies within the executive branch."[480] Instead it is an independent functioning creature *above* the law in most cases.

The Deep State that Trump battled included a vast intellectual underpinning of both "conservative" and liberal intellectuals who had "established a theoretical, or socially constructed, reality that appeared indifferent to reality as it revealed itself in practical or political life."[481] All of Washington's administrative stakeholders were opposed to Trump and required a defense of the Washington establishment. Yet Trump challenged and deprecated the intellectual leadership of not only the liberals, but so-called conservatives as well. "In short," wrote John Marini, "he succeeded in separating parts of the political constituencies of both parties from their organizational and ideological leadership" and "removed political discourse from their hands and placed it directly in the hands of the electorate itself."[482] Trump had mobilized a political constituency that recognized a political reality that, as Marini noted, was still visible to a large segment of America, but which was in stark contrast to the narrative established by the ruling class.

It should come as no surprise that even so-called "conservatives" such as Senator Tim Scott (SC), Senate Minority Leader Mitch McConnell (then Majority Leader), Nebraska Republican senator Ben Sasse and many others either tacitly or openly opposed Trump. After all, from the outset, he was attempting to demystify, defy, and delegitimize the Washington ruling class and challenged the orthodoxy of both parties. In contrast, the Democrats sought to fragment and divide the electorate by race, sex, religious group, and so on to avoid the very notion of a common good that Trump sought to instill. Consequently, many so-called conservatives rejected Trump claiming he was not "conservative," in terms of adhering to an intellectual orthodoxy. Instead, conservatism should be viewed as Lincoln viewed it, as a defense of life based on the authority and goodness of the past. Above all, conservatism is the polar opposite of modern quasi-fascist liberalism and its dictatorship of the bureaucracy and ruling class.

As President Trump settled into office, so-called conservatives who criticized him completely ignored that he was perhaps the most *constitutional* president since Reagan: he routinely called upon Congress, the courts, and governors via federalism to do their jobs before he acted. He repeatedly begged Congress for budgets. He urged Congress to act on DACA (Deferred Action for Childhood Arrivals). Trump insisted the governors end "sanctuary city" politics and cooperate on border control. At every step of the way, Trump *sought* constitutional solutions, only to be rebuffed by the Deep State. Indeed, the greatest criticism of President Trump—outside of some of his questionable personnel decisions—was why the Department of Justice did not intervene in riot-torn hellholes like Chicago or Portland, or why "sanctuary city" mayors or "sanctuary state" governors were not arrested.

Trump's federalism, though he certainly never described it as such, was a return to founding principles of both division of powers among levels of government and separation of powers within government. Even with a Republican House under the leadership of Paul Ryan—a Trump hater—nothing got done. The House refused to consider serious funding for Trump's border wall. When it came to the DACA "Dreamers," Trump virtually begged Congress to deal with the issue. In short, Trump tried to avoid executive orders whenever he could, without success.

He also entered office with a commitment to putting in his cabinet positions achievers, men and women who had been successful in business. Foremost among these was Rex Tillerson, former head of Exxon, as his secretary of state. Many of those appointees would prove less than successful, if not downright disastrous. As Jared Kushner, Trump's son-in-law and advisor, admitted, "He brought in a whole new crop of people. Maybe they didn't have the traditional resumes for doing their jobs, but many of them shared his vision. It took a little bit of time to figure out who were the right people and who were the wrong people."[483] Trump also surrounded himself with military men, whom he greatly respected and thought would run their assigned areas like an efficient military operation. But again, he had badly misjudged who those men were. His worst personnel misjudgment, however, was his most crucial appointment, Attorney General Jeff Sessions.

Looking at how Vladimir Lenin seized control of Russia in 1917, two days after he took power he controlled key parts of Moscow and Leningrad, including police; then in short order shut down the press and closed any newspapers opposed to him; by December had all schools taken from the Church and handed over to the government; and nationalized all factories on the 24th.[484] Certainly Trump was not even remotely involved in such a takeover, but the point remains that taking on a deeply entrenched bureaucracy/network of any kind requires utterly committed people and speed. Trump had neither.

His attorney general selection, Alabama senator Jeff Sessions, seemed like a natural choice for the job. As attorney general of Alabama, he had taken on the Ku Klux Klan and broke it. The DC liberal Deep State seemed no different in its operations, secrecy, and utter hate for conservative ideas. I spent an hour on the phone with Sessions in late 2016 as he headed Trump's transition team. We discussed Reagan's transition, which was hailed as the best ever by Harvard's Business School. Sessions seemed 100 percent committed to the Trump agenda. Although we did not discuss the Deep State, I left with the impression Sessions would not tolerate any insurrectionist nonsense.

Then came a pair of meaningless "conversations" with the Russian ambassador to the United States, Sergey Kislyak. The first time was short, after a public event at the Republican National Convention, and the second time on September 8 when they met in Sessions' office about Russia and Ukraine. Sessions immediately came under scrutiny for "Russian collusion," which didn't take place and which, even if Sessions had spoken to Kislyak, it was perfectly within his purview as head of the transition team to do so. At the time, the investigation into Russian interference was a counterintelligence investigation, *not* a criminal investigation, so there was a third reason Sessions should not have recused himself. Yet he did so on March 2, 2017. He had not even advised Trump that he was under suspicion of any wrongdoing, let alone that he was going to recuse himself. Moreover, the outrageousness of Sessions' action must be seen in light of the fact that he knew the "muh Russia" hoax was going to become a major issue before he accepted the position and had a duty to inform Trump that if the Kislyak meetings came up he would have to recuse, in which case Trump certainly would have—or should have—selected someone else as attorney general. Indeed, Sessions had already taken preliminary steps to recuse himself on his first day in office in January! Again, he did not bother to tell President Trump. Quite the contrary, Sessions in a cowardly manner hid his intentions from Trump.

Gregg Jarrett's definitive studies, *Witch Hunt* and *The Russia Hoax* showed that "neither the facts nor the law required it."[485] As Jarrett noted, the recusal was "illogical and mistaken. There was no legitimate reason for it."[486]

The impact of Sessions' recusal on the entire Trump term of office cannot be overstated. Not only did he hand the matter off to an anti-Trump deputy, Ron Rosenstein—who to this day remains up to his ears in the original Russia hoax as it developed, but who had, according to witnesses, sought to secretly tape President Trump for purposes of removing him through the 25th Amendment.[487] Rosenstein wrote the memo that led to the firing of James Comey.[488] The corrupt FBI director had repeatedly told Trump he was *not* under investigation, and Trump requested that he state that publicly—several times. Yet Comey would not. He should have been fired immediately for insubordination. Finally, on May 9, Trump sacked the pompous FBI director—but that only elevated a more devious and corrupt deputy, Andrew McCabe, into the spot. Neither of them believed in following the law or the Constitution, and their erstwhile supervisor, Jeff Sessions, had taken himself out of the loop.

To restate: Sessions' recusal, and the dishonest way and timing used to deliver it, put Trump's entire fate into the hands of people who hated him. Far from having an attorney general who had his back—his "wingman" as President Barack Obama called his AG Eric Holder—Trump now had a Brutus. That single action meant that Trump would at best have only extremely limited success in draining any of the Deep State Swamp, let alone all of it. Yet Trump—perhaps naively—thought that the people in the high positions at the Department of Justice, the FBI, the CIA, and NSA all were patriots who would put personal feelings or bias aside for the good of the country.

Trump was spectacularly wrong. Tillerson never even tried to get on the Make America Great Again page; Trump's second FBI appointee, Christopher Wray, while probably less overtly corrupt than Comey, was far more sinister by trying to appear reasonable; and the CIA was bounced from do-nothings to a true Deep State obstructionist, Gina Haspel (who as we will see was deeply involved in the January 2021 near-coup). All of these should have been influenced by a solid attorney general, guiding the general anti-"muh Russia" probe.

Firing Sessions immediately would have brought a firestorm of opposition, not the least of which would have been the liberal RINO caucus in the Senate, including Richard Burr, who was the minority chair of the Senate Intelligence Committee, Ben Sasse (a devout Trump hater), Thom Tillis, Lisa Murkowski (a reliable Democrat vote), and Susan Collins. Even in 2017, this may have put Trump close to losing a removal vote in the Senate if the House impeached. Nevertheless, by not removing Sessions, Trump deeply damaged, and may have sabotaged, his entire agenda.

Consider what Sessions did *not* do in the two years prior to his resignation:

- He did not force a single "Sanctuary City" to follow US law and deport illegal aliens. He didn't arrest a single mayor or bring charges against a single governor of a "Sanctuary State."
- Following the post-inaugural riots by the fascist group known as "antifa," Sessions did not demand that the FBI find and arrest the ringleaders or file federal civil rights violations charges against a single rioter.
- Sessions did not weigh in on any of the riots in any of the major cities, nor did he deploy any federal marshals to protect federal property. Neither did he call for the arrest or prosecution of any of those leaders. (Contrast that with the way the Obama administration and Eric Holder immediately waded into the Ferguson, Missouri, case of Michael Brown.)
- Sessions did not bring federal antitrust charges—which Teddy Roosevelt would have done in a month—for the discriminatory treatment of Trump personally and of conservatives nationally on Facebook, Twitter, or other platforms. Quite the contrary, he sat back and allowed Facebook to be seen as aiding the Trump campaign in 2016 by allowing targeted ads (something all politicians and all companies do).

- Sessions did not follow up, nor did he demand that the FBI follow up, on the obvious corruption of the Hillary Clinton campaign and the hundreds of violations of her private email scandal.
- Sessions did not even investigate the constant civil rights violations and threats against almost all conservative speakers on publicly funded universities that accepted federal aid.

This level of incompetence, or cowardice, utterly torpedoed the entire effort to "drain the Swamp" from the outset. Trump's frustration grew over the next two years, knowing that any successor would have to get Senate approval. But the Senate had already held up dozens of Trump appointees and had stalled or wounded several of Trump's cabinet and sub-cabinet level picks.

Trump knew that the tentacles of the Deep State Swamp ran deep. He had no idea how deep. On the campaign trail in October 2016, it was announced that the FBI had sent a letter to Congress informing them that the FBI had discovered still more new emails pertaining to the former secretary of state Hillary Clinton. Trump told a crowd in New Jersey, "They are reopening the case into her criminal an illegal conduct that threatens the security of the United States of America [cheers]."[489] Still under the assumption that the FBI under James Comey would to anything to damage Clinton's chances, Trump praised the FBI: "I have great respect for the fact that the FBI and the Department of Justice are now willing to have the courage to right the horrible mistake they have made. This was a grave miscarriage of justice...."[490] By that time, every crowd had three lines they chanted: "Lock Her Up!" "Build the Wall!" and "Drain the Swamp!"

Not only was the FBI under Comey not going to seriously examine the emails (some staff scanned 33,000 emails in a single weekend) but *already* the FBI had become an accessory in spying on Trump's campaign, wiretapping some of his staffers, and preparing the ground to investigate *him*.

Meanwhile, the "resistance" had started within the Deep State outside the FBI's own treason and the Special Counsel. Institutions fought

Trump through a combination of potentially murderous leaks regarding conversations with foreign leaders, stupid tweets from the National Park Service, and the Environmental Protection Agency's Swamp employees complaining to the *New York Times* that Trump was going to quash an EPA report on the climate change hoax.[491] The EPA's action effectively proved that the bureaucratic Deep State and the Hoax News establishment were completely connected and scarcely different in their political aims. *Politico* grudgingly conceded reality that a large segment of the US government really does operate without much transparency or public scrutiny, and has abused its awesome powers in myriad ways. And sometimes the government bureaucracy really does exercise power over the commander in chief.[492]

Attempting to explain away Swamp activities, *Politico* added that "much of the subversion…Trump faced [was] merely federal employees defending their turf from budget cuts and bone-headed ideas" ("bone-headed ideas" as defined as withdrawing from the eighteen-year-long war in Afghanistan, or pulling out of treaties highly unfavorable to the US). The *Politico* article concluded by noting that it was "not easy to make conservatives distrust law enforcement and intelligence officials," but most Trump supporters would argue that those agencies destroyed their own trust, beginning with the illegal investigation of Trump and the pretzel that FBI director James Comey twisted himself into trying to defend Hillary Clinton from numerous crimes.

In September 2018, a "Senior White House Official" confessed that an anti-Trump cabal leaked stories to try to make Trump appear incompetent and that there was a secret group within the White House working to contain him.[493] Instead of generating sympathy for a group of "patriotic" insiders trying to stop an out-of-control president, the anonymous article merely confirmed what most people already knew: a Deep State existed in Washington, DC, and it was desperate to avoid having its swamp cleaned. Former Democratic congressman Dennis Kucinich admitted a deep state bureaucracy was trying to destroy Trump and his agenda. "The political process of the United States of America [is] under attack by intelligence agencies and individuals in those agencies…. You have politicization of agencies that is resulting in leaks from anonymous, unknown people [to] take down a president.["]494 In fact it was far worse: major outlets such as the *Wall Street Journal* reported that the CIA, on its own, was concealing classified information it did not want Trump to have, and that it flat-out ignored his order on Syria—and that this was "cheered" within the Agency.[495] This was precisely what John Kennedy feared with both the Bay of Pigs and Vietnam.

Despite the efforts of the Hoax News media to conceal, ridicule, or disprove the existence of the Deep State failed. (Interestingly, in researching this book, the Wikipedia page dealing with the Deep State cites no sources providing evidence for the Deep State except through the lens of critical news stories.)[496] As early as April 2017, nearly half of Americans believed a Deep State existed.[497] CNN found in one if its polls that Americans who were skeptical of government were more politically engaged.[498] A repeat survey in March 2018 showed that a majority of the US public believed that the government engaged in widespread monitoring of its privacy and a "large bipartisan majority [felt] national policy is being manipulated or directed by a 'Deep State' of unelected government officials."[499]

Trump entered office somewhat naively thinking that his political enemies would accept defeat and work to better America. Radio host Rush Limbaugh would frequently recount the story of his first golf outing with the president shortly after inauguration and how shocked Trump was that the Democrats had actually intensified their opposition to fixing any of America's problems. That didn't mean that Trump didn't launch serious assaults on the Deep State.

Strategic advisor and former Trump campaign manager Steve Bannon said there were three main areas of focus coming into office: national security (which included dealing with North Korea, ISIS, and Iran), economic nationalism, and deconstruction of the "administrative state." (Bannon hesitated to call it the Deep State.)[500] To that end, Bannon noted, the Supreme Court vacancies that Trump would deal with were instrumental in reining in the administrative state. "[Neil] Gorsuch and [Brett] Kavanaugh were put in their positions for this purpose," he said. "They weren't so much social conservatives" as they were hard-liners in rolling back the bureaucracy, which Bannon recalled, was one of the first questions in their interviews. Nevertheless, Trump hoped that the bureaucracy would do what was best for America.

It didn't take long to find out what the administration was up against. Trump's first two phone calls with the foreign leaders, to the president of Mexico and the prime minister of Australia, were both leaked within five days in full transcript form. Trump had been warned: in April 2017 Mike Higgins gave Bannon and his team the names of sixty Obama holdovers in the national security apparatus who needed to go if Trump's initiatives were to have a chance. The team gave it to Trump, who turned it over to General H. R. McMaster, the National Security Advisor. "McMaster slow-walked it," Bannon said.[501] McMaster didn't get rid of the holdovers right away because "he didn't believe the premise" of the Deep State.

McMaster, however, was not viewed by either Gorka or Bannon that of a full-on enemy, but rather an "administrative state adjacent," as Bannon put it. He would support Trump in most of the minor politics, but, "When you got to the tough decisions, he wasn't there," Bannon observed. Neither Bannon nor Gorka thought McMaster was a particularly original thinker.

Elsewhere, though, Trump had more success against the administrative state, mostly in a program of strategic deregulation. Trump's son-in-law and advisor, Jared Kushner, recalled that "the President rolled back a lot of the overreaches of the federal government," especially in the area of energy.[502] As historian Doug Wead noted, "For the Trump administration, the trick was to eliminate as many of the worst regulations as quickly as possible before the national media, backed by their corporate sponsors, began their [anti-deregulation] campaign."[503] Ironically, Wead argued, the Russian collusion campaign may have diverted the critics from focusing on the regulatory changes.

On many occasions, Trump used a tactic I have called "cheese in the maze," wherein he either originated or allowed to be circulated goofball stories of conflict between Jared, Ivanka, Steve Bannon, or any other number of Trump insiders as a means to deflect serious journalistic investigation of his politics and programs. While reporters chased these baseless, but sensationalistic, stories, Trump's team marched steadily forward where they could.

Some of Trump's early appointees came strongly recommended from virtually all conservative sources. McMaster, who was Trump's first National Security Council advisor, was recommended by virtually everyone including Victor Davis Hanson and myself. Initially, he worked Trump's agenda well, because of Trump's goal of destroying the Islamic terror group known as ISIS. According to Kushner, "McMaster realized the president had a lot of ambition; that there was a lot he wanted to accomplish and quickly. So he took the initiative..." to put the campaign against ISIS into a strategy. Kushner concluded that McMaster "did a very, very good job of doing just that," culminating in the national security presidential memorandum of January 28, 2017, called "Plan to Defeat the Islamic State of Iraq and Syria."[504] All in about four months. Kushner claimed Trump took about a year to put the final product together. Meanwhile, Trump went over every aspect of the plan, including cyberstrategies, international law, and recruitment of coalition powers. Trump won praise from those who later would betray him, including General James "Mad Dog" Mattis: the president "delegated authority to the right level to aggressively and in a timely manner move against enemy vulnerabilities."[505] Trump's actions eliminated layers of permissions for ground troops to get air support, and made for faster decision-making all around. Mattis also identified the strategy of moving ISIS out of safe locations in an attrition fight to surrounding the enemy in strongholds where he could be annihilated. Almost immediately ISIS's recruitment plunged.

Shifting loyalties characterized many of Trump's appointees, including Omarosa Manigault and Anthony Scaramucci (his short-lived director of communications). Both later came back to try to hawk negative stories of the Trump White House for a big payday. As of this writing, none have been successful. Generals Mattis and John Kelly, his later chief of staff, both attacked Trump after they left the administration, always with near orgiastic reception from journalists.

Indeed, Trump's fascination with military men—General Mike Flynn, Mattis, Kelly, McMaster—initially led some to fear he was planning some sort of military state. The logic seemed solid at the time that they might be better choices than civilians: supposedly they were apolitical, goal-oriented, and used to top-down discipline. But that was yesterday's military. The new military, with its "woke" concerns over homosexuals' feelings, transgender rights, and social justice, no longer reflected those values. Sebastian Gorka, the deputy assistant to the president for strategy and part of the "Strategic Initiatives Group" that included Steve Bannon and Jared Kushner, related an experience he had while at the Marine Corps University Foundation where he was conducting an off-site for two dozen colonels and lieutenant colonels, all in the strategic planning sections of the Pentagon. He had asked them to identify what they saw as the top national security threat to the United States, then draft a response to it. More than half identified "Global Warming/Climate Change" as the number one security threat. To Gorka, this was a clear indication that these colonels—all seeking "their first star" (i.e., a generalship)—were not about to risk offending their superiors in the Obama-ized Pentagon.[506] "When they get close to that first star," he noted, "they parrot back what the White House says." In that case, it was what the Obama White House said.

Indeed, probably the biggest failure by America First/conservatives lay in missing the hard leftward tilt of the US military. As Gorka said, prior to 2017, who would have believed what the US military had become under Obama? As Steve Bannon observed about Trump, "He came from a patriotic point of view when it involved the military. His favorite film was 'Victory at Sea.' He revered the military."[507] Trump was hardly alone in failing to notice this radical change in the military in the previous decade.[508] Trump—as were most Americans—was unaware of this radical inversion of the purposes of a military from being an organization designed to fight wars to being an organization oriented toward diversity and fighting climate change. Steve Bannon likewise agreed: "It's a shock to me today. I have a daughter who graduated West Point and served in Afghanistan." The generals were completely politicized. As leftist writer

Tom Engelhardt observed, "Before they manipulate us, they must spend years manipulating themselves."[509]

Nothing makes clearer this self-manipulation and self-deception than the military's radical veer to the left in the Obama years that Trump and his team were largely oblivious to—until it bit them. Consider the testimony of Admiral Michael Gilday before the House Armed Services Committee on June 15, 2121, where he was questioned about "critical race theory" and a book by Ibram X. Kendi, *How to Be an Antiracist*, that white-shamed and argued for "future discrimination" against whites.[510] He repeatedly refused to condemn such whackadoodle and racist statements in the book that claimed US Supreme Court Justice Amy Coney Barrett was a "white colonizer" for adopting black children and said that American whites were responsible for AIDs.

Early on in the administration, Gorka witnessed firsthand the Deep State's tactics for defeating Trump. Gorka was given a special classified project to run, which required "hundreds of guys" he had trained within the intelligence community. Four of those were qualified people at the deputy assistant rank that outranked a four-star general. The White House acted on his request immediately, but the clearances never came. The culprit? The White House head of personnel kept stalling. "We were always told, 'It's coming right away,' or 'You'll have these next week.'"[511] Gorka also identified General John Kelly as responsible for blocking access to the president by anyone he disapproved of, including Trump's former campaign manager Corey Lewandowski. At one point, Lewandowski got in the Oval Office anyway, and upon his exit, Kelly physically accosted him and held him by the coat lapels so tight he ripped the coat. Kelly also tried to force Gorka out.

As part of the National Security Council, Gorka witnessed General Stanley McChrystal (whom Gorka described as "not a creative thinker") approach Trump multiple times about putting more troops into Afghanistan. Each time, Trump rebuffed him. In the final pitch to Trump, McChrystal had a slide show. Every single PowerPoint slide began with "The Federal Government of the Republic of Afghanistan will...." Trump blew up. "What fucking federal government of Afghanistan are you talking about?" No such thing existed in any operational form.[512] Later it was revealed that the drawdown in Afghanistan was expected to significantly affect China, who would have far more Islamic militants to deal with.

On another occasion, a three-star general briefed Trump on our support for South Korea. Trump asked a simple question: "'How much does all this cost?' The general didn't know."[513] "I'd be in a room with the Joint Chiefs of Staff and in two hours none would mention the President. I would remind them that it was his policies they were carrying out. At that point I realized the Deep State was real. To them, the 'writ' was more important than the President."[514]

Kelly had replaced Reince Priebus as White House chief of staff in July 2017. Many thought his organizational skills would help Trump. Little did they know he personally detested Trump and undercut him every step of the way. It was clear from the outset that Kelly and other military leaders were disappointed that Trump had made such inroads with North Korea in his discussions with Kim Jong-un, thereby reducing the need to maintain such large-scale Korean deployments. Later it would become equally obvious the Joint Chiefs would oppose any reduction in the size of the force in Afghanistan, a point that Trump had run on. Kelly used his position to block any MAGA people from coming into the administration, according to Gorka.

Meanwhile, the fix was in for a massive assault on Trump via the "Russia hoax" that began during the primary season as the Clinton forces paid to have a "dossier" compiled to develop a "Russian collusion" narrative. As Gregg Jarrett has written, "Hillary Clinton tried to dismiss her role in paying for the 'dossier' by stating that it was simply 'opposition research.'"[515] Opposition research, however, as Ned Ryun wrote in *The Hill*, "is based on fact, from voting records, court records and public statement.... Fusion GPS's dossier [which Clinton paid for] was misinformation. It was not opposition research because it was not based on fact."[516] Congressional testimony later showed that the "dossier" was entirely concocted from hearsay from *Russian* sources, meaning that if anyone was guilty of Russian collusion, it was the Clinton campaign.

Nevertheless, these charges were wheeled out before Trump took the oath of office, even as the culprits managed to evade the reality that "collusion" was not a crime; that FBI Director James Comey had personally told Trump he was not being investigated; and that the massive, overwhelming genuine criminality of Hillary Clinton was steadily swept aside.

It is worth noting, without reviewing the entire Russia hoax scandal, that Congress found that the FBI deputy director Andrew McCabe admitted no "surveillance warrant would have been sought from the FISC [Foreign Intelligence Surveillance Court] without the Steele dossier; that Christopher Steele himself was deeply compromised and biased against Trump and that his bias was *not* mentioned or reflected in the warrant applications, that Bruce Ohr, another corrupt and anti-Trump FBI agent gave research from his wife, Nellie, who worked at Fusion GPS, to the FBI, and that all these relationships and more were hidden from the court."

Even to the present, there remains debate over whether the entire Russia hoax was designed *merely* to find a way to cover up Clinton's crimes, of if its fabricators genuinely believed they could find some criminal offenses with which to charge Trump. Stripped of any protection by his cowardly attorney general, and with the Department of Justice in the hands of Sessions' subordinate who had (he claimed jokingly) mentioned using the 25th Amendment on Trump, the president was absolutely under siege for over a year.

Trump had no idea how thoroughly corrupt the FBI and the DOJ were. Consensus among conservatives at the time was that while the top ranks might have a few bad apples, the rank-and-file were loyal and patriotic Americans who would follow the law. This was a consistent theme from Rush Limbaugh and Sean Hannity. Even if true, however, as Jack Cashill showed in his study of the TWA 800 downing, everyone doesn't have to be "in on the plot." Information can be contained, manipulated, and controlled by one senior official through whom everything is funneled. In the case of TWA 800, Cashill argued, it was FBI Assistant Director James Kallstrom who, despite the crash being a matter for the Federal Aviation Administration, nevertheless managed to seize control of all evidence and results and dictate conclusions.[517] If Cashill is correct, then the FBI has been a force *against* justice for at least twenty years, perhaps longer (the abuses involving Whitey Bulger come to mind). Bulger was an informant for the FBI. Bulger agreed to be the FBI's "strategist"—he refused to be called an "informant"—and over the next decade he used the FBI to eliminate all his mob rivals. In the process, he gave agent John Connolly $235,000 and airline tickets. At Christmas, he gave corrupt agents and police officers "envelopes bulging with cash."[518] Bulger managed to stay out of jail until 2011, while Connolly was indicted and was sentenced to forty years in prison. Later, Bulger said of the FBI, "I was the guy that did the directing. They didn't direct me."[519]

In a period of less than twenty years, the FBI had been caught deliberately lying about the explosion aboard TWA 800 and had employed a notorious mob boss and removed his enemies based on his identification. Recall that in the JFK assassination investigation, the FBI, which had independent knowledge of many of the details, obediently deferred to the CIA to withhold such information. This was hardly a track record of an agency supposedly involved in "law enforcement." Over that same period, the FBI wrongly identified Richard Jewell as the culprit in the Atlanta Olympic bombing case and wrongfully investigated and slimed Steven Hatfill over its claims he was involved in the 2001 anthrax attacks. (Although Jewell never sued the FBI, he and his estate after his death won a libel settlement from CNN and a payment of a half-million dollars from NBC, as well as settling a separate suit with the *New York Post* for an undisclosed amount; Haftill won a $4.6 million settlement from the US government over the FBI's role).[520]

James Comey's outrageous behavior with Hillary Clinton's emails and the volumes of anti-Trump hate texts that surfaced from members of the Bureau after the Russia hoax investigation began hardly improved the FBI's image. Yet no sooner had Trump dispatched Comey than his replacement, Rod Rosenstein, in June expanded the scope of the Special Counsel's investigation.[521] Then, in an even more breathtaking move, Rosenstein gave Robert Mueller, the Special Counsel, permission to again go after Trump while depriving him of defense by saying that if the investigation were to look at Rosenstein himself (hint, hint) he would recuse himself! The actual "scope memo" itself was not released by the Justice Department until May 2020, and astoundingly despite authorizing Mueller to investigate "any matters that arose or may arise directly from that investigation," not one single Democrat or Clinton supporter was even investigated, including Tony Podesta, who had extensive lobbying activities with foreign powers deemed questionable.[522] And keep in mind, all of this was to be a *counterintelligence* operation with no criminality involved when it started.

In part, what kept the Russia Hoax fueled and moving ahead was Trump's inability to declassify large numbers of key documents. Either the new FBI director—Comey's replacement, another Swamp Creature named Christopher Wray—or the CIA director or Rosenstein would object on grounds of "national security" or "ongoing cases" (usually meaning Mueller's). So the hoax investigation of Trump could not be refuted because of the need to protect...the hoax investigation of Trump! And the common misunderstanding is that a president orders documents declassified, he signs a paper, and the next day they appear. There are constant levels of reviews, protests, redactions, and so on. Had Trump personally overridden those and a single agent in the field was compromised, or, God forbid, killed, Trump would have been impeached immediately and removed for "endangering the lives of agents everywhere," or claims to that effect.

Some argued that Trump's unwillingness to prosecute Hillary Clinton set the tone for the special counsel and the turmoil to come. Trump had said of Clinton, "She's suffered enough." But in fact the decision wasn't entirely Trump's. His chief of staff, Reince Priebus, wanted a coalition with Congress that could pass Trump's agenda. "There was never any sense we had the support to take this on," Bannon said, referring to a prosecution of Clinton. Although White House counsel Don McGahn wanted to do it, "Reince was not into it," and there was very little momentum for it—everything was focused on the economy, ISIS, China." But in retrospect, Bannon mused, "I think Trump today would say different," and would have pursued a prosecution of Clinton.[523]

When the Senate Judiciary Committee finally got around to looking at the investigation, it found that the FBI never corroborated any of
the dossier's main claims; that it presented to the FISA court Steele as a
"reliable" and "credible" source even after learning Steele had lied; that
Comey knew the dossier was unverified yet signed off on warrant applications anyway, and that the FBI knew Clinton associates were feeding
Steele anti-Trump information.[524] In 2021, the investigation of John
Durham, yet another special counsel instructed to investigate the Russia
hoax from the Trump administration's perspective, charged Michael
Sussmann, a lawyer who had ties to the Hillary Clinton campaign, with
lying to the FBI ahead of the 2016 election. Earlier, Durham had charged
a low-level FBI attorney, Kevin Clinesmith, with doctoring an email
designed to permit illegal surveillance of Trump.[525] Yet with his (supposedly) right hand man (Sessions) recused, with Rosenstein in league with
Mueller, and unable to get any documents past the Swamp, Trump was
trapped until Mueller finished his report, which he did in March 2019,
he glumly concluded there was no collusion and despite taking a breathtaking precedent-breaking anti-legal position of saying nothing, Mueller
implied that he found obstruction, but did not cite it.[526]

Throughout the "muh Russia hoax" investigation, Trump supporters
clamored for him to fire Sessions (who finally resigned in November 2018
after having severely damaged the Trump administration).[527] In reality,
Sessions' resignation merely opened the door for the anti-Trump deputy
attorney general, Rod Rosenstein, to step in. Had he been pushed out,
yet other anti-Trumpers awaited in the bureaucracy. It was never as simple as just firing a single individual. One month later, Trump appointed
William Barr who served under President George H. W. Bush (which
should in itself have been a red flag) as the new attorney general. Barr
promptly teased Trump's administration with an apparent show of support, telling a Senate panel he thought "spying" may have taken place
under the auspices of an illegally obtained surveillance warrant.[528] A
week later, after the Special Counsel had finished its report on the Russia
hoax, he issued a statement that again seemed to show his solid support
for the president:

So that is the bottom line. After nearly two years of investigation, thousands of subpoenas, and hundreds of warrants and witness interviews, the Special Counsel confirmed that the Russian government sponsored efforts to illegally interfere with the 2016 presidential election but did not find that the Trump campaign or other Americans colluded in those schemes.[529]

However, over the next year, Barr did nothing to pursue prosecutions against FBI agents who had lied to get FISA warrants. A game of "report waiting" began, where it was assumed Barr would wait for an inspector general's report, which appeared on March 31, 2020, and found "apparent errors or inadequately supported facts" to acquire the wiretaps on Trump's associates, but no action of any sort followed from Barr or the Department of Justice.[530] In fact, that had been a hallmark of Michael Horowitz, the inspector general, who had delivered one report already citing problems but carefully avoiding identifying any behavior that could be prosecuted. In short, it was a giant game of "kick-the-can" in which no one ever got around to indicting any members of the FBI or the rest of the Deep State. (Barr did appoint John Durham as a special counsel to investigate the investigation, and finally in 2021 Durham began to roll out two indictments of low-level players. The jury is still out on whether these were merely the bottom of the chain Durham plans to indict.)

Likewise, at the position of director of national intelligence, Trump named a long-time Republican senator, Dan Coats, as DNI. Coats was considered a long-time "RINO" ("Republican in Name Only") and member of the establishment. Scandal writer Bob Woodward, who supposedly managed an interview with a comatose CIA Director William Casey in the hospital, claimed that Coats thought Trump had "no moral compass" and "couldn't shake the suspicion that Trump must be beholden to Russian President Vladimir Putin."[531] Coats was one generally thought to be active in blocking Trump's attempts to declassify documents from the Russia probe. In fact, Trump had suggested he would declassify large numbers of documents, including all of the JFK assassination documents, only to be thwarted repeatedly by his intelligence services and the FBI. In April 2018, Trump did manage to declassify almost 22,000 documents related to the assassination. Only a handful that fell outside of Section 5 of the President John F. Kennedy Assassination Records Collection Act of 1992 remained withheld, but pending Trump's determination, those also had to be reviewed by October 26, 2021, to determine whether further withholding was warranted. Given that Joe Biden would be president then, it was unlikely any further release would occur.[532]

If releasing documents related to a presidential assassination over fifty years ago was difficult, one can imagine the problems Trump faced in making documents public that would expose current and recent officials as engaging in potentially criminal behavior. Needless to say, the CIA, the FBI, and other parts of the Deep State fought tooth and nail to prevent Trump from making the documents public. When he issued orders, they dragged their heels. They filed protests that had to be processed. They met with him and insisted that such a release would endanger sources and methods. And who was he to argue? They, after all, were the "experts."

Trump found himself opposed by the entire Deep State bureaucracy any time he tried to expose any malfeasance or criminal activity by the Deep State. During the investigation by the Special Counsel, his hands were tied even more. Any perception by squishy Republican senators after January 2019 put Trump in the position of not only being impeached—which everyone expected would happen regardless of the Special Counsel's findings—but also of being convicted by the Senate. Unless Trump did something about twenty Republicans could find (in their minds) dangerous to national security, they had no grounds to publicly abandon him—no matter how much they detested him in private. But had Trump overridden the recommendations by the intelligence agencies and ordered declassification anyway, then those same senators could claim he was "endangering national security," and thus had to be removed. Trump walked the thinnest of lines with virtually no internal support.

The impeachment/removal threat was a central factor when it came to criticisms that Trump should have immediately fired any and all who did not toe the MAGA line. First, as we have seen, the "next man up" in almost every organization would have been as bad as the person Trump removed. In the case of the CIA, where John Brennan—a notorious Trump hater—was succeeded by Mike Pompeo, there was a significant improvement. But Pompeo became secretary of state in April 2018 and his replacement, Gina Haspel, was identified as a member of the Deep State and would later participate in the January 6 "general's coup." When Coats stepped down from the DNI position, a Trumper John Ratcliffe was appointed. His term lasted from May 2020 to January 2021, when he was predictably replaced under the Joe Biden administration by Avril Haines, an Obama apparatchik.

Amanda Milius, who worked in the State Department under Trump, said that trying to shrink our "ridiculously bloated" administration, "they will come for you."[533] "A good portion of the people who are in the administration, even at the executive level, have zero interest in shrinking the federal government," she noted. She also explained a common tactic of picking a low-level administrator, flying him or her around the world and treating the administrator like royalty. When the administrator returned, he or she had been co-opted and instead of eliminating some of these positions, suddenly supporting them. She said that Commerce was viewed as a MAGA department, but others, such as State, had very few Trump supporters. "Once they [other anti-Trump members of the bureaucracy] figure out you're MAGA, they will stab you in the back." Once Bush appointees got back into a department, they quickly brought in as many other "Bushies" as they could. Milius found herself fighting against other members of the Trump administration trying to undermine him.

Peter Navarro, the assistant to the president, director of trade and manufacturing policy, another MAGA appointee, encountered little else but obstruction within the Deep State holdovers. Jeff Rosen at the Department of Transportation, for example, "would give me endless grief" on the administration's "buy America policies." Navarro recalled, "When I tried to fix 'open skies' treaties with Qatar and the [United Arab] Emirates, I got endless grief from DOT."[534] Likewise, when he sought to expedite arms transfers to American allies such as Taiwan or Saudi Arabia, the relevant approval agencies would "sit on the paperwork for months or as long as they could."[535] As Bannon put it, "the 'interagency process' was like medieval times to the Deep State. It was the Holy Grail."[536]

Navarro also found a "big bottleneck" the Department of Justice, which has an office responsible for providing the form and legality language for executive orders, would drag its heels and stall. This stall tactic was apparent throughout the anti-Trump Deep State.

But nothing struck Navarro as starkly as the Food and Drug Administration's refusal to issue a ruling on the new anti-COVID-19 vaccines so that Trump could not claim this as a victory in the 2020 election season. This came, Navarro insisted, at the direct order of Dr. Anthony Fauci, director of the National Institute of Allergy and Infectious Diseases at the National Institute of Health.[537] Navarro argued that this instance of obstruction "killed people directly" and that it "killed people who could have been cured by exposing them to infected people."[538] Navarro conservatively put the estimate of those dead by virtue of the Fauci-directed delay at over 50,000.

One area in which the Deep State completely outflanked Trump was in the area of medicine. Tech magnate Peter Thiel headed a working group to look at ways to reduce the administrative state at the SEC, FEC, and other areas. When it came to the Center for Disease Control and the National Institute of Health, the administration was told by Mitch McConnell, then the majority leader in the Senate, to cease and desist. "They were never going to allow you to get rid of Francis Collins, the head of NIH," Bannon noted. At the time it was a big enough setback, but later, when the COVID-19 China virus hit, the impact of not being able to control the NIH or the CDC produced disastrous problems. Ultimately, due to the influence of Libertarians in the administration, all authority over handling the virus was turned over to the states. What that meant, in fact, was that it was turned over to Dr. Anthony Fauci, because no state had the medical expertise to counter what came out of NIH or the CDC. Thus the Deep State had made an end run around Trump—who almost certainly would have opened the country back up in July of 2020—and allowed anti-Trump governors such as Andrew Cuomo in New York, Gavin Newsom in California, and Gretchen Whitmer in

Michigan to keep their states locked down throughout 2020 and destroy their economies as a way to damage Trump in an election year.

Worse, Trump—in a typical businessman's response—had initiated "Operation Warp Speed" to fix the problem by developing a vaccine for the China virus. Unfortunately, this rushed effort would not allow for sufficient testing. Trump had not thought this solution through. Eventually it would by necessity lead to a mandated vaccine. Without sufficient testing, of course, there would be no way to predict the side effects—which rolled in like waves after the various vaccines were rolled out. This, in turn, led to a major resistance on the part of those with preexisting conditions; those who generally distrusted vaccines (led by Bobby Kennedy's son, Robert Kennedy, Jr.); and by those in the general public who simply did not think that sufficient testing had occurred to make them safe. While Trump claimed credit for "Operation Warp Speed" in 2021, even to the point of urging adults to be vaccinated, increasing evidence surfaced that the vaccines from different companies all had different effects. Some were ineffective, others had severe side effects. By mid-2021, worldwide some 4,000 people had died from the vaccines and thousands of others had fallen ill. Meanwhile increasing numbers of people reported still contracting the disease after being vaccinated.

The government's own VAERS data (Vaccine Adverse Event Reporting System) as of September 10, 2021, showed that there had been 14,506 deaths and 88,171 injuries from the vaccines between December 2020 and September 3, 2021. There were a total of 675,000 (!!) reports of adverse effects from the injections.[539] Trump himself backed off on urging everyone to get vaccinated, and even responded that he "probably won't" get a follow-on booster.[540]

Whether the China virus release was coordinated by the Chinese with elements of the Democrat Party, or whether the Democrats merely took advantage of it, nevertheless the lockdowns damaged Trump in two ways. First, they annihilated small business in the United States. Corporate giants could survive, but gyms, restaurants, movie theaters, and independent businesses of all sorts either closed outright or suffered badly as "at home delivery" was offered by Wal-Mart and Amazon.[541]

Second, Democrats blasted Trump for death totals in their own states that *they* caused, most notably Andrew Cuomo in New York City. Over 9,000 China virus patients were sent to New York City nursing homes, as a Cuomo aide admitted.[542] Meanwhile, the same Democrats and Deep State Republicans who had criticized Trump for acting too quickly in banning travel from China then attacked him for not acting sooner!

Meanwhile, the most malignant of Deep State plots was developing to ensure Trump did not win reelection. This widespread effort involved the intelligence agencies, state elections institutions (including secretaries of state, boards of supervisors, and election officials), the media, and the tech giants. It was breathtaking in its scope. Yet it was so successful, not long after the election *Time Magazine* brazenly admitted that a "shadow campaign" to "fortify" (i.e., steal) the election had taken place.[543]

What was more shocking than what was in the article was the fact *Time* and the Deep State thought they could boast about it with impunity. As Trump said, "It was all very, very strange…. Within days after the election, we witnessed an orchestrated effort to anoint the winner, even while many key states were still being counted."[544] Left-tilting *Time* flat-out labeled this "a conspiracy unfolding behind the scenes, one that both curtailed the protests [by leftist groups] and coordinated the resistance form CEOs."[545] *Time* only slipped up when it called the effort a "vast, cross-partisan campaign to protect the election," when in fact it was a Deep State cross-partisan campaign to steal an election. It was "bipartisan" only in the sense that the Republicans in the Deep State had been as anxious to get rid of Trump as the Democrats. And business? Of course corporate America was all to happy to rid itself of the man who had driven their labor prices up through trade sanctions on China.

Not only did this conspiracy get states to "change voting systems and laws [and] fend off voter-suppression lawsuits…and [get] millions of people to vote by mail," but they "successfully pressured social media companies to take a harder line against disinformation," as *Time* called accurate news about the election.[546] Of course, it went much further than "changing voting systems" before the election: Pennsylvania changed its practices *during* the election in violation of its own state laws. (Predictably, the US Supreme Court refused to hear the challenge on this.) Equally predictably, the so-called architect of this conspiracy was a union advisor to the president of the AFL-CIO, Mike Podhorzer. His union had been terrified of Trump's growing popularity within union ranks, which had done nothing to stop the hordes of illegals or the tsunami of Chinese goods coming into the country over the years.

It became clear that the steal would have to go well beyond the Electoral College. Even a margin of a couple of million California votes, which Hillary Clinton had over Trump, wouldn't be sufficient to again make the argument that Trump was not "popularly elected." To steal the vote, a massive influx of Big Tech corporate capital was needed. The Chan Zuckerberg Initiative coughed up $300 million by itself. Twitter, Facebook, and YouTube all began an aggressive campaign of blocking Trump-supporting ads or posts as being "disinformation." (This author, with a Twitter following of 132,000 on election night, was permanently banned from Twitter for using the word "fraud" in the context of the election. I was certainly not the only one.) Meanwhile, the China virus lockdowns contributed to the steal by ensuring mail-in ballots, which were subject to massive potential fraud, were the preferred form of voting for many people. The conspiracy ran ads about the ease of mail-in voting, and Democrat legislatures attempted to pass laws moving their entire election system to mail-in voting. A Democrat Congress passed the CARES Act with its $400 million in grants to state election administrators to enhance vote fraud. Some thirty-seven states were targeted for an increase in mail voting, aided and abetted by the Voter Participation Center, which conducted focus groups to see who still might be resistant to mail voting. In August and September the Voter Participation Center chipped out 15 million ballots in key states, and eventually half of the electorate voted by mail. The level of fraud has only begun to come out. In Nevada a commissioner's race was found to have more discrepancies than margin of votes, but the state ignored the result and certified the race anyway.[547]

Key to stopping Trump's challenges to potential fraud in Michigan, Georgia, Pennsylvania, Arizona, Nevada, and Wisconsin was the effort to get state legislators to agree to the secretary of state's certification without any examination or review of the process. In some cases (Georgia, with Governor Brian Kemp and Arizona with Governor Doug Ducey) this effort also involved getting the governors to fast track the certification process. Ducey literally signed the state's certification on the day that members of the Arizona State Senate were holding hearings on potential fraud in the balloting. (Since that time, the Arizona legislature has voted to conduct a forensic audit of Maricopa County, which is wrapping up as of this writing and is due to be delivered shortly. Legislators have said that if there is sufficient evidence, they could order an audit of the entire state; and if criminal activity—fraud—is found, order criminal actions by the Attorney General's office.)

In short, the objective was to defeat Trump's clear election-night blowout win with delays until "all" of the votes could be counted; then make sure enough votes were manufactured to offset the Trump margins. Counting in several key states (Wisconsin, Michigan, Pennsylvania, Georgia) was mysteriously stopped in the middle of the night with Trump ahead, only to start back up with massive influxes of Biden ballots. Once they could put Biden in the lead, then the goal was to certify the questionable results as quickly as possible, pressure enough malleable Republicans in the Republican dominated legislatures to vote to submit the certified slates before an investigation could be mounted. It worked like a charm. Biden supposedly had over 81 million votes, or an astonishing *sixteen million more than Hillary Clinton got in 2016.*

Once the accepted vote totals were in, suddenly the tech/media giants flipped the script: now charges of fraud were not permitted. Dozens of major Twitter accounts were suspended permanently (including mine at 132,000) for challenging the results of the election. Facebook and YouTube went into overdrive in squelching any discussion of a stolen election.

Trump was reduced to fighting the fraud with a downsized legal team that was independent from the government, led by Rudy Giuliani. But in the process, lawyers Lin Wood and Sidney Powell began their own efforts, muddying the waters and making claims about Dominion voting machines that were not proven.

Trump's team found itself denied standing or otherwise blocked in state after state. Virtually all of Trump's suits were thrown out on grounds of lack of evidence—when judges refused to actually *hear* the evidence. That said, Rudy's team only nibbled around the edges, fighting small batches of absentee ballots here, some questionable ballots there. They never sought to establish an overall national "conspiracy" anywhere, which worked against their larger claim that the election was stolen across the board. Ultimately, Trump's team did not win any of the cases. Meanwhile, Wood, Powell, and others *were* asserting a large, nationwide "steal" based on the Dominion machines, but faced many of the same problems.

The time and place to challenge those results was before December 14, when the state legislatures certified. It was up to the states to challenge the results and demand a thorough forensic audit. However, in most key states with a Republican legislature, the Trump supporters were an active and vocal minority—except in Arizona, no state had a sufficient number of Trump/ MAGA legislators to institute an audit, let alone override a governor's veto. This was especially true in Pennsylvania, Michigan, and Wisconsin, where a Democrat governor and secretary of state could squelch any talk of a genuine audit. Once the state legislatures signed on, the die was cast.

Trump supporters—and Trump himself—hoped that Vice President Mike Pence would take advantage of an extremely loose reading of his constitutional role of presiding over the Senate to allow protests against the elector slates to move forward and at the very least get the entire fraud issue discussed by the US Senate. Pence consulted over a dozen constitutional lawyers, each of whom told him he did not have the authority to accept a challenge without a state-approved alternative slate of electors. No such state had provided that. (Some *delegations* did, but that was insufficient: the Constitution requires that any and all elector slates be submitted by the entire legislature itself to a judge in the district wherein the legislature is located, to the US Archivist, and to the President of the Senate. None of those entities had received any "competing slate.") Without an actual competing slate (as had been submitted, for example, by Hawaii in 1960 when the judge, the Senate, and the Archivist received *three* competing slates based on recounts), Pence had no flexibility to order the vote to the Senate. (He had, however, clearly misled both Trump and Trump supporters on two occasions, the most notable being an appearance at Turning Point USA just before the election where he promised to count "every legal vote" and prohibit the counting of every illegal vote.)

While that was going on, Trump had encouraged a massive DC rally of over one million people. He delivered a speech as the Senate was gathering to accept the electoral slates. Trump urged his supporters to let their voices be heard peacefully. A break-in at the Capitol occurred, although calling it a "break-in" is inaccurate: in most cases, Capitol police not only allowed the protesters in but *escorted* them in.[548] Then things got out of hand.[549] Some (many suspect FBI or antifa plants) sat in the speaker's chair, occupied open offices, took selfies—all with police watching peacefully and even posing.[550] Meanwhile, representatives, senators, aides, and staff ran like terrified children for bunkers, elevators, or literally cowered under desks and chairs. As of this publishing there is no record of a single person in government inside the building being harmed in any way—but Lt. Michael Byrd, who shot and killed an unarmed grandmother, Ashli Babbitt, was completely exonerated. (Babbitt was *outside* a locked door surrounded by police. Byrd shot through the window with no provocation.) The Swamp has gone to extreme lengths to cover up this shooting, while the "internal investigation" by April cleared the officer of any wrongdoing.[551]

During this time, the chairman of the Joint Chiefs of Staff, Gen. Mark Milley, had made phone calls to a Chinese counterpart to reassure him he would ensure that Trump would not use nuclear weapons against China.[552] This was an outright act of treason, underscoring how fanatical and insane Trump's critics were. This led some observers to ask what else Milley (like the CIA before him) was hiding from Trump or actively undercutting him on.[553] It should be noted that this was the same thoroughly modern Milley that had defended the "critical race theory" texts that were recommended to US officers and stated that the American military was racist.[554]

Over the next few weeks, Nancy Pelosi concocted a second impeachment of Donald Trump, and like the first, it went nowhere in the Senate. She had the rare ignominy of submitting *two* failed impeachment bills to the US Senate. Her role in Milley's treason was still to be determined, but in January 2021 she admitted she spoke to Milley and discussed the nuclear codes episode.[555]

When Trump left office, the new administration of Joe Biden wasted no time going after anyone remotely involved in the Patriot Day protests, many of whom are still in jail as of this writing awaiting trial for taking selfies in the US Capitol building. Trump's business organization was charged with tax violations in New York. The evidence is that not only is the Deep State larger and more powerful than ever, but that it is now being harnessed in ways never before seen in the peacetime USA to attack political enemies. On top of that, the Biden administration has weaponized all medical bureaus to demand Americans accept the untested and dangerous China virus vaccines. Imagining a way to defeat the Deep State Swamp itself is a herculean task. Actually accomplishing it seems out of the realm of human possibility.

Scorecard: Trump and the Deep State Swamp
- Completely unsuccessful in curbing the size or reach of the Deep State, despite two attorney generals, two FBI directors, and two CIA directors.
- Followed the Constitution and clung to federalism, even when it damaged his administration
- Had minimal support from Congress when it came to the fighting the Deep State. Most in both Houses were thoroughly aligned with the Intelligence Services.
- Overall had the most hostile media in American history
- Was hamstrung in his personnel choices to fight the Deep State by...the Deep State!

CONCLUSION: THE DEEP
STATE TRIUMPHANT?

In 1948, historian Richard Hofstadter offered the "consensus" interpretation of American history, namely that there was an enduring consensus among liberals and conservatives from the time of the founding that included a commitment to private property, basic civil rights, the virtues of entrepreneurship, and the rule of law.[556] This consensus began to break down in the 1960s, and its demise continued through the early 2000s. But its collapse accelerated dramatically under Barack Obama and then in opposition to President Donald Trump. As of this writing, virtually all elements of that consensus are under attack and criticized as being "racist," "homophobic," or "exclusive." Predictably, Hofstadter flailed about when an economic explanation failed to provide a cohesive theory, leaving him to embrace a type of ideological critique of conservatism based on "status politics," involving status aspirations based in insecurity.

C. Wright Mills had the right idea, but was on the wrong train track. In 1958, the elitist Ford Foundation asked Hofstadter to write a memo on the "right wing" in America that, in the eyes of the Foundation, presented a threat to the "freedom of thought and expression."[557] One has to wonder how Hofstadter or the Ford Foundation could justify the attacks on the freedom of expression and thought in the "woke" age when the Swamp is ascendant. (It is highly unlikely either would acknowledge that Twitter bans, or YouTube scrubs, or Facebook censoring constituted any kind of restrictions.) After all, in his mind (as in that of all liberals) it is impossible for the left to constrain or restrict expression. Nevertheless, dutifully Hofstadter turned in a piece that described "extremist" thought as "paranoid." He somehow tied together the Democrat organizations such as the Ku Klux Klan, who were the epitome of Democrat politics since Martin Van Buren founded the party, to Richard Nixon and Barry Goldwater, both of whom had an astonishingly insightful grasp of the truly radical and extremist socialistic and Communist left. Hofstadter's mocking of "one world government" seems pathetically silly today, given that the World Health Organization has virtually dictated entire aspects of American policy on the China virus, or that Democrats from Bill Clinton to Joe Biden have rushed to join every globalist internationally governed body they can find. In almost every case, what Hofstadter though he was describing as the right—consumed with "emotional animus"—describes to a T the modern left and its fascist-like violence and use of government tribunals to stop any opposition. Hofstadter's concern about Barry Goldwater's view that the Supreme Court decisions were not necessarily the law of the land looks ironic and pitiful next to modern liberal threats to pack the Supreme Court because its rulings did not meet the left's approval.

Whenever the left needed a respite from the failure of its own policies, a convenient "domestic terror" attack, such as the bombing of the Murrah Federal Building in Oklahoma City in 1995 provided a much-needed distraction. But a full summer of left-wing so-called "antifa" and Black Lives Matter violence in 2019 and 2020 was excused as "peaceful protest," despite fatalities. Bill Clinton's insistence in the wake of the Oklahoma City bombing that "there is nothing patriotic about hating your country" is irrelevant to the America-hating left today because they do not *want* a prosperous, healthy, functioning America. They hate their country precisely because it is the United States of America, not because (in the view of the bomb-murderer Timothy McVeigh) the US had failed to live up to its promise. The only paranoia at work in America today is among Hofstadter's leftist buddies.

His claim that the "paranoid style" is only used by "minority" movements is likely correct, as no polling even in the wake of Donald Trump's 2020 electoral defeat supports *any* of the positions held by Joe Biden or the radical leftists in his party.[558] Trump may have lost (or may have been defrauded) but his *values* absolutely did not lose and remain the majority position, often by large margins depending on the issue. So once again, Hofstadter had the concept right, but the actors wrong.

Possibly the biggest blow to the Deep State, and one that may have delayed our demise by decades, was the arrival of Rush Limbaugh on the national scene as a radio host in 1988. Although there had been some conservative voices (the *Washington Times* and the *Wall Street Journal*), the "Big Three" television networks (CBS, ABC, and NBC) dominated the video and audio spectrum. Rush not only provided a counter to that, but almost succeeded in countering all three of the national networks with his single show. Imitators, some very good, followed, but Rush opened the door. Eventually, Rupert Murdoch opened a television competitor on cable to the news broadcasters with his liberal Fox News (liberal as defined by Hofstadter's consensus).

It is one thing to dig out language in history that has anti-Catholic, anti-monarchist, or anti-elite overtones. Yet when an American senator authors a bill that deliberately undervalues gold by fifty cents an ounce and nearly bankrupts the United States overnight, is it "paranoid" to suggest that he is only guilty of poor judgment? When an American president in the twenty-first century basically removes all impediments to illegal immigrants coming in, is it a "conspiracy"—especially when that is the preferred policy position of the American elites and corporate interests to further their cheap labor policies? Is it a conspiracy or paranoid to think that somehow, the perpetual insertion of a billionaire computer geek into American medical and immunization policies is, to say the least, odd? And when virtually every current policy undertaken by the left—most of whose top leadership have powerful personal economic and financial ties to Communist China—*benefits* Communist China, is that "paranoid"... or common sense?

When both leftist writers such as Tom Engelhardt and conservatives such as Tucker Carlson acknowledge the operations of a shadow government, that's one thing; but when the American public has in its hands extensive email and text chains between the perpetrators of the "Russia hoax," that is an entirely different level. Who's paranoid now?

It remains to be seen if Trump merely bought us four years or was the herald of a new, slow burn against the administrative state. Since the November 2020 election, state after state has passed new election integrity laws that would control the fraud of 2020; more states have passed concealed carry laws; states have passed or started the process to pass laws banning "vaccine passports" for the China virus; and a host of other anti-Deep State bills. There is only so much states can do, however. Attacking and dismantling the Deep State will take decades of dedicated work. It didn't get here overnight, nor will it disappear overnight.

The Administrative State, the Deep State, the Swamp—whatever name it goes by, it has continued to grow since Trump's election. Over time, each agency got its own police force and armed agents. Bannon summed it up as follows: "From the very beginning we were at war. They won round one."[559] The question yet to be answered is, "Will there be a round two?"

ENDNOTES

Introduction

1   Edmund Morgan, *American Slavery, American Freedom: The Ordeal of Colonial Virginia* (New York: W.W. Norton, 1975), 276.

2   Declaration of Independence, July 4, 1776, https://www.archives.gov/founding-docs/declaration-transcript.

3   Larry Schweikart, *The Hypersonic Revolution: Case Studies in the History of Hypersonic Technology: Volume III, The Quest for the Orbital Jet: The National Aero-Space Plane Program* (Washington, DC: United States Air Force, 2003).

Chapter 1

4   Harry Jaffa, *Crisis of the House Divided* (Chicago: University of Chicago Press, 1982), 30.

5   Ibid., 36.

6   James Oakes, *Freedom National: The Destruction of Slavery in the United States, 1861–1865* (New York: Norton, 2013), 191.

7   Ibid., 190.

8   James G. Randall, *The Civil War and Reconstruction* (New York: D. C. Heath, 1937), 145.

9   Ibid.

10   Roy P. Basler, *Collected Works of Abraham Lincoln*, 9 vols. (New Brunswick, NJ: Rutgers University Press, 1953–55), II:318.

11   Stephen B. Oates, *With Malice Toward None: The Life of Abraham Lincoln* (New York: Mentor/New American Library, 1977), 136.

12 Howard Ohline, "Republicanism and Slavery: Origins of the Three-Fifths Clause in the United States Constitution," *William & Mary Quarterly*, 28, 1971, 563–84; William Wiecek, *The Sources of Antislavery Constitutionalism in America, 1760–1848* (Ithaca, NY: Cornell University Press, 1977).

13 "Political Power of Free and Slave States," *Wooster Republican*, February 2, 1859, reproduced at https://en.wikipedia.org/wiki/Slave_Power#Background.

14 "The Nation's Great Triumph," *Philadelphia Press*, April 10, 1865.

15 Allan Nevins, *The Emergence of Lincoln: Prologue to Civil War* (New York: Charles Scribner's, 1950), 465.

16 Cincinnati *Philanthropist*, September 17, 1839; *The Emancipator*, February 6, 1838.

17 Russel B. Nye, "The Slave Power Conspiracy: 1830–1860," *Science & Society*, 10, Summer 1946, 262-74 (quotation citing Anonymous, *Five Years' Progress of the Slave Power* [Boston, 1852], 2, quotation on 263). Nye concluded that if the Slave Power did not exist as Phillips or Garrison portrayed it (because the Southern states were never as united as claimed), he nevertheless admitted that the threats abolitionists warned about were indeed real. The abolitionists, he concluded, "were not so far wrong in believing that [the Slave Power's] existence seriously jeopardized…the American tradition" with its intentions toward American personal rights and free speech liberties (274).

18 Phillips in *The National Antislavery Standard*, June 14, 1859. This theme was also found in *Five Years' Progress*, 25–31.

19 *The Anti-Slavery Bugle*, November 9, 1850.

20 Oakes, *Freedom National*, 54.

21 William C. Davis, *Jefferson Davis: The Man and His Hour* (New York: HarperCollins, 1991), 251; Jeffrey Rogers Hummel, *Emancipating Slaves, Enslaving Free Men: A History of the American Civil War* (Chicago: Open Court, 1996), 96.

22 Hummel, *Emancipating Slaves*, 96.

23 Cincinnati *Weekly Herald and Philanthropist*, May 7, 1844; *The National Era*, August 23, 1855; *The Anti-Slavery Bugle*, September 15, 1855; and *The National Anti-Slavery Standard*, December 20, 1856.

24 Nye, "Slave Power Conspiracy," 264.

25 *New York Herald*, March 9, 1854.

26 William Walker, *The War in Nicaragua* (New York: S. H. Goetzel, 1860); William O. Scroggs, *Filibusters and Financiers: The Story of William Walker and his Associates* (New York: Macmillan, 1916); Harrison Brady, *William*

Walker and the Imperial Self in American Literature (Athens, GA: University of Georgia Press, 2004); and Michel Gobat, *Empire by Invitation: William Walker and Manifest Destiny in Central America* (Cambridge, MA: Harvard University Press, 2018).

27 Ibid., 266.

28 David M. Potter, *The Impending Crisis, 1848–1861*, completed and edited by Don E. Fehrenbacher (New York: Harper, 1976), 198.

29 Cincinnati *Freeman* quoted in *The National Antislavery Standard*, January 4, 1844 and *The Anti-Slavery Bugle*, August 30, 1856.

30 John Elliott Cairnes, *The Slave Power: Its Character, Career, and Probable Designs* (New York: Carelton, 1862); William E. Gienapp, "The Republican Party and the Slave Power," in Robert Abzug and Stephen Maizlish, eds., *New Perspectives on Race and Slavery in America* (Lexinton, KY: University Press of Kentucky, 1986), 51–78; and David Brion Davis, *The Slave Power Conspiracy and the Paranoid Style* (Baton Rouge, LA: Louisiana State University Press, 1970).

31 The edifice of research on slaver profitability seems overwhelming now, to the point it is surprising the proposition was ever doubted. See Alfred Conrad and John Meyer, "The Economics of Slavery in the Antebellum South," *Journal of Political Economy*, 66, 1958, 95–130; Robert Fogel and Stanley Engerman, *Time on the Cross*, revised ed., (New York: Norton, 2013 [1974]); and Jeremy Atack and Peter Passell, *A New Economic View of American History*, 2nd ed. (New York: W. W. Norton, 1994). It is true that Southern manufacturing paid higher rates of return, but there were a host of reasons ranging from social to risk-averse business concerns about manufacturing in the South. (See Fred Bateman and Thomas Weiss, *A Deplorable Scarcity: The Failure of Industrialization in the Slave Economy* [Chapel Hill, NC: University of North Carolina Press, 1981].)

32 Eric Foner, *Free Soil, Free Labor, Free Man: The Ideology of the Republican Party Before the Civil War* (New York: Oxford, 63).

33 Ulrich Bonnell Phillips, *American Negro Slavery* (New York: D. Appleton & Company, 1918) and his "The Economic Cost of Slave Holding in the Cotton Belt," *Political Science Quarterly*, 20, 1905, 257–75; and Charles Sydnor, *Slavery in Mississippi* 9, New York Appleton-Century, 1933).

34 Paul Johnson, *A History of the American People* (New York: HarperCollins, 1997), 433.

35 Ibid.

36 Larry Schweikart and Michael Allen, *A Patriot's History of the United States*, 15th Anniversary ed. (New York: Sentinel, 2019), 272.

37 James Huston, *Calculating the Value of the Union: Slavery, Property Rights, and the Economic Origins of the Civil War* (Chapel Hill, NC: University of North Carolina Press, 2003), 25; James Huston, "Property Rights in Slavery and the Coming of the Civil War," *Journal of Southern History*, 65, May 1999, 248–86.

38 Huston, *Calculating the Value of the Union*, 24.

39 Ibid., 25.

40 Ibid., table 2.3, 28.

41 Huston, *Calculating the Value of the Union*, 25.

42 Houston, "Property Rights in Slavery," 279.

43 Schweikart and Allen, *Patriot's History*, 272.

44 George Fitzhugh, *Cannibals All! Or, Slaves Without Masters* (Cambridge, MA: Belknap Press, 2006 [1857]) and *Sociology for the South, or the Failure of Free Society* (London: Forgotten Books, 2017 [1854]). See also a critique of Fitzhugh precisely from the perspective of his similarities to modern liberals in Robert J. Loewenberg, *Freedom's Despots: The Critique of Abolition*, (Durham, NC: Carolina Academic Press, 1986).

45 Oates, *With Malice Toward None*, 137.

46 T. R. R. Cobb, *Historical Sketch of Slavery, From the Earliest Periods* (London: Forgotten Books, 2017 [1853]).

47 Ibid.

48 Nye, "Slave Power Conspiracy," 270–71.

49 Johnson, *History of the American People*, 458.

50 Ibid., 455–56.

51 Among the numerous biographies and Lincoln literature, see Louis A. Warren, *Lincoln's Youth: Indiana Years, Seven to Twenty-One* (New York: G. P. Putnam's Sons, 1916); Kenneth Thompson, ed., *Essays in Lincoln's Faith and Politics* (Lanhan, MD: University Press of America, 1983); David Donald, *Lincoln Reconsidered* (New York: Vintage, 1961); Richard N. Current, *The Lincoln Nobody Knows* (New York: Hill and Wang, 1958); Henry B. Rankin, *Personal Recollections of Abraham Lincoln* (New York: G. P. Putnam's Sons, 1916); Don E. Fehrenbacher, *Prelude to Greatness: Lincoln in the 1850s* (Stanford, CA: Stanford University Press, 1962); Albert Beveridge, *Abraham Lincoln, 1809–1858*, 4 vols. (New York: Houghton Mifflin, 1928); David Herbert Donald, *Lincoln* (New York: Simon & Schuster, 2011); Carl Sandburg, *Abraham Lincoln: the Prairie Years and the War Years*, 6 vols. (New York: Harcourt Brace, 1939), and of course the aforementioned Stephen Oates' *With Malice Toward None*. Lincoln's writings

are in Roy P. Basler, *The Collected Works of Abraham Lincoln*, 9 vols. (New Brunswick, NJ: Rutgers University Press, 1953–55).

[52] Schweikart and Allen, *Patriot's History*, 299. For further information on Lincoln's depression, see Joshua Shenk's psychological analysis of Lincoln, *Lincoln's Melancholy* (New York: Mariner, 2005).

[53] Reinhard H. Luthin, "Abraham Lincoln and the Tariff," *American Historical Review*, 49, July 1944, 609–20 (quotation on 610).

[54] Abraham Lincoln, "Speech Delivered at Springfield, Illinois, at the Close of the Republican State Convention by which Mr. Lincoln had been Named as Their Candidate for United States Senator, June 16ʻ858," in T. Harry Williams, ed., *Selected Writings and Speeches of Abraham Lincoln* (New York: Hendricks House, 1943), 53.

[55] Johnson, *History of the American People*, 440–41.

[56] Robert Johannsen, *Stephen A. Douglas* (Oxford: Oxford University Press, 2973).

[57] Johnson, *History of the American People*, 445.

[58] Paul Finkelman, "*Scott v. Sandford*: The Court's Most Dreadful Case and How it Changed History," *Chicago-Kent Law Review*, 82, 3–48. One interesting element of the case is that John Sanford, Mrs. Emerson's brother, had been handling the case for his sister when she moved out of state to marry again. Yet Sanford was not *legally* authorized either in Iowa or in Missouri to handle the Emerson estate. He merely did so. Thus, the worst-decided case in American history may have been wrongfully brought in the first place. See Walter Ehrlich, "Was the Dred Scott Case Valid?" New light is shed on many of the unanswered questions from Don Fehrenbacher's book (see note 60) by David Hardy, *Dred Scott: the Inside Story* (Columbia, SC: np, 2019).

[59] *Scott v. Emerson*, 15 Mo. 576 (Mo. 1852).

[60] The literature on the *Dred Scott* case is extensive. See Don Fehrenbacher, *The Dred Scott Case: Its Significance in American Law and Politics* (New York: Oxford, 1978) and David Konig, Paul Finkleman, and Christopher Bracey, eds. *The Dred Scott Case: Historical and Contemporary Perspectives on Race and Law* (Columbus, OH: Ohio State University Press, 2010) for just two of the many works.

[61] Rodney Davis and Douglas Wilson, eds., *The Lincoln-Douglas Debates* (Urbana and Chicago: Knox College Lincoln Studies Center and University of Illinois Press, 2008, 31, 113, 198, 286; Oates, *Freedom National*, 45–6.

[62] Oates, *Freedom National*, 19.

[63] Oates, *Freedom National*, passim.

64 Charles Calomiris and Larry Schweikart, "The Panic of 1857: Origins, Transmission, and Containment," *Journal of Economic History*, 51, December 1991, 807–34.

65 David M. Potter, *The Impending Crisis, 1848–1861*, completed and edited by Don E. Fehrenbacher (New York: Harper Torch Books, 1976), 337.

66 Roy F. Nichols, *The Disruption of American Democracy* (New York: Free Press, 1948), 221.

67 *New York Times*, June 23, 1857.

68 *Collected Works of Abraham Lincoln*, III: 312–15.

69 Howard Zinn, *A People's History of the United States* (New York: Harper Collins, 2003), 187.

70 Ibid., 188.

71 Ibid.

72 Jaffa, *Crisis of the House Divided*, 43.

73 Roy P. Basler, ed., *The Collected Works of Abraham Lincoln* (Rutgers, N.J.: Rutgers University Press, 1953), I:75.

74 Basler, *Collected Works*, III:231.

75 Ibid., II:278.

76 Stephen B. Oates, *With Malice Toward None: The Life of Abraham Lincoln* (New York: Mentor/New American Library, 1977), 137.

77 Paul Johnson, *A History of the American People* (New York: HarperCollins, 1997), 442.

78 Ibid.

79 Ibid., 138.

80 Richmond papers quoted in *The National Antislavery Standard*, October 11, 1856 and *The Anti-Slavery Bugle*, November 3, 1855.

81 Abraham Lincoln, "Address Before the Young Men's Lyceum of Springfield, Illinois, January, 1838," in Williams, *Selected Writings and Speeches*, 8.

82 Abraham Lincoln, "First Inaugural Address of Abraham Lincoln," March 4, 1861, at https://avalon.law.yale.edu/19th_century/lincoln1.asp.

83 Oakes, *Freedom National*, 59.

84 Oakes, *Freedom National*, 54.

85 Ibid.

86 New Orleans *Daily True Delta*, October 12, 1860.

87 Phillip Paludan, in "The American Civil War Considered as a Crisis in Law and Order," (*American Historical Review*, 77, October 1972, 1013–1034) argued that the thirst for order could be seen in two key developments as settlers moved into new western territories: their first act was to form a local church, and they also established "Claims Clubs" that adjudicated the land

claims that, due to the slowness of the federal surveys, the US government was slow to do. Farther west, miners' clubs performed the same function with mine titles.

[88]   Walter Dean Burnham, "The Changing Shape of the American Political Universe," *American Political Science Review*, 59, 1965, 7–28.

[89]   Charleston *Evening News*, May 18, 1854.

[90]   Allan Nevins, *Emergence of Lincoln: Douglas, Buchanan, and Party Chaos, 1857–1859* (New York: Charles Scribner's Sons, 1950), 299–301.

[91]   Allan Nevins, *Ordeal of the Union: A House Dividing, 1852–1857* (New York: Charles Scribner's Sons, 1947), 158.

[92]   Dale Watts, "How Bloody Was Bleeding Kansas? Political Killings in Kansas Territory, 1854–1861," *Kansas History: A Journal of the Central Plains*, 18, Summer 1995, 116–29, argues that "Bleeding Kansas" wasn't as bloody as antislave forces claimed, with only 50 dead instead of 200. Also see Louis Decaro, *"Fire from the Midst of You": A Religious Life of John Brown* (New York: New York University Press, 2005), and David Reynolds, *John Brown, Abolitionist: The Man who Killed Slavery, Sparked the Civil War, and Seeded Civil Rights* (New York: Vintage, 2005).

[93]   Calomiris and Schweikart, "Panic of 1857," passim.

[94]   Nevins, *Ordeal of the Union*, 383.

[95]   Abraham Lincoln, "Peoria Speech, October 16, 1854," https://www.nps.gov/liho/learn/historyculture/peoriaspeech.htm.

[96]   "Speech of William H. Seward," *Congressional Globe*, 36th Congress, 2nd Session, 246–344.

[97]   David Grimsted, *American Mobbing, 1828-1861: Toward Civil War* (Cambridge, MA: Oxford University Press, 1998).

[98]   Paludan, "The American Civil War Considered," passim.

[99]   Nevins, *Emergence of Lincoln: Prologue to Civil War*, 225.

[100] Ibid., 329.

[101] Ibid., 331.

[102] Ibid., 331.

[103] Irving Bartlett, ed., *Wendell & Ann Phillips: The Community of Reform, 1840–1880* (New York: W. W. Norton, 1979), 52.

[104] Ibid., 462.

[105] Allan Nevins, *The War for the Union: The Improvised War, 1861–1862* (New York: Charles Scribner's Sons, 1959), 53.

[106] Oates, *With Malice Toward None*, 258.

[107] Oakes, *Freedom National*, 112.

108 Michael Burlingame and John Ettlinger, eds., *Inside Lincoln's White House: The Complete Civil War Diary of John Hay* (Carbondale, Illinois: Southern Illinois University Press, 1997), 20.

109 *Congressional Globe*, 37th Congress, 1st Session, 269.

110 *Congressional Globe*, 37th Congress, 1st Session, 216–7.

111 Oakes, *Freedom National*, 121.

112 Ibid.

113 Ibid., 322.

114 Schweikart and Allen, *Patriot's History of the United States*, 344.

115 Oates, 334.

116 Schweikart and Allen, *Patriot's History of the United States*, 344.

117 Zinn, *People's History*, 191–2.

118 Ibid., 192; Irwin Unger, *These United States: The Questions of Our Past*, concise ed., combined vol. (Upper Saddle River, NJ: Pearson, 2007), 344.

119 Larry Schweikart, *48 Liberal Lies About American History: (That You Probably Learned in School)* (New York: Sentinel, 2009), 127–129.

120 Schweikart and Allen, *Patriot's History of the United States*, 347.

121 Michael Burlingame, *Abraham Lincoln: A Life*, 2 vols. (Baltimore: Johns Hopkins University Press, 2008), 2:462–473.

122 *Congressional Globe*, 38th Congress, 1st Session, 1203.

Chapter 2

123 Robert Remini, *Martin Van Buren and the Making of the Democratic Party* (New York: Columbia University Press, 1959); Robert Pierce Forbes, *the Missouri Compromise and It's Aftermath* (Chapel Hill, NC: University of North Carolina Press, 2007); and the classic article, Richard H. Brown, "The Missouri Crisis, Slavery, and the Politics of Jacksonianism," in Stanley N. Katz and Stanley I. Kutler, eds. *New Perspectives on the American Past, vol. 1, 1607–1877* (Boston: Little, Brown, 1969), 241–255. Also see Larry Schweikart, *Seven Events that Made America America* (New York: Sentinel, 2010), 5–33.

124 Thomas Jefferson to John Holmes, Thomas Jefferson Library of Congress Exhibition, US Library of Congress, www.loc.gov/exhibits/jefferson/159.html.

125 Jim Kuypers, *Partisan Journalism: A History of Media Bias in the United States* (Lanham, MD: Rowman & Littlefield, 2014).

126 H. Paul Jeffers, *An Honest President: The Life and Presidencies of Grover Cleveland* (New York: William Morrow, 2000), 221.

[127] Abraham Lincoln to William B. Preston, May 16, 1849, in Roy P. Basler, ed., *The Collected Works of Abraham Lincoln*, vol. II (Rutgers, NJ; Rutgers University Press, 1953), 48-49.

[128] Allan Nevins, *The War for the Union: The Improvised War, 1861–1862* (New York: Charles Scribner's Sons, 1959), 34.

[129] Mark E. Neely, Jr., *The Abraham Lincoln Encyclopedia* (New York: McGraw Hill, 1981), 234.

[130] "Mr. Lincoln and Friends," http://www.mrlincolnandfriends.org/presidential-patronage/#:~:text=Patronage%20involved%20a%20balancing%20act,%2C%E2%80%9D%20wrote%20biographer%20Carl%20Sandburg.

[131] William O. Stoddard, *Abraham Lincoln: The Man and the War President* (New York: Fords, Howard, and Hulbert, 1888), 203–4.

[132] Rufus Rockwell Wilson, *Intimate Memories of Lincoln* (Elmira, NY: Primavera Press, 1945), 33–34.

[133] Basler, *Collected Works*, V:379, 397.

[134] Michael Burlingame, ed., Noah Brooks, *Lincoln Observed: The Civil War Dispatches of Noah Brooks* (Baltimore: Johns Hopkins University Press, 1998), 216–217.

[135] Noah Brooks, *Abraham Lincoln: The Nation's Leader in the Great Struggle* (Washington, DC: National Tribune, 1888), 425.

[136] Thurlow Weed, "Mr. Lincoln and Three Friends in Council," *Galaxy*, February 11, 1871, in Don E. and Virginia Fehrenbacher, *Recollected Words of Abraham Lincoln* (Stanford, CA: Stanford University Press, 1996), 255.

[137] John Hay, *Century Magazine*, November 1890, in Rockwell, *Intimate Memories of Lincoln*, 401.

[138] Scott S. Greenberger, *The Unexpected President: The Life and Times of Chester A. Arthur* (New York: Da Capo, 2017), 132.

[139] Ibid., 134.

[140] J. Martin Klotsche, "The Star Route Cases," *The Mississippi Valley Historical Review*, 22, December 1935, 407–418.

[141] Allan Peskin, *Garfield: A Biography* (Kent, OH: Kent State University Press, 1978), 578.

[142] Kenneth D. Ackerman, *Dark Horse: The Surprise Election and Political Murder of James A. Garfield* (New York: Avalon, 2003), 335.

[143] Zachary Karabell, *Chester Alan Arthur* (New York: Times Books, 2004), 55.

[144] Ibid., 56.

[145] *New York Times*, September 21, 1881.

146   Louis Lang, ed., *The Autobiography of Thomas Collier Platt* (New York: B. W. Dodge and Co., 1910), 180.

147   Greenberger, *Unexpected President*, 182.

148   Henry Adams to Henry Cabot Lodge, November 15, 1881, in Worthington Chauncey Ford, ed., *Letters of Henry Adams, 1858-1891* (Cambridge, MA: Riverside Press, 1930), 331.

149   Ibid., 332.

150   Karabell, *Chester Alan Arthur*, 89.

151   Thomas C. Reeves, *Gentleman Boss: The Life of Chester Alan Arthur* (New York: Alfred A. Knopf, 1975), 273–4.

152   Ibid., 274.

153   Allan Nevins, *Grover Cleveland: A Study in Courage* (Tokyo: Ishi Press International, 2018), 178.

154   Ibid., 190.

155   Jeffers, *An Honest President*, 127.

156   Grover Cleveland, First Inaugural Address, March 4, 1885. Miller Center: Presidential Speech Archive, http://millercenter.org/president/speeches/detail/3571.

157   *New York World*, September 10, 1885.

158   Ibid., 130.

159   Ibid., 143.

160   Ibid.

161   Ibid.

162   Alyn Brodsky, *Grover Cleveland: A Study in Character* (New York: St. Martin's Press, 2000), 214.

163   Nevins, *Grover Cleveland*, 235.

164   Ibid.

165   Ibid.

166   Ibid., 248.

167   Ibid., 239.

168   Ibid., 247.

169   Ibid., 256.

170   Ibid., 240.

171   Ron Chernow, *Titan: The Life of John D. Rockefeller* (New York: Vintage, 1998), 291.

172   Ibid., 215.

173   Ibid., 219.

174   Ibid., 220.

175   Ibid., 326.

176 Stefanie Haeffele-Balch and Virgil Henry Storr, "Grover Cleveland Against the Special Interests," *The Independent Review*, 18, Spring 2014, 581–596.

177 Brodsky, *Grover Cleveland*, 183.

178 Ibid.

179 Grover Cleveland, Veto Message: May 8, 1886. American Presidency Project, compiled by Gerhard Peters and John T. Woolley, at http://www.presidency.ucsb.edu/ws/index.php?pid=71292&st=groverþcleveland&st1=.

180 "Veto of Military Pension Legislation," February 11, 1887, https://millercenter.org/the-presidency/presidential-speeches/february-11-1887-veto-military-pension-legislation.

181 Ibid.

182 Ibid.

183 Robert Higgs, "Why Grover Cleveland Vetoed the Texas Seed Bill," *The Independent Institute*, July 1, 2003, http://www.independent.org/publications/article.asp?id=1329.

184 Nevins, *Grover Cleveland*, 233.

185 Larry Schweikart, *Encyclopedia of American Business History and Biography: Banking and Finance to 1913* (New York: Facts on File, 1990); Vincent P. Carosso, *Investment Banking in America: A History* (Cambridge, MA: Harvard University Press, 1970); and Lance Davis and Robert Gallman (*Evolving Financial markets and the International Capital Flows: Britain, the Americas, and Australia, 1865–1914* (Cambridge: Cambridge University Press, 2001.

186 Nevins, *Grover Cleveland*, 515.

187 *New York Evening Post*, March 13, 1893.

188 *Public Opinion*, May 13, 1893; Jeffers, *An Honest President*, 262.

189 Nevins, *Grover Cleveland*, 519.

190 Richard Timberlake, Jr., "Panic of 1893," in David Glasner and Thomas Cooley, eds. *Business Cycles and Depressions: an Encyclopedia* (New York: Garland, 1997), 516–7; Charles Hoffmann, "The Depression of the Nineties," *Journal of Economic History*, 16, 137–164; and Samuel Rezneck, "Unemployment, Unrest, and Relief in the United States During the Depression of 1893–97," *Journal of Political Economy*, 61, 324–345.

191 See Ron Chernow, *The House of Morgan: An American Banking Dynasty and the Rise of Modern Finance* (New York: Atlantic Monthly Press, 1990) and Vincent P. Carosso, *The Morgans: Private International Bankers, 1854–1913* (Cambridge, MA: Harvard University Press, 1987).

192 Haeffele-Balch and Storr, "Grover Cleveland," 594.

193   John M. Pafford, *The Forgotten Conservative: Rediscovering Grover Cleveland* (Washington, DC: Regnery, 2013), 69.

194   Paul Johnson, *Modern Times: From the Twenties to the Nineties* (New York: HarperCollins, 1991), 217.

195   Stephen E. Ambrose, *Nixon, vol. 2: The Triumph of a Politician, 1962–1972* (New York: Simon & Schuster, 1989).

196   "Weinberger Faces 5 Counts in Iran-Contra Indictment," *New York Times*, June 17, 1992.

Chapter 3

197   Larry Schweikart and Lynne Doti, *American Entrepreneur* (New York: Amacom, 2010), 81–113.

198   Ibid., 114–150; Alfred D. Chandler, *Visible Hand: The Managerial Revolution in American Business* (Cambridge, MA: Belknap, 1977).

199   Burton Folsom, Jr., *The Myth of the Robber Barons* (Reston, VA: Young America's Foundation, 2018), 83.

200   Ibid.

201   Chandler, *Visible Hand*, passim; Vincent Carosso, *The Morgans: Private International Bankers, 1854–1913* (Cambridge, MA: Harvard University Press, 1987).

202   See Folsom, *Myth*, passim.

203   Ibid., 96.

204   Ibid.

205   Ron Chernow, *Titan: The Life of John D. Rockefeller, Sr.* (New York: Vintage, 2004), 224–25.

206   Ibid., 225.

207   Ibid., 226.

208   Ibid., 289.

209   *The World*, May 19, 1887.

210   Folsom, *Myth*, 92.

211   Robert J. Gordon, *The Rise and Fall of American Growth* (Princeton, NJ: Princeton University Press, 2016), 119.

212   Chernow, *Titan*, 257.

213   Ibid., 211.

214   Chernow, *Titan*, 257.

215   Susan Berfield, *The Hour of Fate: Theodore Roosevelt, J. P. Morgan, and the Battle to Transform American Capitalism* (New York: Bloomsbury, 2020), 47.

216   Chernow, *Titan*, 259.

[217] *Munn v. Illinois*, 94 U.S. 113.

[218] The Interstate Commerce Act, 1887, https://www.ourdocuments.gov/doc.
php?flash=false&doc=49&page=pdf.

[219] Chernow, *Titan*, 267.

[220] Ibid., 268.

[221] *New York Herald Tribune*, March 17, 1940.

[222] Allan Nevins, *John D. Rockefeller: The Heroic Age of American Enterprise*, 2
vols. (New York: Charles Scribner's Sons, 1940), II: 123; Ida Tarbell, *The
History of Standard Oil Company*, 2 vols. (Glouchester, Mass.: Peter Smith,
1963), II: 131.

[223] Stuart Bruchey, *The Wealth of the Nation: An Economic History of the United
States* (New York: Harper & Brothers, 1958), 132. On antitrust laws, see
Robert H. Bork, *The Antitrust Paradox: A Policy at War with Itself* (New
York: Basic Books, 1978); Yale Brozen, "Does Concentration Matter,"
Antitrust Bulletin, 19, 1974, 381–99; and Dominick T. Armentano, *Antitrust
and Monopoly: Anatomy of a Policy Failure*, 2nd ed. (New York: Holmes &
Meier, 1990). For a debate of more recent antitrust policy, see Dennis W.
Carlton and Ken Heyer, "The Revolution in Antitrust: An Assessment," *The
Antitrust Bulletin*, August 20, 2020, 608–27, and William Comanor, "The
Antitrust Revolution," ibid., September 4, 2020, 547–67.

[224] Gordon, *Rise and Fall of American Growth*, 2–129; Schweikart and Doti,
American Entrepreneur, chapter 8.

[225] Schweikart and Doti, *American Entrepreneur*, 167–178.

[226] Gordon, *Rise and Fall of American Growth*, 80–81.

[227] George Rogers Taylor, *The Transportation Revolution, 1815–1860* (New
York: Holt, Rinehart, 1962); Folsom, *Myth of the Robber Barons*, 1–15;
Nathan Rosenberg and L. E. Birdsell, Jr., *How the West Grew Rich:
The Economic Transformation of the Industrial World* .(New York: Basic
Books, 1986).

[228] Robert Sobel, *The Big Board: A History of the New York Stock Market* (New
York: Macmillan, 1970); Harold Evans, *They Made America: From the Steam
Engine to the Search Engine: Two Centuries of Innovators* (Boston: Little
Brown, 2004).

[229] Berfield, *Hour of Fate*, 33.

[230] Ibid., 34.

[231] Douglas Brinkley, *The Wilderness Warrior: Theodore Roosevelt and the
Crusade for America* (New York: Harper, 2010), 153.

[232] Ibid., 194.

233 Theodore Roosevelt, "Citizenship in a Republic," speech at the Sorbonne, Paris, April 23, 1910.

234 Ibid., 41.

235 Berfield, *Hour of Fate*, 46.

236 Chernow, *Titan*, 336.

237 Leroy Dorsey, "Theodore Roosevelt and Corporate America, 1901–1909," *Presidential Studies Quarterly*, 25, 725–9.

238 Theodore Roosevelt, "Wise and Unwise Methods for Remedying Trust Evils, September 2, 1902," in William Griffith, ed., *The Roosevelt Policy: Speeches, Letters and State Papers, Relating to Corporate Wealth and Closely Allied Topics*, 3 vols. (New York: Kraus Reprint Co., 1971), 1:52, 55.

239 Roosevelt, "Wise and Unwise," 1:51–52; Theodore Roosevelt, "Necessity of Establishing Federal Sovereignty over 'Trusts,' August 23, 1902," in *Roosevelt Policy*, 1:32,38; Theodore Roosevelt, "Progress Made Toward Federal Control of Corporations, April 3, 1903," ibid., 1:120.

240 Dorsey, "Theodore Roosevelt and Corporate America," 727.

241 Henry Pringle, *Theodore Roosevelt: A Biography* (New York: Harcourt, Brace & World, 1956), 300.

242 James Ceaser, et. al., "The Rise of the Rhetorical Presidency," *Presidential Studies Quarterly*, 11, 1981, 158–171 and Jeffrey Tulis, *The Rhetorical Presidency* (Princeton, NJ.: Princeton University Press, 1987). The scholarship on how much, if any, presidential rhetoric influences public opinion is hotly debated. One study found that in foreign policy it had no effect, but a small effect on domestic policy (George Edwards, III and Matthew Eshbaugh-Soha, "Presidential Persuasion: Does the Public Respond?" Paper presented at the annual meeting of the Southern Political Science Association, November 2000), while another suggests that the only real beneficiary is the president himself in terms of slightly better approval numbers in polls (James Druckman and Justin Holmes, "Does Presidential Rhetoric Matter? Priming and Presidential Approval," *Presidential Studies Quarterly*, 34, December 2004, 755–778.

243 Theodore Roosevelt, "National Supervision of Great Combinations of Capital and Labor, April 9, 1902," in Griffith, *The Roosevelt Policy*, 1:25.

244 Larry Schweikart and Michael Allen, *A Patriot's History of the United States: From Columbus's Great Discovery to the Age of Entitlement, 15th Anniversary Ed.* (New York: Sentinel, 2019), 490.

245 Edmund Morris, *The Rise of Theodore Roosevelt* (New York: Ballantine, 1979), 446.

246 Ibid., 314.

247 Schweikart and Allen, *Patriot's History*, 491.

248 Marc Winerman, "The Origins of the FTC: Concentration, Cooperation, Control, and Competition," *Antitrust Law Journal*, 17, 2003, 1–97.

249 Ibid., 17.

250 Richard Hofstadter, *The American Political Tradition and the Men Who Made It* (New York: Alfred A. Knopf), 1967, 224.

251 Edmund Morris, *Theodore Rex* (New York: Modern Library, 2002), 60.

252 Ibid., 72.

253 Ibid., 72–76.

254 Ibid., 137.

255 Transcript of Speech, August 23, 1902, in Morris, *Theodore Rex*, 138–9.

256 *New York Times*, August 24, 1902.

257 Hans Thorelli, *Federal Antitrust Policy* (Baltimore: Johns Hopkins Press, 1955), 555–60.

258 Theodore Roosevelt, "The Square Deal, April 5, 1905," *Roosevelt Policy*, 1:256.

259 Theodore Roosevelt, "Enforcement of Law and the Railways, October 4, 1907," ibid., 2:632.

260 Theodore Roosevelt, "False Standards Resulting from Swollen Fortunes," ibid., 1:284–85.

261 Theodore Roosevelt," "False Standards," 1:284–5 and "Corporate Activity and 'Law Honesty,' October 20, 1905," in ibid., 1:311.

262 Theodore Roosevelt, "Federal Supervision of Railways as an Executive not a Judicial Function, June 22, 1905," ibid., 1:276, and "There Will be no Change in Policy, August 20, 1907," ibid., 2:569–70.

263 Theodore Roosevelt, "The Campaign Against Special Privilege, January 31, 1908," ibid., 2:725.

264 Special Message on the Hepburn Bill, 1908, cited in Winerman, "Origins of the FTC," 20.

265 Theodore Roosevelt, "The Trusts, the People, and the Square Deal," *Outlook*, 99, November 18, 1911), 649–56.

266 James Rill and Stacy Turner, "Presidents Practicing Antitrust: Where to Draw the Line," *Antitrust Law Journal*, 79, 2014, 577–599 (580).

267 David Graham Phillips, "The Treason of the Senate: Aldrich, the Head of it All," *Cosmopolitan*, March 1906, http://www.starkman.com/hippo/history/aldrich/phillips.html.

268 Ibid.

269 Morris, *Theodore Rex*, 434.

270 Ibid., 436.

271 Ibid., 446.
272 Larry Schweikart, *The Entrepreneurial Adventure* (Ft. Worth, TX: Harcourt Brace, 2000), 273–4.
273 Ibid., 499.
274 Mark Sullivan, *Our Times: 1900–1925* (Six volumes), (New York: Charles Scribners' Sons, 1926–1940), III: 34.
275 Chernow, *Titan*, 553.
276 *Standard Oil Co. of New Jersey v. United States*, 221 U.S. 1 (1911).
277 *United States v. American Tobacco Company*, 221 U.S. 106 (1911).
278 *Chicago Board of Trade v. United States*, 246 U.S. 231 (1918).
279 Paolo Coletta, *The Presidency of William Howard Taft* (Lawrence, KS: University Press of Kansas, 1973), 157–59.
280 Chernow, *Titan*, 430.
281 Ibid., 431.
282 Ibid., 433.

Chapter 4

283 Jeff Deist, "Truman Was Right About the CIA," Mises Institute, March 8, 2017, https://mises.org/wire/truman-was-right-about-cia.
284 Peter Fenn, "Heed Truman's Call to Rein in the CIA," *US News & World Report*, January 28, 2015, https://www.usnews.com/opinion/blogs/peter-fenn/2015/01/28/truman-was-right-to-warn-against-cia-power.
285 Robarge, "First 'First Customer.'"
286 Arthur Krock, "The President's Secret Daily 'Newspaper,'" *New York Times*, July 16, 1946.
287 Harry S. Truman, *Memoirs, Vol. 2: Years of Trial and Hope* (Garden City, NY: Doubleday, 1956), 58.
288 Allen W. Dulles, William H. Jackson, and Mathias F. Correa, "The Central Intelligence Agency and National Organization for Intelligence: A Report to the National Security Council," January 1, 1949, 85–86.
289 David Robarge, "The First 'First Customer': Harry Truman," https://www.cia.gov/readingroom/docs/THE%20FIRST%20FIRST%20CUSTOMER%20%5B15452307%5D.pdf.
290 "Truman Never Intended C.I.A. as a Cloak and Dagger Outfit," *New York Times*, December 1, 1963, https://www.nytimes.com/1995/10/01/opinion/l-truman-never-intended-cia-as-a-cloak-and-dagger-outfit-295895.html.

291 "Remarks of the President to the Final Session of the CIA's Eighth Training Orientation Course...," November 21, 1952, in Michael Warner, ed., *The CIA Under Truman* (Washington, DC: CIA History Staff, 1994), 471.

292 Renee Parsons, "President Harry Truman and the CIA," December 15, 2016, *Huffpost*, https://www.huffpost.com/entry/president-harry-truman-and-the-cia_b_5852cd5ae4b05f567d8bd71f.

293 Irwin Gellman, *The President and the Apprentice: Eisenhower and Nixon, 1951–1961* (New Haven, CT: Yale University Press, 2015), 98.

294 Chester Pach, Jr., "Dwight D. Eisenhower: Foreign Affairs," https://millercenter.org/president/eisenhower/foreign-affairs.

295 Gellman, *President and the Apprentice*, 163.

296 Philip Taubman, *Secret Empire: Eisenhower, the CIA, and the Hidden Story of America's Space Espionage* (New York: Simon & Schuster, 2003).

297 *New York Times*, October 6, 16, 21, 1960; Gellman, *President and the Apprentice*, 552.

298 Transcript of John F. Kennedy's Inaugural Address (1961), https://www.ourdocuments.gov/doc.php?flash=false&doc=91&page=transcript.

299 L. Fletcher Prouty, *JFK: The CIA, Vietnam, and the Plot to Assassinate John F. Kennedy* (New York: Carol Publishing, 1996), 100.

300 Lamar Waldron and Thom Hartmann, *Legacy of Secrecy: the Long Shadow of the JFK Assassination* (Berkeley, CA: Counterpoint Press, 2013).

301 "The Bay of Pigs Invasion: A Comprehensive Chronology of Events," in Peter Kornbluh, ed., *Bay of Pigs Declassified* (New York: New Press, 1998), 305.

302 "Inspector General's Survey of the Cuban Operation and Associated Documents," February 1962, https://nsarchive2.gwu.edu/NSAEBB/NSAEBB341/IGrpt1.pdf; Irwin Gellman, *The President and the Apprentice: Eisenhower and Nixon, 1952–1961* (New Haven, CT: Yale University Press, 2015).

303 "Inspector General's Survey," 75.

304 Ibid., 77.

305 "Church Committee: Interim Report—Alleged Assassination Plots Involving Foreign Leaders, Current Section: 1. The Assassination Plots, 72, https://www.maryferrell.org/showDoc.html?docId=1156#relPageId=86.

306 Paul Johnson, *Modern Times: A History of the World from the Twenties to the Nineties*, rev. ed. (New York: HarperCollins, 1991), 625.

307 Humberto Fontova, May 14, 2021, "A Woke CIA? Old News," *FrontPageMagazine.com*, https://www.frontpagemag.com/fpm/2021/05/woke-cia-old-news-just-ask-hipsters-fidel-and-che-humberto-fontova/.

308 Ibid. See Humberto Fontova, *The Longest Romance: The Mainstream Media and Fidel Castro* (New York: Encounter Books, 2013).

309 Fontova, "A Woke CIA."

310 Ibid.

311 Central Intelligence Agency, "Official History of the Bay of Pigs Operation, Volume III, Evolution of CIA's Anti-Castro Policies, 1959–January 1961," 8, declassified, https://nsarchive2.gwu.edu/NSAEBB/NSAEBB355/bop-vol3.pdf#page=13&zoom=auto,-89,735.

312 Ibid., 9ff.

313 Ibid., 12–13.

314 Ibid., 27.

315 Ibid., 16–17.

316 Ibid., 26.

317 Ibid., 29–30ff.

318 H. R. McMaster, *Dereliction of Duty: Lyndon Johnson, Robert McNamara, the Joint Chiefs of Staff, and the Lies that Led to Vietnam* (New York: Harper, 1997) 5.

319 Ibid., 6–7.

320 Edwin Guthman and Jeffrey Shulman, *Robert Kennedy in His Own Words* (New York: Bantam, 1988) 245.

321 "C.I.A. Maker of Policy, or Tool?" *New York Times*, April 25, 1966.

322 Arthur M. Schlesinger, Jr., *Robert Kennedy and His Times* (New York: Ballantine Books, 1978), 486.

323 James G. Blight and Peter Kornbluh, eds., *Politics of Illusion: The Bay of Pigs Invasion Reexamined* (Boulder, CO: Lynne Rienner, 1999), 125.

324 Joint Chiefs of Staff, "Memorandum for the Secretary of Defense: Subject: Justification for US Military Intervention in Cuba (TS)," March 13, 1962, https://nsarchive2.gwu.edu//news/20010430/doc1.pdf.

325 "Report on Plots to Assassinate Fidel Castro (1967 Inspector General's Report), 14, https://www.maryferrell.org/showDoc.html?docId=9983#relPageId=14&tab=page.

326 Jorge Dominguez, "The @#$%& Missile Crisis: (Or, What Was 'Cuban' About the U.S. Decisions during the Cuban Missile Crisis?)," *Diplomatic History*, 24, Spring 2000, 305-316.

327 Graham Allison and Philip Zelikow, *Essence of Decision: Explaining the Cuban Missile Crisis* (New York: Addison Wesley Longman, 1999), 94–95.

328 D. Douglas Dalgleish and Larry Schweikart, "What You Don't Know About SDI," *Dayton Engineer*, July 1988, pp. 1, 4, 8, 11 and August 1988, pp. 1, 4.

329 Schlesinger, *Robert Kennedy*, 504-5, quoted in Johnson, *Modern Times*, 625.

[330] Marc Leif and Larry Schweikart, "Rockin' the Wall," 2010.

[331] Robert Kennedy, *Thirteen Days: A Memoir of the Cuban Missile Crisis* (New York: W. W. Norton, 1971), 14.

[332] James Douglass, *JFK and the Unspeakable* (New York: Touchstone, 2008), 21.

[333] There are two conflicting sets of transcripts for this incident: Ernest May and Philip Zelikow, eds., *The Kennedy Tapes* (Cambridge, MA: Harvard University Press, 1997), and Sheldon Stern, "What JFK Really Said," *Atlantic Monthly*, 285, May 2000, 122–28, and "Source Material: The 1997 Published Transcripts of the JFK Cuban Missile Crisis tapes: Too Good to be True?" *Presidential Studies Quarterly*, 30, September, 2000, 586–93. May, et. al., produced a revised set of transcripts in 2001 (*The Presidential Recordings: John F. Kennedy: Volumes 1-3, the Great Crises* [New York: Norton, 2001) and Stern's challenge to this in "The JFK Tapes: Round Two," *Reviews in American History*, 30 (2002), 680–88. See also Stern, *Averting "The Final Failure": John F. Kennedy and the Secret Cuban Missile Crisis Meetings* (Stanford: Stanford University Press, 2003).

[334] H. R. Kohn and J. P. Harahan, "Strategic Air Power, 1948-1962. Excerpts from an Interview with Generals Curtis LeMay, Leon W. Johnson, David A. Bruchinal, and Jack J. Catton," *International Security*, 12, 78–95.

[335] Sergo Mikoyan, *The Soviet Cuban Missile Crisis: Castro, Mikoyan, Kennedy, Khrushchev, and the Missiles of November* (Stanford: Stanford University Press, 2012), 148.

[336] James Blight and Janet Lang, *The Armageddon Letters: Kennedy, Khrushchev, Castro in the Cuban Missile Crisis* (Lanham, MD: Rowman & Littlefield), 2013.

[337] Sheldon Stern, *The Week the World Stood Still: Inside the Secret Cuban Missile Crisis* (Stanford: Stanford University Press, 2005), 146.

[338] Johnson, *Modern Times*, 627.

[339] Mikoyan, *Soviet Cuban Missile Crisis*.

[340] Johnson, *Modern Times*, 627.

[341] Larry Schweikart, *Reagan: The American President* (New York: Post Hill Press, 2019), 365–368.

[342] John F. Kennedy's Berlin Speech, June 26, 1963, http://news.bbc.co.uk/2/hi/europe/3022166.stm.

[343] During the crisis, Robert Kennedy told Soviet Ambassador to the US, Anatoly Dobrynin, that "the President is not sure that the military will not overthrow him and seize power" (Edward Crankshaw, ed., *Khrushchev Remembers* [Boston: Little, Brown, 1970], 498). However, it was entirely

likely that Bobby was using language that only the Soviet communists would understand. To them a military coup would be a perfectly natural reaction. Far from a statement of truth (or likelihood) it may well have been a bargaining chip.

344   *The Pentagon Papers: The Defense Department History of the United States: Decision Making on Vietnam, Senator Gravel Edition*, 5 vols. (Boston: Beacon Press, 1972), II:22.

345   Ibid., II:56–7.

346   See the newly released documents on land reform that substantially increased the number of dead from about 40,000 that was accepted at the time. (http://www.lib.washington.edu/southeastasia/vsg/elist_2007/Newly released documents on the land reform .html).

347   McMaster, *Dereliction of Duty*, 10.

348   Ibid., 41.

349   Ibid., 43.

350   See "IV.B. Evolution of the War 4. Phased Withdrawal of U.S. Forces in Vietnam, 1962–64," Report of the Office of the Secretary of Defense, Washington, DC, May 4, 2015. http://media.nara.gov/research/pentagon-papers/Pentagon-Papers-Part-IV-B-4.pdf.

351   Max Hastings, *Vietnam: An Epic Tragedy, 1945–1975* (New York: HarperCollins, 2018). And almost all other general histories accept the 16,000 number. Kennedy himself, however, alluded to a much higher number.

352   Director of Operations, Joint Chiefs of Staff, "Southeast Asia Situation Report," May 16, 1962, file Top Secrets—FE 5000-5599, Bureau of Eastern Affairs, Assistant Secretary of State for Far East Asia, Top Secret Files of the Regional Planning Advisor 1955–1963, Box 1, Record Group 59, United States National Archives; Arne Kislenko, "A Not So Silent Partner: Thailand's Role in Covert Operations, Counter-Insurgency, and the Wars in Indochina," *Journal of Conflict Studies*, 24.

353   Douglass, *JFK and the Unspeakable*, 122.

354   Schweikart and Allen, *A Patriot's History of the United States*, 15th Anniversary Edition 702.

355   Douglass, *JFK and the Unspeakable*, 125.

356   Kenneth O'Donnell and David Powers, *"Johnny, We Hardly Knew Ye"* (Boston: Little, Born, 1970), 16.

357   "Memorandum by Assistant Secretary of State-designate Roger Hilsman to Frederick G. Dutton, Assistant Secretary of State for Congressional Affairs, *Foreign Relations of the United States, 1961–1963*, III 208-11; Francis

Winters, *The Year of the Hare: America in Vietnam, January 25, 1963– February 14, 1964* (Athens, GA: University of Georgia Press), 26.

[358] "Viet-Nam Wants 50% of GIs Out," *Washington Post*, May 12, 1963.

[359] O'Donnell and Powers, *"Johnny, We Hardly Knew Ye,"* 18.

[360] Ellen Hammer, *A Death in November* (New York: Oxford, 1987), 197.

[361] Stanley Karnow, "The Fall of the House of Ngo Dinh," in Milton Bates, et. al., eds., *Reporting Vietnam, Part One: American Journalism, 1959–1969* (New York: Library of America, 1998), 94.

[362] Douglass, *JFK and the Unspeakable*, 168.

[363] H. R. McMaster, *Dereliction of Duty: Johnson, McNamara, the Joint Chiefs of Staff, and the Lies that Led to Vietnam* (New York: Harper Perennial Library, 1998).

[364] Lawrence Wittner, *Cold War America from Hiroshima to Watergate* (New York: Praeger, 2000), 229.

[365] "National Security Action Memorandum No. 263, South Vietnam," October 5, 1963, https://www.jfklibrary.org/asset-viewer/archives/ JFKNSF/342/JFKNSF-342-007, and "Memorandum From the Chairman of the Joint Chiefs of Staff (Taylor) and the Secretary of Defense (McNamara) to the President," October 2, 1963, *Foreign Relations of the United States, 1961–1963, Volume IV, Vietnam,* August-December 1963, https://history. state.gov/historicaldocuments/frus1961-63v04/d167.

[366] Douglass, *JFK and the Unspeakable*, 180.

[367] Charles Bartlett, "Portrait of a Friend," in Kenneth Thompson, ed., *The Kennedy Presidency: 17 Intimate Perspectives of John F. Kennedy* (Lanham, MD: University Press of America, 1985), 16.

[368] John Farrell, *Tip O'Neill and the Democratic Century* (Boston: Little, Brown, 2001), 193.

[369] Wayne Morse interview, *Boston Globe*, June 24, 1973.

[370] *Foreign Relations of the United States, 1961–63*, IV: 252–54.

[371] David Ratcliffe, *Understanding Special Operations and Their Impact of the Vietnam War Era* (Santa Cruz, CA: rat haus reality press, 1999), 71–72, interview with Col. Fletcher Prouty (one of the leading conspiracists).

[372] *Public Papers of the Presidents: JFK*, 1963, 651–2.

[373] Ibid., 660.

[374] *Foreign Relations of the United States, 1961–63*, 374.

[375] Ibid., 385–86.

[376] Douglass, *JFK and the Unspeakable*, 192.

[377] Marguerite Higgins, *Our Vietnam Nightmare* (New York: Harper & Row, 1965), 208.

378 Herbert S. Parmet, *JFK: The Presidency of John F. Kennedy* (New York: Dial Press, 1983), 334–45.

379 Edwin Black, "The Plot to Kill JFK in Chicago November 2, 1963," *Chicago Independent*, November 1975., cited in Douglass, *JFK and the Unspeakable*, 200.

380 John Davis, *Mafia Kingfish: Carlos Marcello and the Assassination of John F. Kennedy* (New York: McGraw-Hill, 1988); Sam Giancana, *Double Cross: The Explosive Inside Story of the Mobster Who Controlled America* (New York: Warner Books, 1992); Lamar Waldron, *Legacy of Secrecy: The Long Shadow of the JFK Assassination* (Berkeley, CA: Counterpoint, 2009).

381 "JFK Assassination System, Transcript of Cablegram Dated October 1967," docid-32165833.pdf.

382 "CIA Wondered if Oswald Sought Visas as Part of Escape Plan," CNN, November 5, 2017, https://www.archives.gov/files/research/jfk/releases/docid-32165833.pdf.

383 Douglass, *JFK and the Unspeakable*, passim; Mark Lane, *Plausible Denial: Was the CIA Involved in the Assassination of JFK?* (New York: Skyhorse Publishing, 2011).

384 Bonar Menninger, *Mortal Error: The Shot that Killed JFK* (New York: St. Martin's, 1992).

385 Gerald Posner makes a compelling case that Oswald acted alone and, for the first time, explained the "magic bullet's" not-so-magical trajectory. See *Case Closed: Lee Harvey Oswald and the Assassination of JFK* (New York: Random House, 1993).

386 Menninger, *Mortal Error*, passim.

Chapter 5

387 John Marini, *Unmasking the Administrative State* (New York: Encounter Books, 2019), 65–67 and passim; Marini, *The Crisis of American Politics in the Twenty-First Century*, edited by Ken Masugi (New York: Encounter Books, 2019).

388 Ibid., 46.

389 *Public Papers of the Presidents of the United States, Richard M. Nixon, 1972* (Washington, DC: Government Printing Office, 1974), 1088.

390 Marini, *Unmasking the Administrative State*, 136.

391 Alan Olmstead and Paul Rhode, *Arresting Contagion: Science, Policy, and Conflicts over Animal Disease Control* (Cambridge: Harvard University Press, 2015).

392 Ibid., 7.

393 Ibid., 18.

394 Ibid., 76.

395 Ulysses Grant Houck, *The Bureau of Animal Industry of the United States Department of Agriculture: Its Establishment, Achievements and Current Activities* (Washington, DC: Hayworth Printing Company, 1924), 44–47.

396 Franklin Roosevelt, State of the Union Address, January 21, 1944, 1945http://www.fdrlibrary.marist.edu/archives/stateoftheunion.html.

397 Ronald Reagan, "A Time for Choosing," October 27, 1964, https://www.reaganlibrary.gov/reagans/ronald-reagan/time-choosing-speech-october-27-1964#:~:text=%22The%20Speech%22%20is%20what%20Ronald,his%20acting%20career%20closed%20out.

398 Marini, *Unmasking the Administrative State*, 205.

399 Ronald Reagan, "Ronald Reagan's Announcement for Presidential Candidacy," January 13, 1979, Reagan Presidential Library, https://www.reaganlibrary.gov/archives/speech/ronald-reagans-announcement-presidential-candidacy-1979.

400 Ibid.

401 Ibid.

402 Ronald Reagan, "Televised Campaign Address, 'A Vital Economy: Jobs, Growth, and Progress for Americans,'" https://www.reaganlibrary.gov/archives/speech/televised-campaign-address-vital-economy-jobs-growth-and-progress-americans.

403 Ronald Reagan, "Election Eve Address, 'A Vision for America,'" https://www.reaganlibrary.gov/archives/speech/election-eve-address-vision-america.

404 Ronald Reagan, "First Inaugural Address," January 20, 1981, https://avalon.law.yale.edu/20th_century/reagan1.asp.

405 Ibid.

406 Larry Schweikart, *Reagan: The American President* (New York: Post Hill Press, 2019), 197.

407 Ibid.

408 Memorandum from Anthony R. Dolan to Ed Meese and Bob Barrick, January 7, 1981, in Transition Papers, 1979–81, Box 5, Reagan Presidential Library (RL).

409 Transition Timmons Papers, 1980 Transition Papers, 1979–1981, Series III: Deputy Director for Executive Branch Management (William Timmons), Series III, Subseries B, Reports, Box 35, RL.

410 Interview with Joseph Wright, June 15, 2015.

411   Edwin Meese III, *With Reagan: The Inside Story* (Washington: Regnery, 1992), 74–5.

412   Franklin D. Roosevelt, "Message to Congress on Social Security, January 17, 1935," https://www.ssa.gov/history/fdrstmts.html#message2.

413   Lou Cannon, *President Reagan: The Role of a Lifetime* (New York: Simon & Schuster, 1991), 243.

414   Ibid., 247.

415   Ibid., 251.

416   "Annual Averages," July 6, 1981, in Anderson, Martin Files, Series 1, Subject Files, Congressional Budget Office, "Council of Economic Advisers," Box 9 (1 of 3), C. Folder "Issues" (5), RL.

417   Ronald Reagan, *The Reagan Diaries*, ed., Douglas Brinkley, single vol. ed. (New York: HarperCollins, 2007), September 21, 1981, 39.

418   Ibid., 40.

419   Cannon, *President Reagan*, 155.

420   Schweikart, *Reagan*, 250–51.

421   Steven Hayward *The Age of Reagan: The Conservative Counterrevolution, 1980–1989* (New York: Three Rivers Press, 2009), 84.

422   Ibid.

423   David Stockman, *The Triumph of Politics: Why the Reagan Revolution Failed* (New York: Harper and Row, 1986), 54.

424   Daniel Patrick Moynihan, *Came the Revolution: Argument in the Reagan Era* (San Diego: Harcourt, Brace, Jovanovich, 1988), 6.

425   Hayward, *Age of Reagan: Conservative Counterrevolution*, 85.

426   William Greider, *The Education of David Stockman and Other Americans*, rev. updated ed. (New York: New American Library, 1986), 25.

427   Ibid., 7.

428   Ibid., 16.

429   Ibid.

430   Ibid., 26.

431   Ibid., 153.

432   Ibid., 152.

433   Ibid., 154.

434   Philip Hamburger, *The Administrative Threat* (New York: Encounter Books, 2017), 39.

435   H. W. Brands, *Reagan: The Life* (New York: Doubleday, 2015), 322–3.

436   Reagan, *Presidential Diaries*, 96.

437   Schweikart, *Reagan*, 418.

438   Brands, *Reagan*, 265.

439   Dinesh D'Souza, *Ronald Reagan: How an Ordinary Man Became an Extraordinary Leader* (New York: Touchstone, 1997), 96–7.

440   Greider, *Education of David Stockman*, 22–23.

441   Acting Secretary of Commerce to James C. Miller III, April 15, 1988, in Crippen, Dan Files, Office of the Chief of Staff, Series 1: Subject File, Box 8, "Park Package(s)" (5), RL.

442   Schweikart, *Reagan*, chapters 10, 12, 14.

443   Hamburger, *The Administrative Threat*, passim.

444   Hayward, *Age of Reagan: Conservative Counterrevolution*, 163.

445   Ibid., 218.

446   Ronald Reagan, "Second Inaugural Address," January 21, 1985, https://avalon.law.yale.edu/20th_century/reagan2.asp.

447   Schweikart, *Reagan*, 326–7.

448   Ibid., 345.

449   Caspar Weinberger, *Fighting for Peace* (New York: Time Warner, 1991), 363–4; George Shultz, *Turmoil and Triumph: My Years as Secretary of State* (New York: Charles Scribner's Sons, 1993), 793–94; and *Report of the Congressional Committees Investigating the Iran-Contra Affair* (Washington, DC: Congressional Budget Office, 1988), passim.

450   Reagan, *Reagan Diaries*, 384.

451   Ronald Reagan, remarks to the American Bar Association, July 8, 1985; Michael Ledeen, *Perilous Statecraft* (New York: Scribners, 1988), 27.

452   Don Regan, *For the Record: From Wall Street to Washington* (New York: Harcourt Brace Jovanovich, 1988), 38.

453   US House Committee on Science and Technology, "Investigation of the Challenger Accident; Report of the Committee on Science and Technology, House of Representatives" (Washington, DC: US Government Printing Office, 1986).

454   Hayward, *Age of Reagan: Conservative Counterrevolution*, 635.

455   Ibid.

Chapter 6

456   Edward-Isaac Dovere, *Battle for the Soul: Inside the Democrats' Campaigns to Defeat Trump* (New York: Viking, 2021), 7.

457   Ibid., 8.

458   Angelo Codevilla, "America's Ruling Class—And the Perils of Revolution," *American Spectator*, July-August 2010, http://spectator.org/articles/39326/americas-ruling-class-and-perils-revolution.

459   C. Wright Mills, *The Power Elite*, new ed. (Cambridge, MA: Oxford University Press, 2000).

460   Charles Murray, *Coming Apart: The State of White America, 1960–2010* (New York: Crown, 2012), 57.

461   "Private Schools Have Become Truly Obscene," *The Atlantic*, April 2021, https://www.theatlantic.com/magazine/archive/2021/04/private-schools-are-indefensible/618078/.

462   Tom Engelhardt, *Shadow Government* (Chicago: Haymarket Books, 2014), 3.

463   John Marini, *Unmasking the Administrative State* (New York: Encounter Books, 2019), 145.

464   Engelhardt, *Shadow Government*, 6.

465   Ibid., 31.

466   Ibid., 84.

467   Ibid., 89.

468   Trump Calls to 'Drain the Swamp' of Washington," *USA Today*, October 18, 2016.

469   "How Might Trump 'Drain the Swamp'?" https://www.bbc.com/news/election-us-2016-37699073.

470   "Here's What Trump Means When He Says 'Drain the Swamp'" https://www.businessinsider.com/what-does-drain-the-swamp-mean-was-dc-built-on-a-swamp-2016-11.

471   "The Turkish Origins of the 'Deep State,'" *JSTOR Daily*, April 10, 2017, https://daily.jstor.org/the-unacknowledged-origins-of-the-deep-state/. Mike Lofgren on "Moyers & Company," February 21, 2014, https://www.pbs.org/video/moyers-company-deep-state-hiding-plain-sight. Moyers and Lofgren, however, cited the Deep State as "how we had deregulation, financialization of the economy…." without noting that both of those had extensive popular support. Such was not the case with the resistance to Trump.

472   "As Leaks Multiply, Fears of a 'Deep State' in America," *New York Times*, February 16, 2017.

473   "Deep State: How a Conspiracy Theory Went From Political Fringe to Mainstream," *Newsweek*, August 2, 2017, https://www.newsweek.com/deep-state-conspiracy-theory-trump-645376.

474   "Five Myths About the 'Deep State,'" *Washington Post*, March 10, 2017.

475   "The Deep State is a Very Real Thing," *Huffpost*, March 15, 2017, https://www.huffpost.com/entry/the-deep-state_b_58c94a64e4b01d0d473bcfa3.

476 "Justice Watchdog Can't Pinpoint FBI Leaks Prior to 2016 Election," *Politico*, August 5, 2021, https://www.politico.com/news/2021/08/05/fbi-2016-election-leaks-502554.

477 "The Deep State is Real: But it Might Not Be What You Think," *Politico Magazine*, September/October, 2017, https://www.politico.com/magazine/story/2017/09/05/deep-state-real-cia-fbi-intelligence-215537/.

478 Ibid.

479 "Preview, The Fourth Branch of Government," *The Conservative Treehouse*, July 4, 2021, https://theconservativetreehouse.com/blog/2021/07/04/preview-the-fourth-branch-of-government/.

480 Ibid.

481 John Marini, *Unmasking the Administrative State* (New York: Encounter Books, 2019), 275.

482 Ibid.

483 Doug Wead, *Inside Trump's White House: The Real Story of His Presidency* (New York: Center Street, 2019), 248.

484 Paul Johnson, *Modern Times: A History of the World from the Twenties to the Nineties*, rev. ed. (New York: HarperCollins, 1991), 65–66.

485 Gregg Jarret, *Witch Hunt: The Story of the Greatest Mass Delusion in American Political History* (New York: Broadside, 2019), 156.

486 Jarrett, *Witch Hunt*, 156.

487 "Rod Rosenstein Suggested Secretly Recording Trump and Discussed 25th Amendment," *New York Times*, September 21, 2018, https://www.nytimes.com/2018/09/21/us/politics/rod-rosenstein-wear-wire-25th-amendment.html.

488 "Rod Rosenstein's Letter Recommending Comey be Fired," BBC News, May 10, 2017, https://www.bbc.com/news/world-us-canada-39866767.

489 Joel Pollack and Larry Schweikart, *How Trump Won: The Inside Story of a Revolution* (Washington, DC: Regnery, 2017), 69.

490 Ibid.

491 "Exclusive—Deep State Teams with Fake News: Email Evidence Proves New York Times Soliciting Anti-Trump Bureaucracy Leakers," *Breitbart*, August 8, 2017, https://www.breitbart.com/the-media/2017/08/08/exclusive-deep-state-teams-fake-news-email-evidence-proves-new-york-times-soliciting-anti-trump-bureaucracy-leakers/.

492 "Deep State is Real: but it Might Not Be What You Think."

493 "Senior White House Official Confesses Anti-Trump Cabal in Newspaper Trump Reads," *The National Interest*, September 5, 2018, https://nymag.com/intelligencer/amp/2018/09/senior-white-house-official-confesses-anti-trump-cabal.html.

494 "Kucinich: 'Deep State' Trying to Take Down Trump, 'Our Country is Under Attack Within,'" *RealClearPolitics*, May 18, 2017, https://www.realclearpolitics.com/video/2017/05/18/kucinich_deep_state_trying_to_take_down_trump_our_country_is_under_attack_within.html.

495 "Spies Keep Intelligence From Donald Trump on Leak Concerns," *Wall Street Journal*, February 16, 1017, https://www.wsj.com/articles/spies-keep-intelligence-from-donald-trump-1487209351.

496 See Wikipedia: "Deep State in the United States, https://en.wikipedia.org/wiki/Deep_state_in_the_United_States#cite_note-29.

497 "Nearly Half of Americans Think There's a 'Deep State': Poll," ABC News, April 27, 2017, https://abcnews.go.com/Politics/lies-damn-lies-deep-state-plenty-americans-poll/story?id=47032061.

498 "Americans Skeptical of Government, More Politically Engaged, Poll Finds," March 19, 2018, https://www.cnn.com/2018/03/19/politics/americans-skeptical-government-poll/index.html.

499 "Bi-Partisan Concern that Government is Tracking U.S. Citizens," Monmouth University Polling Institute, March 19, 2018, https://www.monmouth.edu/polling-institute/reports/monmouthpoll_us_031918/.

500 Interview with Steve Bannon, June 16, 2021.

501 Ibid.

502 Wead, *Inside Trump's White House*, 241.

503 Ibid., 242.

504 Ibid., 258.

505 Robin Simcox, " Did Trump Really Beat ISIS?" Heritage Foundation, January 29, 2018, https://www.heritage.org/middle-east/commentary/did-trump-really-beat-isis.

506 Interview with Sebastian Gorka, June 14, 2021.

507 Interview with Steve Bannon, June 16, 2021.

508 "After Capitol Riot, Pentagon Announces New Efforts to Weed Out Extremism Among Troops," *New York Times*, April 13, 2021, https://www.google.com/search?q=Pentagon+announces+new+anti-racism+efforts&oq=Pentagon+announces+new+anti-racism+efforts&aqs=chrome..69i57.15911j0j1&sourceid=chrome&ie=UTF-8. In the interest of accuracy, there was no "riot," none of the protesters were armed, the only people who died did so after the fact of natural causes except for Ashli Babbitt who, unarmed, was shot by an unidentified as of this writing, Capitol policeman.

509 Engelhardt, *Shadow Government*, 6.

510 House Armed Services Committee, "Department of the Navy Fiscal Year 2022 Budget Request," https://armedservices.house.gov/hearings?ID= A0C361D6-51C0-48A2-95E7-269B80E69D83.

511 Interview with Sebastian Gorka, June 14, 2021.

512 Ibid.

513 Ibid.

514 Ibid.

515 Gregg Jarrett, *The Russia Hoax: The Illicit Scheme to Clear Hillary Clinton and Frame Donald Trump* (New York: HarperCollins, 2018), 146.

516 "There is Nothing Normal About the Fusion GPS Dossier," *The Hill,* November 3, 2017.

517 Jack Cashill, *TWA 800: The Crash, the Cover-Up, and the Conspiracy* (Washington, DC: Regnery, 2016), passim.

518 "How Whitey Bulger Manipulated the FBI Into Locking Up His Enemies," History.com, July 25, 2018, https://www.history.com/news/ whitey-bulger-fbi-informant.

519 Ibid.

520 "Jewell Sues Newspapers, Former Employer for Libel," CNN, January 28, 1997; "Commentary: Don't Name 'Person of Interest,'" CNN, September 17, 2009; "Richard Jewell Files Suit Against the Post," *New York Times,* July 24, 1997; "Scientist is Paid Millions by U.S. in Anthrax Suit," *New York Times,* June 28, 2008.

521 "Special Counsel on Russia Probe to Expand Scope," *The Times of Israel,* June 3, 2017, https://www.timesofisrael.com/special-counsel-on-russia- probe-expanding-scope/.

522 "Read: 2017 Rod Rosenstein 'Scope Memo' Detailing Parameters of Mueller Probe," Fox News, May 6, 2020, https://www.foxnews.com/politics/read- 2017-rod-rosenstein-scope-memo-detailing-parameters-of-mueller-probe.

523 Interview with Steve Bannon, June 16, 2021.

524 Jarrett, *Russia Hoax,* 157.

525 "Ex-FBI Lawyer Sentenced to Probation for Actions During Russia Investigation," NPR, January 29, 2021, https://www.npr. org/2021/01/29/962140325/ex-fbi-lawyer-sentenced-to-probation-for- actions-during-russia-investigation; "The Trump Russia Probe's Special Counsel Has Charged a Lawyer With Lying to the FBI," NPR, September 16, 2021, https://www.npr.org/2021/09/16/1038035231/the-trump-russia- probe-special-counsel-has-charged-a-lawyer-with-lying-to-the-fbi.

526 Gregg Jarrett, *Witch Hunt: The Story of the Greatest Mass Delusion in American Political History* (New York: HarperCollins, 2019), 399–410;

Robert Mueller, "Report on the Investigation Into Russian Interference in the 2016 Presidential Election," March 2019, https://www.justice.gov/archives/sco/file/1373816/download.

527 "Read Jeff Sessions' Resignation Letter," CNN, November 7, 2018, https://www.cnn.com/2018/11/07/politics/sessions-resignation-letter/index.html.

528 "Barr Says, 'I Think Spying Did Occur' Against Trump Campaign," AP, April 10, 2019.

529 "Attorney General William P. Barr Delivers Remarks on the Release of the Report on the Investigation into Russian Interference in the 2016 Presidential Election," April 18, 2019, https://www.justice.gov/opa/speech/attorney-general-william-p-barr-delivers-remarks-release-report-investigation-russian.

530 "Justice Department IG Finds Widespread Problems With FBI's FISA Applications," NPR, March 31, 2020, https://www.npr.org/2020/03/31/824510255/justice-department-ig-finds-widespread-problems-with-fbis-fisa-applications.

531 "Woodward Book: Former Intelligence Head Dan Coats Thought It Useless to Speak Out Against Donald Trump," USA Today, September 15, 2020, https://www.usatoday.com/story/news/politics/2020/09/15/woodward-book-former-intelligence-director-dan-coats-concluded-would-useless-speak-out-against-donal/5803115002/.

532 National Archives, "New Group of JFK Assassination Documents Available to the Public," April 26, 2018, https://www.archives.gov/press/press-releases/nr18-45.

533 Amanda Milius on Jack Murphy Live Podcast, #39, https://jackmurphylive.com/podcast/.

534 Interview with Peter Navarro, June 15, 2021.

535 Ibid.

536 Interview with Steve Bannon, June 16, 2021.

537 Ibid.

538 Ibid.

539 "Reports of Injuries, Deaths After COVID Vaccines Hit New Highs, as Biden Rolls Out Plan to Force 100 Million More Americans to Get Vaccinated," The Defender, September 10, 2021, https://childrenshealthdefense.org/defender/vaers-injuries-deaths-covid-vaccines-new-highs-biden-mandates/.

540 "Trump Says He 'Probably Won't' Get COVID-19 Booster Shot," The Hill, September 3, 2021, https://thehill.com/homenews/administration/570781-trump-says-he-probably-wont-get-covid-19-booster-shot.

541 "Data from Yelp Shows 60% of All Businesses that Shut Down During COVID are now Permanently Closed," Gateway Pundit, September 19, 2021, https://www.thegatewaypundit.com/2021/09/data-yelp-shows-60-businesses-closed-covid-now-permanently-gone/.

542 "Thousands of Covid Patients Sent to NY Nursing Homes; Cuomo Aide Acknowledges Concealing Data," KHN Morning Briefing, February 12, 2021, https://khn.org/morning-breakout/thousands-of-covid-patients-sent-to-ny-nursing-homes-cuomo-aide-acknowledges-concealing-data/.

543 "The Secret History of the Shadow Campaign That Saved the 2020 Election," *Time Magazine*, February 4, 2021, https://time.com/5936036/secret-2020-election-campaign/.

544 Ibid.

545 Ibid.

546 Ibid.

547 "Clark County Calls for Re-Vote in Commission Race Decided by 10 Ballots; Discrepancies Outnumber Victory Margin," *Nevada Independent*, November 16, 2020, https://thenevadaindependent.com/article/clark-county-calls-for-re-vote-in-commission-race-decided-by-10-ballots-discrepancies-outnumber-victory-margin.

548 "In New Defense, Dozens of Capitol Rioters Say Law Enforcement 'Let Us In' to the Building," February 19, 2021, https://abcnews.go.com/US/defense-dozens-capitol-rioters-law-enforcement-us-building/story?id=75976466.

549 "Woman Dies After Shooting in U.S. Capitol; D.C. National Guard Activated After Mob Breaches Building," *Washington Post*, January 7, 2021, https://www.washingtonpost.com/dc-md-va/2021/01/06/dc-protests-trump-rally-live-updates/.

550 "Police Officer Filmed Posing for Selfie with Pro-Trump Rioter Inside U.S. Capitol," https://www.independent.co.uk/news/world/americas/us-politics/police-officer-selfie-rioter-us-capitol-trump-b1783760.html; "Officers Calmly Posed for Selfies and Appeared to Open Gates for Protesters During the Madness of the Capitol Building Insurrection," *Business Insider*, January 8, 2021, https://www.businessinsider.com/capitol-building-officers-posed-for-selfies-helped-protesters-2021-1.

551 "Officer Cleared in the Shooting Death of Ashli Babbitt During Capitol Riot," NPR, April 14, 2021, https://www.npr.org/2021/04/14/987425312/officer-cleared-in-the-shooting-of-ashli-babbitt-during-capitol-riot.

Conclusion

552 "Gen. Milley Reportedly Took Steps to Limit Trump's Nuclear Strike Powers after Jan. 6," *Forbes*, September 14, 2021, https://www.forbes.com/sites/andrewsolender/2021/09/14/gen-milley-reportedly-took-steps-to-limit-trumps-nuclear-strike-powers-after-jan-6/?sh=276431cf409a.

553 "Joe Concha: What Else did Gen. Milley Keep Trump, Pence in the Dark On?" Fox News, September 20, 2021, https://www.foxnews.com/media/joe-concha-gen-milley-trump-pence-in-the-dark-washington-post.

554 "No Place for Racism, Discrimination in U.S. Military, Milley Says," US Department of Defense, July 9, 2020, https://www.defense.gov/Explore/News/Article/Article/2269438/no-place-for-racism-discrimination-in-us-military-milley-says/.

555 "Pelosi Says She Spoke to Gen. Milley About Trump and the Nuclear Codes," CNN, January 8, 2021, https://www.cnn.com/2021/01/08/politics/house-speaker-joint-chiefs-milley/index.html.

556 Richard Hofstadter, *The American Political Tradition: And the Men Who Made It* (New York: Vintage, 1989 [1948]).

557 Richard Hofstadter, *The Paranoid Style in American Politics* (New York: Vintage, 2008), foreword by Sean Wilenz, xviii.

558 Ibid., 7.

559 Interview with Steve Bannon, June 17, 2021.